FINLAND

RUSSIAN FEDERATION

Helsinki
Tallinn ESTONIA
Riga LATVIA
Vilnius LITHUANIA
Minsk
BELARUS
Moscow

SLOVAKIA UKRAINE
EP. MOLDOVA
Budapest Chisinau
HUNGARY
SERBIA ROMANIA
Belgrade Bucharest
OS. Sofia BULGARIA
ALBANIA Pristina GEORGIA Tbilisi
MAC. Skopje ARMENIA AZERBAIJAN
GREECE Ankara Yerevan Baku
TURKEY
CYPRUS Nicosia SYRIA
LEBANON Beirut Damascus
ISRAEL Amman
Jerusalem JORDAN
Cairo
EGYPT

Astana
KAZAKHSTAN

Bishkek
UZBEKISTAN Tashkent KYRGYZSTAN
TURKMENISTAN Dushanbe
Asgabat TAJIKISTAN
Tehran Kabul
IRAQ IRAN AFGHANISTAN Islamabad
Baghdad
Kuwait
KUWAIT PAKISTAN New Delhi
BAHRAIN QATAR
Riyadh Manama Doha Abu Dhabi
SAUDI UAE Muscat
ARABIA OMAN INDIA

MONGOLIA
Ulan Bator

CHINA
Beijing

NORTH
KOREA
Pyongyang JAPAN
Seoul
SOUTH Sejong City Tokyo
KOREA

NEPAL Thimphu
Kathmandu BHUTAN
BANGLADESH
Dhaka
BURMA
(MYANMAR)
Nay Pyi Taw

Taipei
TAIWAN

Midway
Islands
(US)

SUDAN
Khartoum ERITREA
Asmara YEMEN
Sana
DJIBOUTI
Djibouti
Addis Ababa
ETHIOPIA
CENTRAL
REPUBLIC
SOUTH
SUDAN
Juba
ngui

Socotra
(Yemen)

OMAN

Laccadive Islands
(India)
Colombo
SRI LANKA
Sri Jayewardenapura
Kotte
Nicobar
Islands
(India)

Andaman
Islands
(India)
Bangkok
THAILAND
Vientiane LAOS
CAMBODIA
Phnom Penh

Hanoi
VIETNAM

Manila
PHILIPPINES

Wake Island (US)

Northern
Mariana
Islands
(US)

Guam
(US)

UGANDA
Kampala
Kigali RWANDA Nairobi
EM. REP. BURUNDI
CONGO Bujumbura
Dodoma
TANZANIA

KENYA
Mogadishu
SOMALIA

MALDIVES Male

SEYCHELLES
Victoria

BRUNEI
Bandar Seri Begawan
Kuala Lumpur
MALAYSIA
Putrajaya
SINGAPORE
Singapore

PALAU
Ngerulmud

MICRONESIA
Palikir

MARSHALL ISLANDS

Majuro

Baker &
Howland Islands
(US)

NAURU
Bairiki

KIRIBATI

ZAMBIA MALAWI
Lusaka Lilongwe
Harare
ZIMBABWE
BOTSWANA
aborone Pretoria
Mbabane
emfontein SWAZILAND
Maseru
OUTH LESOTHO
AFRICA

COMOROS
Moroni
Mayotte
(France)

MADAGASCAR
Antananarivo

British Indian
Ocean Territory
(UK)

MAURITIUS
Port Louis

Réunion
(France)

Christmas Island
(Australia)
Cocos (Keeling) Island
(Australia)

Ashmore & Cartier Islands
(Australia)

Maputo
MOZAMBIQUE

INDONESIA
Jakarta

Dili
EAST
TIMOR

PAPUA NEW GUINEA
Port Moresby
Honiara

SOLOMON
ISLANDS

Coral Sea
Islands
(Australia)

New
Caledonia
(France)

VANUATU
Port-Vila

TUVALU
Fongafale

Tokelau
(NZ)
Apia
Wallis
& Futuna
(France)
SAMOA

FIJI Suva
TONGA
Nuku'alofa

Amsterdam Island
(France)

St-Paul Island
(France)

WESTERN
AUSTRALIA

NORTHERN
TERRITORY

QUEENSLAND

AUSTRALIA
SOUTH
AUSTRALIA

NEW SOUTH
WALES

Norfolk Island
(Australia)

Kermadec Islands
(New Zealand)

Crozet Islands
(France)

Prince Edward
Islands
(South Africa)

Kerguelen
(France)

VICTORIA
Canberra
AUSTRALIAN
CAPITAL
TERRITORY
TASMANIA

NEW ZEALAND
Wellington

Chatham Islands
(New Zealand)

Bounty Islands
(New Zealand)

Auckland Islands
(New Zealand)

Macquarie Island
(Australia)

Country abbreviations

BEL.	Belgium
BOS. & HERZ.	Bosnia and Herzegovina
CZECH REP.	Czech Republic
KOS.	Kosovo
LIECH.	Liechtenstein
LUX.	Luxembourg
MAC.	Macedonia
MON.	Montenegro
NETH.	Netherlands
NZ	New Zealand
RUSS. FED.	Russian Federation
SM	San Marino
SLVN.	Slovenia
SWITZ.	Switzerland
UAE	United Arab Emirates
UK	United Kingdom
US	United States of America
VAT. CITY	Vatican City

ANTARCTICA

WHAT HAPPENED WHEN in the WORLD

HISTORY AS YOU'VE NEVER SEEN IT BEFORE

DK London
Senior editor Rob Houston
Senior art editor Rachael Grady
Editors Suhel Ahmed, Joanna Edwards,
Chris Hawkes, Anna Limerick, Susan Reuben, Fleur Star
Designers David Ball, Carol Davis, Mik Gates,
Spencer Holbrook, Steve Woosnam-Savage
Illustrators Adam Benton,
Stuart Jackson-Carter, Arran Lewis
Creative retouching Steve Willis
Cartography Simon Mumford, Encompass Graphics
Consultants Reg Grant, Philip Parker

Jacket editor Claire Gell
Jacket designer Mark Cavanagh
Jacket design development manager Sophia MTT
Picture research Sakshi Saluja

Producer, pre-production Adam Stoneham
Senior producer Mandy Inness

Managing editor Gareth Jones
Managing art editor Philip Letsu
Publisher Andrew Macintyre
Publishing director Jonathan Metcalf
Associate publishing director Liz Wheeler
Art director Phil Ormerod

DK Delhi
Senior art editor Anis Sayyed
Assistant art editor Tanvi Sahu
Managing editor Kingshuk Ghoshal
Managing art editor Govind Mittal

First published in Great Britain in 2015
by Dorling Kindersley Limited
80 Strand, London WC2R 0RL

Copyright © 2015 Dorling Kindersley Limited

A Penguin Random House Company

10 9 8 7 6 5 4 3 2
005–193419–04/15

A CIP catalogue record for this book
is available from the British Library.

ISBN: 978-1-4093-5659-2

Printed and bound in Hong Kong

CONTENTS

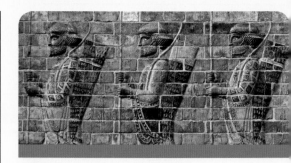

The ancient world

"Lion Man" ivory figurine

**Bison carved
from mammoth
ivory**

The medieval world

**Chinese monk
Xuanzang**

The modern world

**Kissing bug captured
by Charles Darwin**

The 20th and 21st centuries

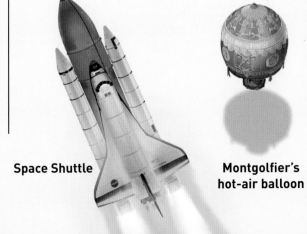

Space Shuttle   **Montgolfier's
hot-air balloon**

The ancient world

The Immortals
These figures are from the palace of the emperor of Persia. They are thought to show the emperor's bodyguards, known as "the Immortals". The guards seemed immortal because if one died, he was replaced before anyone noticed.

Upright man

Homo erectus, ancestor of modern humans, evolved longer legs and shorter arms, helping it to walk upright. Its brains and intelligence developed, allowing it to use finely crafted tools to catch food.

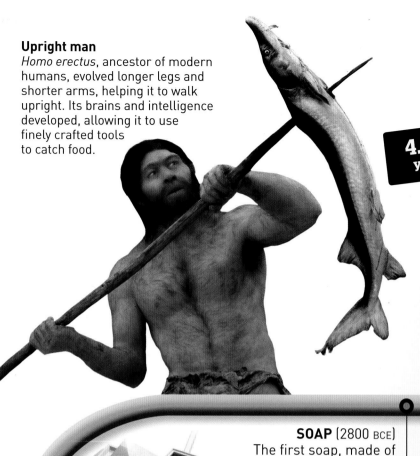

BIRTH OF EARTH (4.6 billion years ago) Planet Earth forms.

STONE TOOLS (2.5 mya) Early human ancestors called *Homo habilis* ("able man") make tools for the first time. Most are made of stone.

4.6 billion years ago

UPRIGHT MAN (1.8 mya) *Homo erectus* ("upright man") appears. It is the first human ancestor that is similar to modern humans.

ANCIENT EGYPT (3100 BCE) The civilization of ancient Egypt begins to grow around the River Nile. »pp22–23

BRONZE (3200 BCE) People in Egypt and Mesopotamia learn to make the hard-wearing metal, bronze. »pp24–25

SOAP (2800 BCE) The first soap, made of oil and salt, is used for washing fabric, not people. »pp46–47

WHEELED TRANSPORT (3200 BCE) Two-wheeled carts – the earliest known wheeled vehicles – are made in what is now Slovenia. »pp46–47

WRITING (3400 BCE) The first forms of writing are created in Sumer (in Mesopotamia) and Egypt. »pp20–21

The Great Pyramid at Giza

THE GREAT PYRAMID (2500 BCE) The pyramid tomb of the pharaoh Khufu is completed in Giza, Egypt. »pp22–23; 44–45

PACIFIC SETTLERS (2000 BCE) Lapita people become the first of five waves of settlers moving to islands in the Pacific. »pp42–43

OLMECS AND CHAVÍN (1200 BCE) The Olmecs are the first civilization in Mexico, while the Chavín culture dominates Peru. »pp26–27

ANCIENT GREECE (700–400 BCE) The ancient Greek civilization becomes the most influential power in the Mediterranean region. »pp28–29

Greek vase showing a temple

Ancient times

Humans have come a long way since their ancestors walked the planet 2.5 million years ago (mya). For many thousands of years, people lived simple lives as hunter-gatherers, who spent their time looking for food and defending themselves from wild animals. Then, with the advent of farming, civilizations grew. Inventions and discoveries – the wheel, irrigation, and writing – were slow at first, but progress has sped up ever since.

MOCHE CULTURE (100 CE) The Moche people of northern Peru create sophisticated art and textiles. »pp26–27

600 CE

SPREADING CHRISTIANITY (60 CE) Paul the Apostle sets up churches across the Roman Empire. »pp40–41

IF THE 4.6 BILLION YEARS OF EARTH'S HISTORY IS REPRESENTED AS

FIRE! (790,000 years ago)
The first evidence of humans using controlled fire dates to this time. »pp46–47

THE SECOND MIGRATION
(65,000 years ago) Modern humans leave Africa. They reach Asia and Australia 15,000 years later. »pp8–9

MODERN HUMANS
(195,000 years ago) Modern humans, *Homo sapiens* ("thinking man"), evolve in Africa. »pp8–9

THE FIRST MIGRATION
(100,000 years ago) The first modern humans leave Africa towards the Middle East, but do not survive long. »pp8–9

CAVE ART (40,000 years ago)
The earliest known paintings are made in Spain, France, and Australia. »pp12–13

Cave art of fish from Ubirr, Australia

GLASS (3500 BCE)
People in Mesopotamia (modern-day Iraq) make the first glass. »pp46–47

MEGALITHIC EUROPE
(5000–2000 BCE) Now settled, people build huge stone temples, tombs, and ceremonial sites. »pp16–17

ICE AGE (20,000 years ago)
The most recent of Earth's ice ages reaches its peak. »pp10–11

CITY LIVING (4500 BCE)
The world's first cities are established, in Mesopotamia. »pp18–19

NEOLITHIC REVOLUTION
(9000 BCE) People begin to settle in places and start to farm, leading to a change also known as the Agricultural Revolution. »pp14–15

EARLY MUSIC (40,000 years ago)
The earliest known musical instruments – flutes crafted from animal bones – are made in what is now Germany. »pp46–47

COINS (610 BCE)
The first coins are made in the kingdom of Lydia (in modern-day Turkey). »pp46–47

EXILE FROM ISRAEL
(597–539 BCE) The Babylonian king, Nebuchadnezzar, exiles the Jews from the kingdom of Judah to Babylon. »pp40–41

ALEXANDER THE GREAT
(334–323 BCE) Alexander III of Macedonia expands his Greek empire through Asia and northern Africa. »pp32–33

Temple of Artemis
The remains of this 2,000-year-old Greek temple to Artemis, the goddess of hunting, stand in modern-day Selçuk, Turkey.

HANGING GARDENS OF BABYLON (600 BCE)
The spectacular stepped gardens in Babylonia are one of the wonders of the ancient world. »pp44–45

PERSIAN EMPIRE
(550–330 BCE) Cyrus the Great establishes an Asian empire centred in Persia (modern-day Iran). »pp30–31

DEATH OF JESUS CHRIST
(c.30 CE) After Jesus is killed by the Romans, his followers call him Christ and establish the Christian religion. »pp40–41

GREAT WALL OF CHINA
(221 BCE) Qin Shi Huangdi unites the states of China and joins their small defensive walls into one Great Wall. »pp34–35

ROMAN EMPIRE (27 BCE)
Octavian declares himself "Emperor Augustus" and the Roman Republic becomes an empire. »pp38–39

PUNIC WARS (264–146 BCE)
The Roman Republic expands after destroying the powerful state of Carthage during the Punic Wars. »pp36–37

ONE YEAR, THE FIRST HUMANS APPEAR AT 11.35PM ON 31 DECEMBER!

Lagar Velho, Portugal
The 24,000-year-old remains of a child found in this rock shelter have made the cave famous.

Pestera cu Oase, Romania
These caves yielded some of the oldest remains of *Homo sapiens* in Europe, at 30,000–34,000 years old. At this time, another human species, called Neanderthals, greatly outnumbered *Homo sapiens*.

Tianyuan Cave, China
The oldest *Homo sapiens* remains discovered in eastern Asia are 37 bone fragments found in this cave. They belonged to a single person and are dated to 37,000–42,000 years old.

Mugharet es-Skhul and Qafzeh, Israel
Human remains that are 90,000–110,000 years old have been found here. They suggest that a first wave of *Homo sapiens* migration happened earlier than 100,000 years ago.

EUROPE

40,000 years ago

ASIA

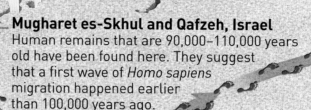

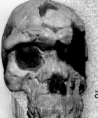

Homo sapiens skull, Herto

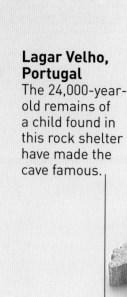

MIDDLE EAST

125,000 years ago

60,000 years ago

40,000 years ago

50,000 years ago

Herto, Ethiopia
The 160,000-year-old skulls found here show some features of human ancestors, such as heavy, or "robust", face bones.

195,000 years ago

Niah Caves, Malaysia
Human remains including a skull dating to 40,000 years ago, have been found here

Omo Kibish, Ethiopia
The human bones discovered here in 1967–74 have been dated to 195,000 years old, making them the earliest known in the world.

AFRICA

Stone tool, Klasies River

Fa Hien Cave, Sri Lanka
Bones from this cave show that humans had arrived in Sri Lanka around 33,000 years ago.

1,500 years ago

Malakunanja, Australia
Archaeologists have discovered that humans were living in the protection of this rock shelter 40,000 years ago.

50,000 years ago

Bone tools, Lake Mungo

AUSTRALASIA

120,000 years ago

Blombos Cave, South Africa
This cave contains engraved objects, shell beads, and fine tools of stone and bone, all up to 100,000 years old.

Lake Mungo, Australia
The oldest human remains found in Australia (around 40,000 years old) were discovered here in 1974.

The story told by DNA
Scientists study the DNA of modern people from around the world to show how closely related they are. This data can shed light on how their remote ancestors might have spread across the globe.

Klasies River, South Africa
The caves at this site have revealed that humans were living here 125,000 years ago.

DNA is a complex molecule shaped like a spiral ladder. The order of chemicals along the rungs of the ladder forms the unique DNA code of every human.

KEY

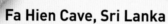 Spread of humans

 Date of first arrival, based on both archaeological and DNA evidence

● Site of major archaeological finds

65,000 years ago

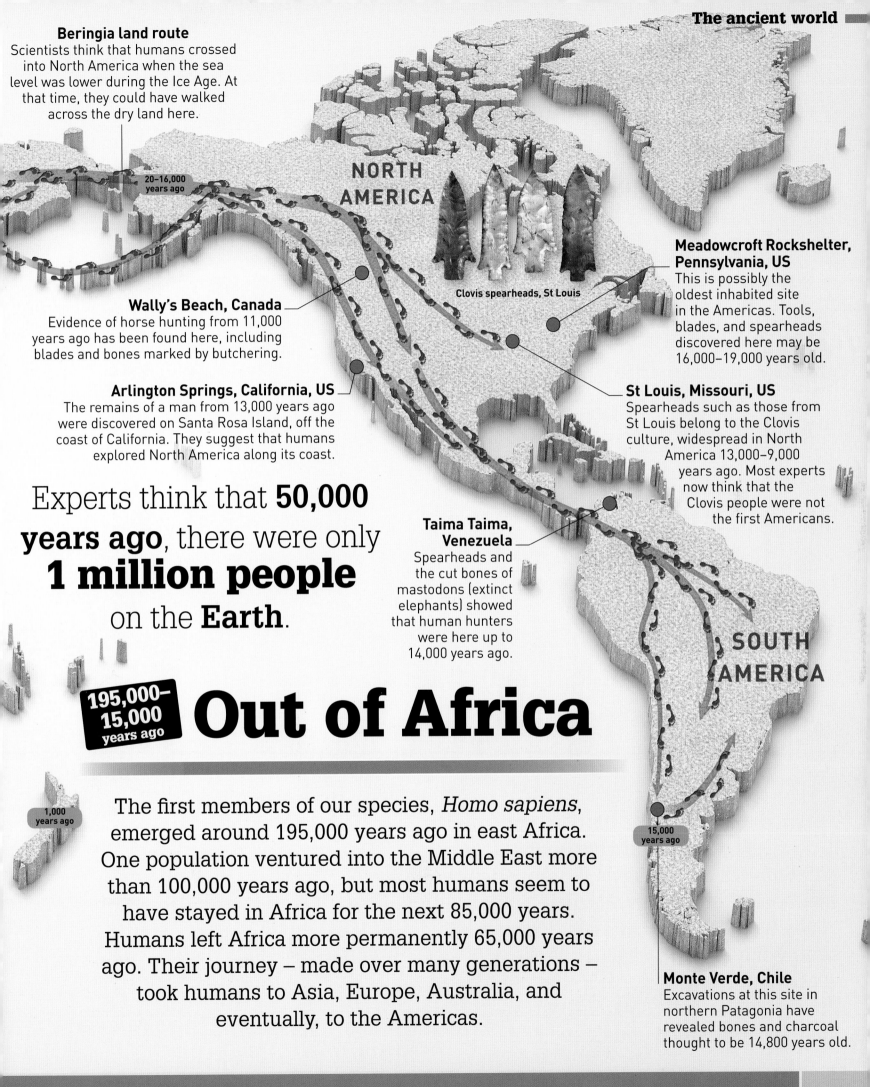

Beringia land route
Scientists think that humans crossed into North America when the sea level was lower during the Ice Age. At that time, they could have walked across the dry land here.

20–16,000 years ago

NORTH AMERICA

Clovis spearheads, St Louis

Wally's Beach, Canada
Evidence of horse hunting from 11,000 years ago has been found here, including blades and bones marked by butchering.

Arlington Springs, California, US
The remains of a man from 13,000 years ago were discovered on Santa Rosa Island, off the coast of California. They suggest that humans explored North America along its coast.

Meadowcroft Rockshelter, Pennsylvania, US
This is possibly the oldest inhabited site in the Americas. Tools, blades, and spearheads discovered here may be 16,000–19,000 years old.

St Louis, Missouri, US
Spearheads such as those from St Louis belong to the Clovis culture, widespread in North America 13,000–9,000 years ago. Most experts now think that the Clovis people were not the first Americans.

Experts think that **50,000 years ago**, there were only **1 million people** on the **Earth**.

Taima Taima, Venezuela
Spearheads and the cut bones of mastodons (extinct elephants) showed that human hunters were here up to 14,000 years ago.

SOUTH AMERICA

195,000– 15,000 years ago **Out of Africa**

1,000 years ago

15,000 years ago

The first members of our species, *Homo sapiens*, emerged around 195,000 years ago in east Africa. One population ventured into the Middle East more than 100,000 years ago, but most humans seem to have stayed in Africa for the next 85,000 years. Humans left Africa more permanently 65,000 years ago. Their journey – made over many generations – took humans to Asia, Europe, Australia, and eventually, to the Americas.

Monte Verde, Chile
Excavations at this site in northern Patagonia have revealed bones and charcoal thought to be 14,800 years old.

SPECIES, SUCH AS NEANDERTHALS AND HOMO ERECTUS, DIED OUT.

Laurentide Ice Sheet
This ice sheet was 3.2 km (2 miles) thick at its centre. It scraped huge hollows as it crept over the land. When it melted, the hollows became the Great Lakes.

Greenland Ice Sheet

Short-faced bear

Bering Land Bridge

Laurentide Ice Sheet

Cordilleran ice sheet

NORTH AMERICA

Cordilleran Ice Sheet
The Rocky Mountains region of Canada was covered by a giant glacier called the Cordilleran Ice Sheet.

Smilodon

American mastodon

British Isles
The British Isles were joined to the rest of Europe, and northern England, Wales, and all of Scotland were covered by ice.

Bridge to Europe
Lower sea levels meant that Europe and Africa were joined.

When the **Ice Age** was **at its height**, ice covered **one-third** of the Earth's surface.

Glyptodon

SOUTH AMERICA

Giant ground sloth

Patagonian Ice Sheet

Sea ice
During the Ice Age, sea ice extended further from the Antarctic continent than it does today. However, sea ice is never more than a few metres thick, so it is insignificant compared to the great sheets of ice covering the land.

20,000 years ago The Ice Age

Ice ages happen when global temperatures drop a few degrees and ice builds up in great sheets. Since water is trapped in the ice sheets, the oceans shrink, turning areas of sea bed into land. The last ice age, called simply the Ice Age, reached its peak 20,000 years ago. After this, the ice began to melt. Today, the largest remaining ice sheets are over Antarctica and Greenland.

ANTARCTICA

THE WORLD'S SEA LEVELS FELL SOME 120 M (390 FT) DURING THE ICE

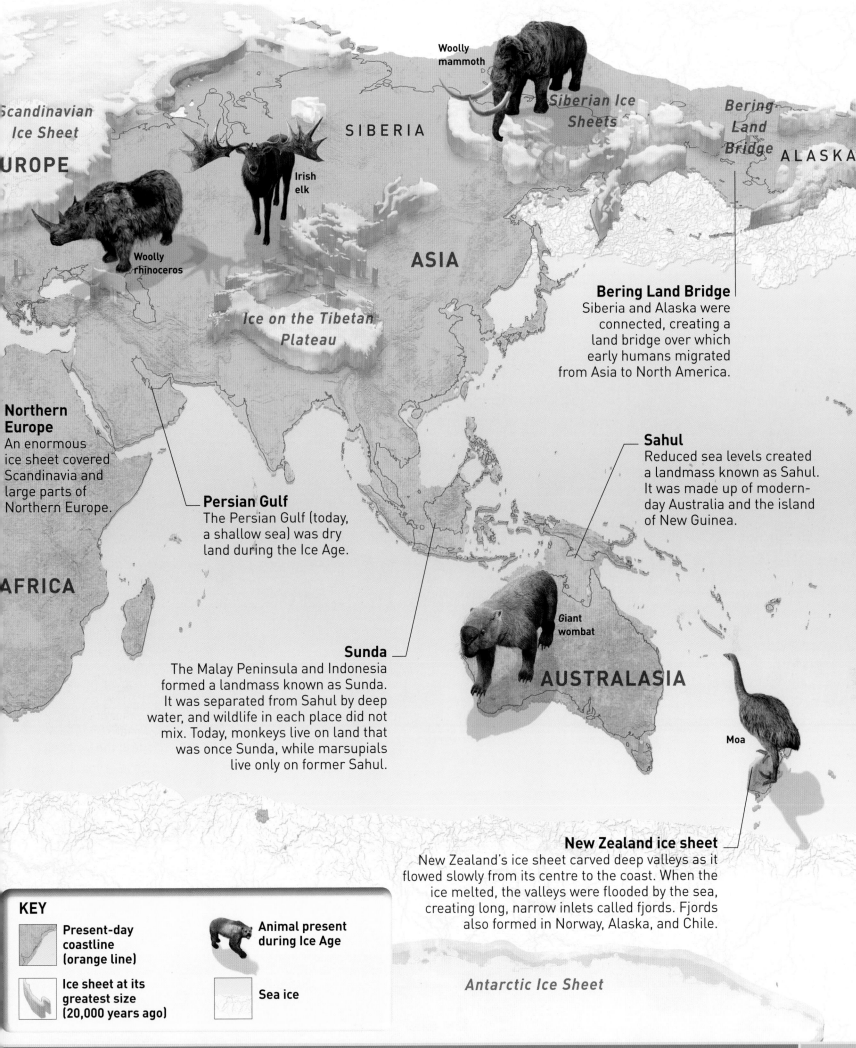

Woolly
mammoth

*Siberian Ice
Sheets*

*Bering
Land
Bridge*

*Scandinavian
Ice Sheet*

EUROPE

SIBERIA

ALASKA

Irish
elk

Woolly
rhinoceros

ASIA

*Ice on the Tibetan
Plateau*

Bering Land Bridge
Siberia and Alaska were
connected, creating a
land bridge over which
early humans migrated
from Asia to North America.

Northern
Europe
An enormous
ice sheet covered
Scandinavia and
large parts of
Northern Europe.

Sahul
Reduced sea levels created
a landmass known as Sahul.
It was made up of modern-
day Australia and the island
of New Guinea.

Persian Gulf
The Persian Gulf (today,
a shallow sea) was dry
land during the Ice Age.

AFRICA

Giant
wombat

Sunda
The Malay Peninsula and Indonesia
formed a landmass known as Sunda.
It was separated from Sahul by deep
water, and wildlife in each place did not
mix. Today, monkeys live on land that
was once Sunda, while marsupials
live only on former Sahul.

AUSTRALASIA

Moa

New Zealand ice sheet
New Zealand's ice sheet carved deep valleys as it
flowed slowly from its centre to the coast. When the
ice melted, the valleys were flooded by the sea,
creating long, narrow inlets called fjords. Fjords
also formed in Norway, Alaska, and Chile.

KEY
Present-day
coastline
(orange line)

Animal present
during Ice Age

Ice sheet at its
greatest size
(20,000 years ago)

Sea ice

Antarctic Ice Sheet

AGE, UNCOVERING PARTS OF THE SEA BED, WHICH BECAME DRY LAND.

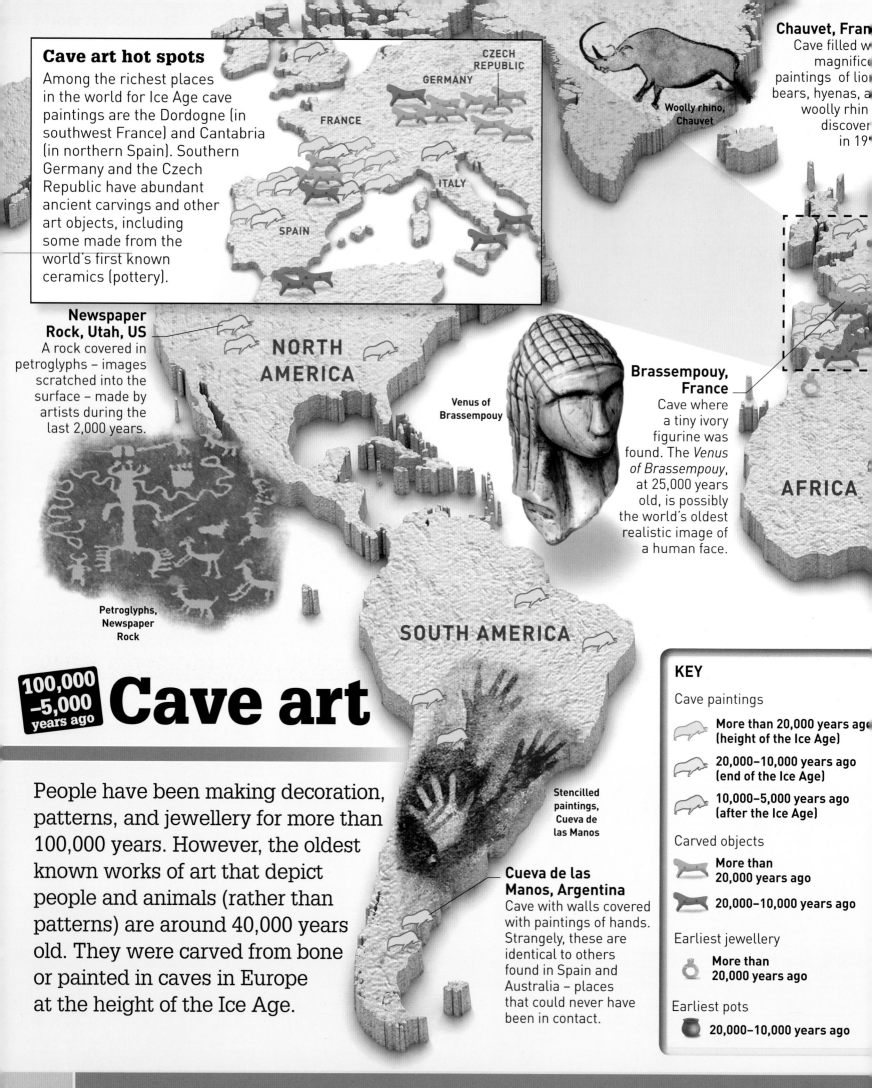

Cave art hot spots

Among the richest places in the world for Ice Age cave paintings are the Dordogne (in southwest France) and Cantabria (in northern Spain). Southern Germany and the Czech Republic have abundant ancient carvings and other art objects, including some made from the world's first known ceramics (pottery).

GERMANY

CZECH REPUBLIC

FRANCE

ITALY

SPAIN

Chauvet, Fran
Cave filled w
magnifice
paintings of lio
bears, hyenas, a
woolly rhin
discover
in 19

Woolly rhino, Chauvet

Newspaper Rock, Utah, US
A rock covered in petroglyphs – images scratched into the surface – made by artists during the last 2,000 years.

NORTH AMERICA

Petroglyphs, Newspaper Rock

Venus of Brassempouy

Brassempouy, France
Cave where a tiny ivory figurine was found. The *Venus of Brassempouy*, at 25,000 years old, is possibly the world's oldest realistic image of a human face.

AFRICA

SOUTH AMERICA

100,000 –5,000 years ago

Cave art

People have been making decoration, patterns, and jewellery for more than 100,000 years. However, the oldest known works of art that depict people and animals (rather than patterns) are around 40,000 years old. They were carved from bone or painted in caves in Europe at the height of the Ice Age.

Stencilled paintings, Cueva de las Manos

Cueva de las Manos, Argentina
Cave with walls covered with paintings of hands. Strangely, these are identical to others found in Spain and Australia – places that could never have been in contact.

KEY

Cave paintings

More than 20,000 years ago (height of the Ice Age)

20,000–10,000 years ago (end of the Ice Age)

10,000–5,000 years ago (after the Ice Age)

Carved objects

More than 20,000 years ago

20,000–10,000 years ago

Earliest jewellery

More than 20,000 years ago

Earliest pots

20,000–10,000 years ago

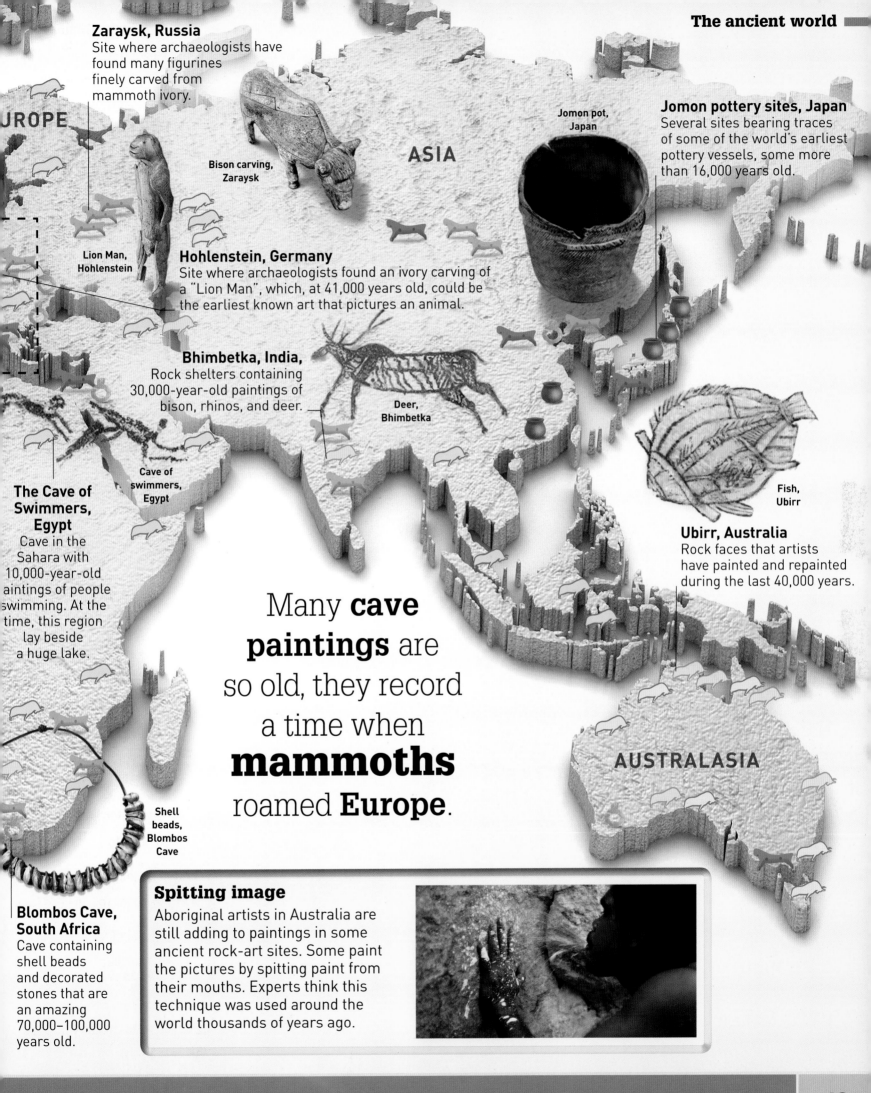

Zaraysk, Russia
Site where archaeologists have found many figurines finely carved from mammoth ivory.

Bison carving, Zaraysk

EUROPE

ASIA

Jomon pot, Japan

Jomon pottery sites, Japan
Several sites bearing traces of some of the world's earliest pottery vessels, some more than 16,000 years old.

Lion Man, Hohlenstein

Hohlenstein, Germany
Site where archaeologists found an ivory carving of a "Lion Man", which, at 41,000 years old, could be the earliest known art that pictures an animal.

Bhimbetka, India,
Rock shelters containing 30,000-year-old paintings of bison, rhinos, and deer.

Deer, Bhimbetka

The Cave of Swimmers, Egypt
Cave in the Sahara with 10,000-year-old paintings of people swimming. At the time, this region lay beside a huge lake.

Cave of swimmers, Egypt

Fish, Ubirr

Ubirr, Australia
Rock faces that artists have painted and repainted during the last 40,000 years.

Many **cave paintings** are so old, they record a time when **mammoths** roamed **Europe**.

AUSTRALASIA

Shell beads, Blombos Cave

Blombos Cave, South Africa
Cave containing shell beads and decorated stones that are an amazing 70,000–100,000 years old.

Spitting image
Aboriginal artists in Australia are still adding to paintings in some ancient rock-art sites. Some paint the pictures by spitting paint from their mouths. Experts think this technique was used around the world thousands of years ago.

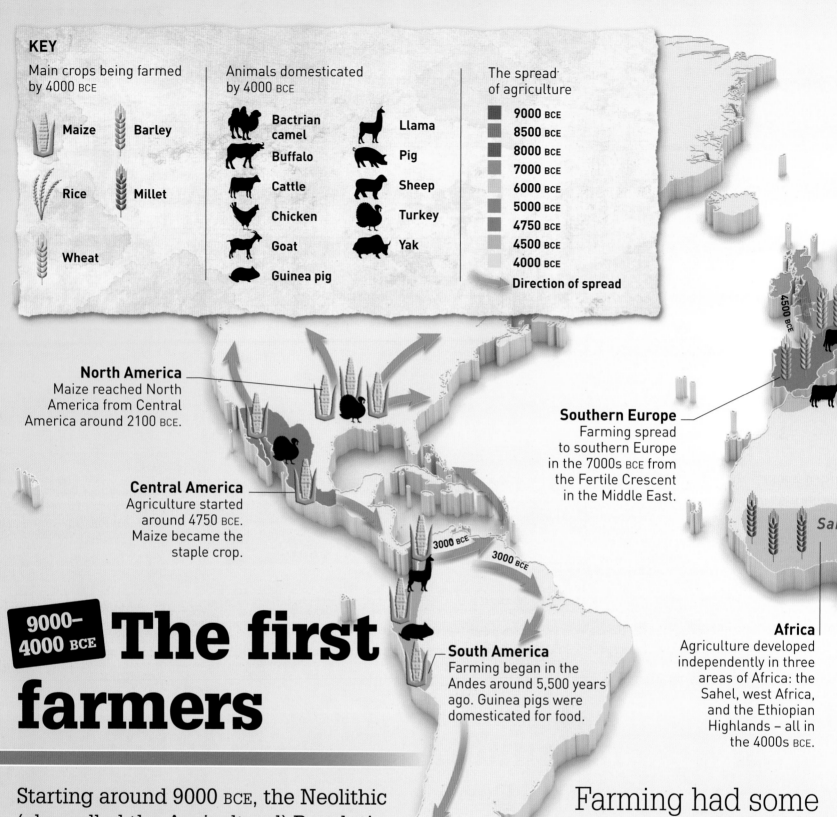

KEY

Main crops being farmed by 4000 BCE

Maize   Barley

Rice   Millet

Wheat

Animals domesticated by 4000 BCE

Bactrian camel   Llama

Buffalo   Pig

Cattle   Sheep

Chicken   Turkey

Goat   Yak

Guinea pig

The spread of agriculture

- 9000 BCE
- 8500 BCE
- 8000 BCE
- 7000 BCE
- 6000 BCE
- 5000 BCE
- 4750 BCE
- 4500 BCE
- 4000 BCE

→ Direction of spread

North America
Maize reached North America from Central America around 2100 BCE.

Central America
Agriculture started around 4750 BCE. Maize became the staple crop.

Southern Europe
Farming spread to southern Europe in the 7000s BCE from the Fertile Crescent in the Middle East.

3000 BCE

3000 BCE

South America
Farming began in the Andes around 5,500 years ago. Guinea pigs were domesticated for food.

Africa
Agriculture developed independently in three areas of Africa: the Sahel, west Africa, and the Ethiopian Highlands – all in the 4000s BCE.

Sahel

4500 BCE

9000–4000 BCE The first farmers

Starting around 9000 BCE, the Neolithic (also called the Agricultural) Revolution transformed the way humans lived. People grew crops and kept animals for the first time, produced greater amounts of food, and started to live in permanent farming villages. In the end, farming led to people living in towns and cities.

Farming had some drawbacks. It led to an **increase** in **disease**. Smallpox, influenza, and measles all spread from **animals** to **humans**.

Domestication

All crops and farm animals are descended from wild plants and animals, which people have changed through selective breeding over many generations. People would sow only the seeds of plants that produced the largest grains and breed only from animals that were both strong and tame. This process is called "domestication".

Early cattle might have looked like this ancient breed, the heck cow.

Northern China

Agriculture developed independently in northern China around 8000 BCE.

Northern Europe

Farming began in northern Europe around 4500 BCE.

The Middle East

The Neolithic Revolution started in an area known as the Fertile Crescent around 9000 BCE.

Central Asia

The Bactrian camel was first domesticated (tamed) in central Asia around 2500 BCE.

5000 BCE

Ethiopian Highlands

East Asia

Domesticated rice was grown as early as 8500 BCE in China's Yangtze Valley.

Indus Valley

Agriculture was well established in the Indus Valley by around 6000 BCE.

1000 BCE

2500 BCE

1000 BCE

1000 BCE

The Fertile Crescent

Farming is thought to have started around 9000 BCE in an arc-shaped area of land known as the Fertile Crescent. Stretching from the Persian Gulf in the east to Egypt in the west, the soil in the region was watered by several important rivers, including the Tigris, the Euphrates, and the Nile.

KEY

The Fertile Crescent

Caspian Sea

Anatolia

Mesopotamia

Mediterranean Sea

River Jordan

River Euphrates

River Tigris

Egypt

Sinai

River Nile

Red Sea

Arabian Desert

Persian Gulf

GRASSES, INCLUDING PRIMITIVE VARIETIES OF BARLEY AND WHEAT.

Newgrange, Ireland
Burial chamber at the end of a narrow passage of giant stone slabs, built 5,200 years ago and buried in an earth mound.

Stoplesteinan

Ales Stones

Goseck Circle, Germany
Circular enclosure built in 4800 BCE as a Sun observatory. Its gates align with sunrise and sunset on the summer and winter solstice (the longest and shortest days of the year).

Vera Island

EUROPE

Grand Menhir d'Er Grah

Stonehenge, England
The world's most famous stone circle, built from 3100 to 1600 BCE. No one knows exactly what it was used for.

Bulls of Guisando

Hot Stones

Antequera

Giants' Graves

Almendres Cromlech

Mzoura

Göbleki Tepe, Turk
Ancient ruins in Turk that may be remains the world's oldest ter dating back to 9000 B

Atlit Yam

Temples of Malta
11 complex and spectacular temples built as long ago as 3000 BCE on the islands of Malta and Gozo.

Nabta Playa

Stone circles of Senegambia (The Gambia and Senegal)
93 stone circles and many burial mounds in a wide area of sacred land along the Gambia River.

AFRICA

Tiya

Bouar

9000 BCE –1300 CE Megaliths

During the megalithic ("giant stone") period, people in many places built structures (megaliths) from huge stone blocks. These structures included tombs, temples, ceremonial sites, and observatories – used to measure the position of the Sun, Moon, and stars. The megalithic period in Europe started 7,000 years ago, but later megalithic traditions began in east Asia 3,000 years ago, and in west Africa 1,000 years ago.

MANY OF THE STONES USED TO BUILD STONEHENGE WERE TRANSPORTED

KEY
This map shows the global pattern of megaliths. Megalithic cultures developed where people settled in communities that were big enough to organize grand building projects.

■ Areas of megalithic culture
● Major megalithic monuments
Ⅱ Other important megalithic sites

Ganghwa Dolmens, South Korea
More than 120 dolmens (tombs) in the mountains of the island of Ganghwa. Built in 1000–800 BCE, these are some of the oldest dolmens in Korea.

Deer stones, Mongolia
More than 550 granite stones carved with pictures of deer, dating to 1000 BCE.

ASIA

Burzahom

Plain of Jars, Laos
Several hundred huge stone jars, dating from 500 BCE to 200 CE, spread over more than 90 separate sites.

Mozu Kofungun

Furuichi Kofungun

Kochang

Hwasun

Birbir

Chokahatu

Chang Kuang

Ishibutai Kofun, Japan
Largest megalithic tomb in Japan, built in the Asuka Period, 592–710 CE.

Dolmens of Kerala, India
Mushroom-shaped burial monuments dating from 300 BCE to 200 CE.

Marayoor

Ibbankatuwa

Dong Nai

Nias

Megaliths in the Americas
The Americas are home to megaliths, too, including those in eastern Canada, Central America, Peru, and Bolivia. Some are up to 3,400 years old. The giant stone blocks (right) of the Pumapunku temple complex in Bolivia date to around 600 CE.

Gunung Padang

Sumba

Lore Lindu, Indonesia
Over 400 megaliths, some carved in the shape of humans. They date from 3000 BCE to 1300 CE.

FROM 240 KM (150 MILES) AWAY. THE LARGEST WEIGH OVER 40 TONNES.

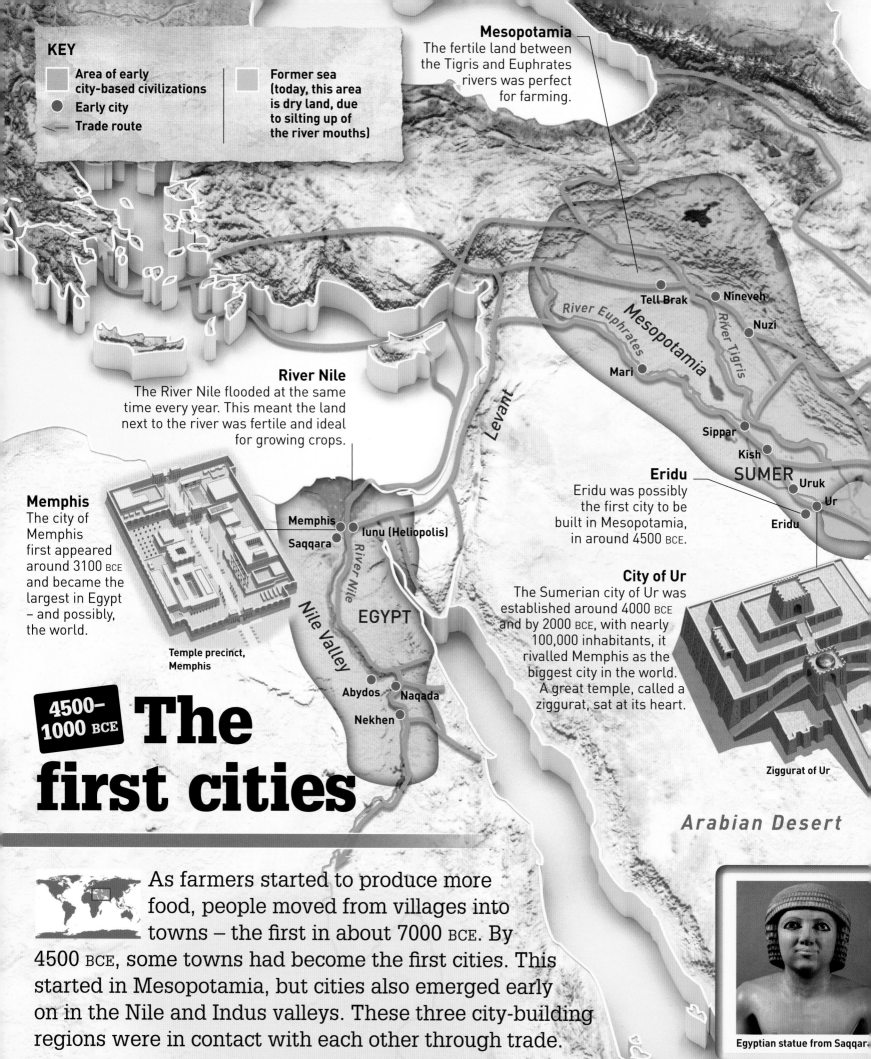

KEY

- ☐ Area of early city-based civilizations
- ● Early city
- — Trade route
- ☐ Former sea (today, this area is dry land, due to silting up of the river mouths)

Mesopotamia
The fertile land between the Tigris and Euphrates rivers was perfect for farming.

River Nile
The River Nile flooded at the same time every year. This meant the land next to the river was fertile and ideal for growing crops.

Memphis
The city of Memphis first appeared around 3100 BCE and became the largest in Egypt – and possibly, the world.

Temple precinct, Memphis

Eridu
Eridu was possibly the first city to be built in Mesopotamia, in around 4500 BCE.

City of Ur
The Sumerian city of Ur was established around 4000 BCE and by 2000 BCE, with nearly 100,000 inhabitants, it rivalled Memphis as the biggest city in the world. A great temple, called a ziggurat, sat at its heart.

Ziggurat of Ur

Tell Brak · Nineveh
River Euphrates · Mesopotamia · River Tigris · Nuzi
Mari
Levant
Sippar
Kish · SUMER · Uruk
Ur
Eridu

Memphis · Iunu (Heliopolis)
Saqqara
River Nile
Nile Valley · EGYPT
Abydos · Naqada
Nekhen

Arabian Desert

4500–1000 BCE The first cities

As farmers started to produce more food, people moved from villages into towns – the first in about 7000 BCE. By 4500 BCE, some towns had become the first cities. This started in Mesopotamia, but cities also emerged early on in the Nile and Indus valleys. These three city-building regions were in contact with each other through trade.

Egyptian statue from Saqqara

Early cities worldwide

In time, cities started to spring up independently in other parts of the world. In South America, the city of Caral, and other cities of Peru's Norte Chico civilization, appeared in 2600–2000 BCE; in Asia, around 1800 BCE, city-based kingdoms grew around China's Yellow River; and in Mesoamerica, the Olmec civilization had taken root by 1000 BCE.

NORTH AMERICA

Olmec civilization

Mesoamerica

Norte Chico civilization

Peru

SOUTH AMERICA

EUROPE

ASIA

Yellow River Valley

Chinese civilization

AFRICA

KEY

Sites of Chinese and American city-based civilizations, 3000–1000 BCE

Harappa street layout

Zagros Mountains

Irrigation (controlling the flow of water to grow crops) was invented in the Zagros Mountains. The idea soon spread to Mesopotamia and Egypt and became a vital part of the city-based civilizations there.

Zagros Mountains

River Indus

The mighty River Indus gave rise to the first cities in Asia.

Rakhigarhi

Harappa

River Indus

Indus Valley

Mohenjo-Daro

Mohenjo-Daro existed from around 2500 BCE and had a population of more than 50,000. As in Harappa, every house had both running water and plumbing to carry away waste.

Mohenjo-Daro

Chanhu-Daro

Harappa

At its height in 2500–1900 BCE, Harappa had a population of up to 40,000 people. Like other Indus cities, it was laid out on a precise grid pattern of streets.

Dholavira

Lothal

Rojadi

City walls, built for **defence**, were common in **Mesopotamia** by 2900 BCE.

le Valley

e cities of the Nile Valley came part of the Old ngdom of Egypt. Egyptians veloped medicine, maths, tronomy, and a 365-day-a-r calendar. Their number stem was based on 10s, t as ours is today.

Sumerian statue from Mari

Mesopotamia

In Mesopotamia, the earliest cities were built in Sumer. Sumerians developed the world's first writing, used accurate calendars, and were the first people to create laws to govern many people living together.

Priest-king from Mohenjo-Daro

Indus Valley

The Indus Valley civilization appeared around 2600 BCE, but by 1700 BCE, most cities had been mysteriously abandoned. The people left some artefacts, such as this statue, which is known as the "priest-king".

IN MESOPOTAMIA HAD A POPULATION OF AROUND 80,000 PEOPLE.

The first alphabet

Alphabets, used today to write many languages, were originally an idea of people (below) living in Canaan and Egypt's Sinai Desert around 1800 BCE. They adapted Egyptian hieroglyphs and Sumerian cuneiform writing to stand for the sounds in their language, inventing the Proto-Canaanite script. The alphabet idea was passed on to the Phoenicians, then the Greeks, and then the Romans. Each time, people changed slightly the shape and order of the symbols.

Germanic runes, 150 CE

Runes were the writing symbols used in Germany and Scandinavia. They were also called *futhark*, after the sounds of the first six symbols in the runic alphabet (above).

EUROPE

Olmec glyphs, 900 BCE

Writing in North America may have begun with the Olmecs. Their writing was first found when road builders discovered the Cascajal Block in the 1990s. It was covered in Olmec picture symbols, or glyphs.

NORTH AMERICA

AFRICA

Quipu knots, 650 CE

People used this method of record keeping, also known as "talking knots", in the Inca Empire and older civilizations in ancient Peru. Information was coded by the colour and pattern of knots in threads of llama or alpaca wool.

3400 BCE –650 CE The origins of writing

SOUTH AMERICA

People began recording things by writing them down more than 5,000 years ago, in Sumer (in modern Iraq), and Egypt. Later, in China and the Americas, other groups of people invented totally different systems of writing.

In **Chinese legend**, the day the first writing symbols were born marked the **second beginning** of the world

Phaistos disc script, 1800 BCE
is disc from Crete,
ece, carries a unique
oglyphic script that
not been decoded.

Phoenician alphabet, 1100 BCE
Traders of the eastern Mediterranean, called
the Phoenicians, had their own alphabet,
which they passed on to the Greeks.

Indus Valley script, 2600 BCE
Experts have not yet cracked the
code of these mysterious symbols,
written by people of the long-lost
Indus Valley civilization.

KEY
Colours show
the date by which
writing had arrived.

- **3000 BCE**
- **2000 BCE**
- **1250 BCE**
- **500 BCE**
- **500 CE**
- ● **Location of a key form of writing**

ASIA

Canaan

Sinai Desert

Chinese Shang Dynasty oracle bone script, 1500 BCE
The earliest recognizable
Chinese writing was carved
on bones and turtle shells
by oracles (fortune tellers).

Indian Brahmi script, 500 BCE
Brahmi appeared on announcements
of the emperor Ashoka (left, from the
200s BCE) throughout India. Its origins
are unknown, but it is the ancestor of
dozens of writing systems in India
and southeast Asia.

Sumerian pictographs, 3400 BCE
Merchants in Sumer (southern
Mesopotamia) developed the earliest
known writing. They recorded quantities
of goods by scratching pictographs
(picture symbols, above) on clay tablets.
Over centuries, the symbols evolved into
simple "cuneiform" (wedge-shaped)
marks pressed into the clay.

AUSTRALASIA

Ethiopic script, 300s CE
When writing arrived in Ethiopia,
scribes adapted it to write the Geʿez
language used in church. People
now write modern Ethiopian
languages with this script.

The Rosetta Stone
Egyptian hieroglyphs might be
meaningless to us if it weren't
for the Rosetta Stone. It bears
an inscription in three scripts
– hieroglyphics, demotic (another
form of Egyptian writing), and
Ancient Greek. Since experts
could read the Greek, the stone
provided the key to breaking
the code of the hieroglyphs.

Egyptian hieroglyphs, 3100 BCE
A unique type of picture writing called
hieroglyphics developed in Egypt.
Some of the pictures, or hieroglyphs,
stood for sounds, but others acted
as words, or parts of words.

Rosetta Stone
Stone slab, carved with three different scripts, which provided the key to deciphering hieroglyphs in the 19th century.

Bastet
Cat goddess who represented the power of the Sun to ripen crops. People worshipped statues of her at Bubastis.

Karnak Temple
Largest temple complex in Egypt, dating from the Middle Kingdom.

Sinai

Colossus of Memnon
One of two great statues of Pharaoh Amenhotep III, built about 1350 BCE.

Great Pyramid
One of the Seven Wonders of the World, this is the largest and oldest pyramid at Giza.

Lower Egypt

Tanis
Avans
Bubastis
Rosetta
Heliopolis
Giza
Memphis
Saqqara

Crocodilopolis

Nefertiti
Queen of Egypt in 1353–36 BCE, when her husband Akhenaten moved the capital to Amarna. Nefertiti is famous for a beautiful sculpture of her, now in a museum in Berlin.

Upper Egypt

Hermopolis
Amarna
Thebes

Sphinx
Great statue of a lion with a human head, built 4,500 years ago.

Sobek
In Crocodilopolis, people prayed to statues like this, which shows Sobek, the Crocodile god of rivers and lakes.

Valley of the Kings
Burial ground of pharaohs of the New Kingdom. Tutankhamun's tomb was found, untouched, containing the golden mask of his mummy, in 1922.

Thoth
Baboon god of wisdom whose cult centre was at the ancient city of Hermopolis, where people prayed to statues like this.

Narmer Palette
Decorated stone that depicts the victories of King Narmer, th pharaoh who firs united Egypt

"If anyone would know **how great I am**, let him surpass one of my works."

Pharaoh Ramesses II, inscription in his memorial temple, the Ramesseum, 13th century BCE

3100–30 BCE Land of the pharaohs

Egypt was a narrow strip of fertile land along the River Nile, surrounded by desert. It was in the Nile Valley that the Egyptians built their immense pyramids, colossal temples, and secret tombs, containing mummies of thei dead, cut deep into hillsides. Pharaohs were the rulers of Egypt for more than 3,000 years, from around 3100 BCE until the country became a province of Rome in 30 BCE.

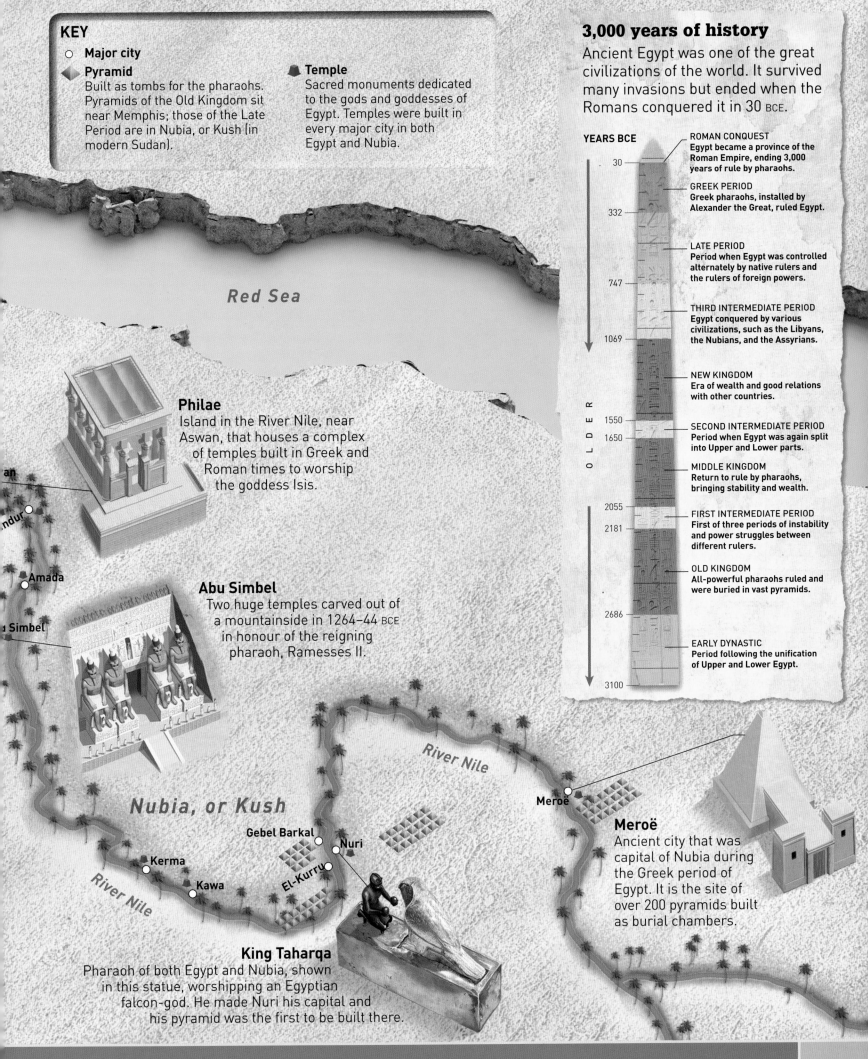

KEY

○ **Major city**

◆ **Pyramid**
Built as tombs for the pharaohs. Pyramids of the Old Kingdom sit near Memphis; those of the Late Period are in Nubia, or Kush (in modern Sudan).

🔺 **Temple**
Sacred monuments dedicated to the gods and goddesses of Egypt. Temples were built in every major city in both Egypt and Nubia.

3,000 years of history

Ancient Egypt was one of the great civilizations of the world. It survived many invasions but ended when the Romans conquered it in 30 BCE.

YEARS BCE

30 — ROMAN CONQUEST
Egypt became a province of the Roman Empire, ending 3,000 years of rule by pharaohs.

332 — GREEK PERIOD
Greek pharaohs, installed by Alexander the Great, ruled Egypt.

— LATE PERIOD
Period when Egypt was controlled alternately by native rulers and the rulers of foreign powers.

747 —

1069 — THIRD INTERMEDIATE PERIOD
Egypt conquered by various civilizations, such as the Libyans, the Nubians, and the Assyrians.

— NEW KINGDOM
Era of wealth and good relations with other countries.

1550 —
1650 — SECOND INTERMEDIATE PERIOD
Period when Egypt was again split into Upper and Lower parts.

— MIDDLE KINGDOM
Return to rule by pharaohs, bringing stability and wealth.

2055 —
2181 — FIRST INTERMEDIATE PERIOD
First of three periods of instability and power struggles between different rulers.

— OLD KINGDOM
All-powerful pharaohs ruled and were buried in vast pyramids.

2686 —

— EARLY DYNASTIC
Period following the unification of Upper and Lower Egypt.

3100 —

OLDER

Red Sea

Philae
Island in the River Nile, near Aswan, that houses a complex of temples built in Greek and Roman times to worship the goddess Isis.

Amada

Simbel

Abu Simbel
Two huge temples carved out of a mountainside in 1264–44 BCE in honour of the reigning pharaoh, Ramesses II.

River Nile

Nubia, or Kush

Meroë

Meroë
Ancient city that was capital of Nubia during the Greek period of Egypt. It is the site of over 200 pyramids built as burial chambers.

Gebel Barkal
Nuri
Kerma
Kawa
El-Kurru

River Nile

King Taharqa
Pharaoh of both Egypt and Nubia, shown in this statue, worshipping an Egyptian falcon-god. He made Nuri his capital and his pyramid was the first to be built there.

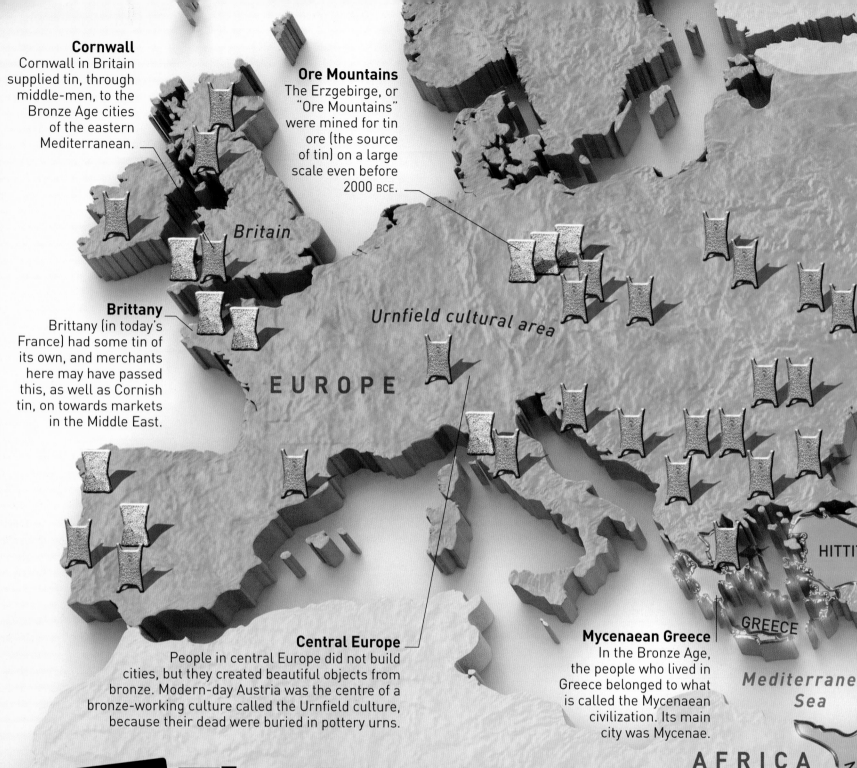

Cornwall
Cornwall in Britain supplied tin, through middle-men, to the Bronze Age cities of the eastern Mediterranean.

Ore Mountains
The Erzgebirge, or "Ore Mountains" were mined for tin ore (the source of tin) on a large scale even before 2000 BCE.

Britain

Urnfield cultural area

Brittany
Brittany (in today's France) had some tin of its own, and merchants here may have passed this, as well as Cornish tin, on towards markets in the Middle East.

E U R O P E

HITTIT

Central Europe
People in central Europe did not build cities, but they created beautiful objects from bronze. Modern-day Austria was the centre of a bronze-working culture called the Urnfield culture, because their dead were buried in pottery urns.

Mycenaean Greece
In the Bronze Age, the people who lived in Greece belonged to what is called the Mycenaean civilization. Its main city was Mycenae.

GREECE

Mediterrane Sea

A F R I C A

NEW K OF EGYPT

3200–1200 BCE The Bronze Age

In around 3200 BCE, people in Egypt and Mesopotamia (now Iraq) first added tin to copper at high temperatures to form a hard-wearing metal called bronze. This new metal could make tools, weapons, armour, and beautiful jewellery. In Mesopotamia and the Middle East, cities and civilizations grew, and bronze working spread widely. The cities' hunger for rare tin reserves increased, and by 1250 BCE, the world's biggest powers needed a long trade network to maintain the tin supply.

IN AROUND 1200 BCE, THE BRONZE AGE POWERS OF EGYPT, GREECE, AND

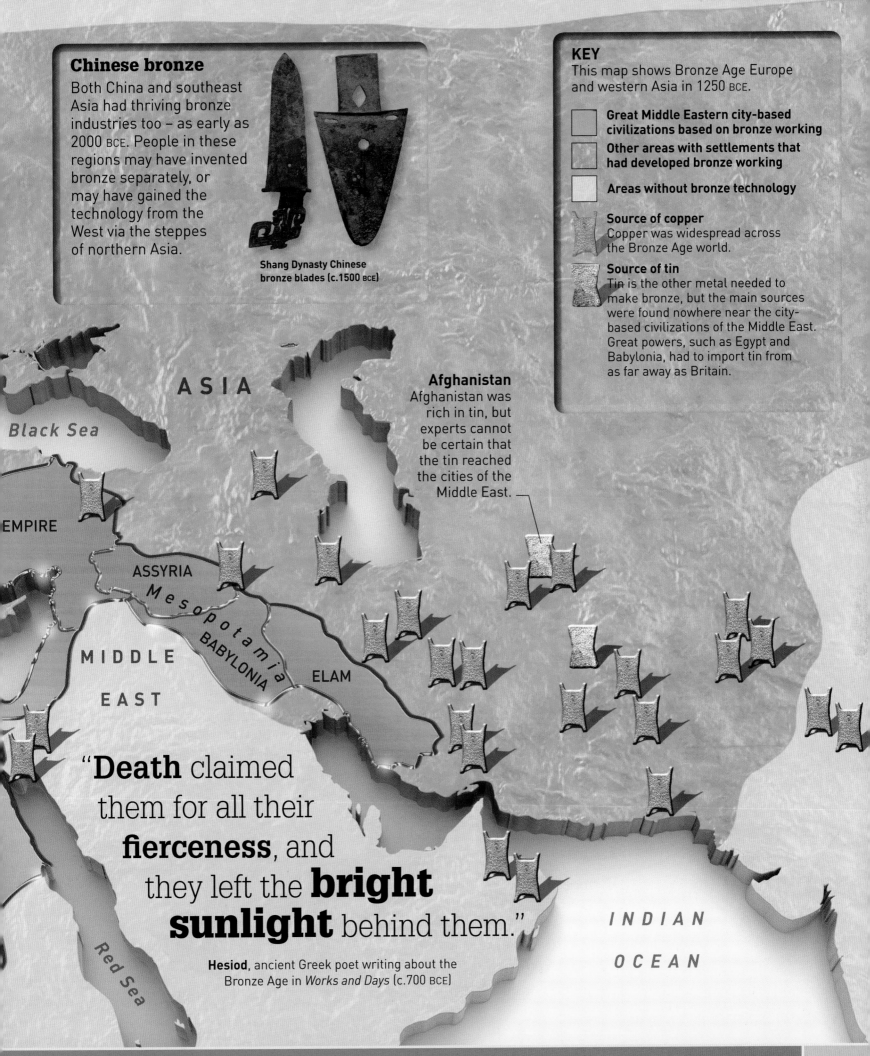

Chinese bronze

Both China and southeast Asia had thriving bronze industries too – as early as 2000 BCE. People in these regions may have invented bronze separately, or may have gained the technology from the West via the steppes of northern Asia.

Shang Dynasty Chinese bronze blades (c.1500 BCE)

KEY

This map shows Bronze Age Europe and western Asia in 1250 BCE.

Great Middle Eastern city-based civilizations based on bronze working

Other areas with settlements that had developed bronze working

Areas without bronze technology

Source of copper
Copper was widespread across the Bronze Age world.

Source of tin
Tin is the other metal needed to make bronze, but the main sources were found nowhere near the city-based civilizations of the Middle East. Great powers, such as Egypt and Babylonia, had to import tin from as far away as Britain.

Afghanistan

Afghanistan was rich in tin, but experts cannot be certain that the tin reached the cities of the Middle East.

ASIA

Black Sea

EMPIRE

ASSYRIA
M e s o p o t a m i a
BABYLONIA
ELAM

MIDDLE
EAST

Red Sea

INDIAN
OCEAN

"**Death** claimed them for all their **fierceness**, and they left the **bright sunlight** behind them."

Hesiod, ancient Greek poet writing about the Bronze Age in *Works and Days* (c.700 BCE)

BABYLONIA ALL COLLAPSED, LEAVING LITTLE RECORD OF WHAT HAPPENED.

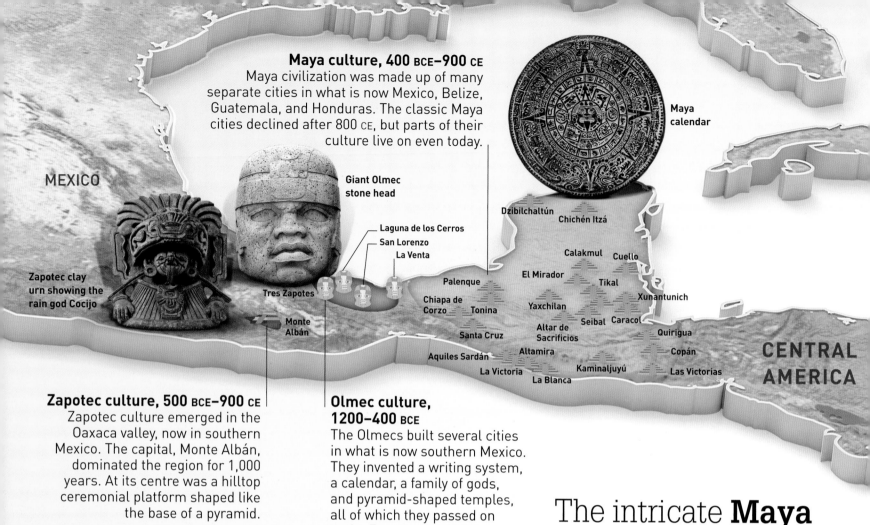

Maya culture, 400 BCE–900 CE
Maya civilization was made up of many separate cities in what is now Mexico, Belize, Guatemala, and Honduras. The classic Maya cities declined after 800 CE, but parts of their culture live on even today.

Maya calendar

MEXICO

Giant Olmec stone head

Laguna de los Cerros
San Lorenzo
La Venta

Tres Zapotes

Zapotec clay urn showing the rain god Cocijo

Monte Albán

Dzibilchaltún
Chichén Itzá
Calakmul
Cuello
El Mirador
Palenque
Tikal
Xunantunich
Chiapa de Corzo
Tonina
Yaxchilan
Seibal
Caracol
Santa Cruz
Altar de Sacrificios
Quirigua
Aquiles Sardán
Altamira
Copán
La Victoria
Kaminaljuyú
Las Victorias
La Blanca

CENTRAL AMERICA

Zapotec culture, 500 BCE–900 CE
Zapotec culture emerged in the Oaxaca valley, now in southern Mexico. The capital, Monte Albán, dominated the region for 1,000 years. At its centre was a hilltop ceremonial platform shaped like the base of a pyramid.

Olmec culture, 1200–400 BCE
The Olmecs built several cities in what is now southern Mexico. They invented a writing system, a calendar, a family of gods, and pyramid-shaped temples, all of which they passed on to the Zapotecs and Maya.

The intricate **Maya calendar** includes the Long Count dating system, which lasts **5,126 years**.

1200 BCE –900 CE Ancient Americas

More than 3,000 years ago, city-based civilizations were developing in two different areas of the Americas. In what is now southern Mexico, the Olmecs became experts in growing maize. They grew wealthy and began to build great ceremonial centres with pyramid temples. At the same time, fishing and farming people in Peru developed a civilization called the Chavín. Their cities, too, were centred on temples in the shape of flat-topped pyramids.

Maya writing
The Maya developed advanced astronomy, maths, and medicine, and a complex writing system. It was made up of 500 or so symbols called glyphs. They were arranged in glyph blocks organized in pairs. You had to read the glyphs in a zigzag pattern down each pair of columns.

WEALTHY MAYA PEOPLE TIED BOARDS TO CHILDREN'S HEADS TO

The Mound Builders

At the same time as the Maya were building their pyramid temples, people in North America were building mysterious monuments – mounds of various shapes and patterns – in the Mississippi and Ohio river valleys. Some were burial mounds, but the reason most were built is still unknown. Together, these peoples are called Mound Builders, but they belonged to several different cultures.

Serpent Mound, Ohio, US – a Hopewell culture monument

KEY
Hopewell and Adena mound sites

Mounds of the Hopewell and Adena cultures, 700 BCE–400 CE

ATLANTIC OCEAN

SOUTH AMERICA

Moche culture, 100–800 CE

The Moche people flourished on the northern desert coast of Peru. They were skilled weavers and goldsmiths, and created pottery in many shapes and designs, sometimes as portraits and often with stirrup spouts.

Moche earring

PACIFIC OCEAN

Chavín tenon head

Nazca culture, 350 BCE–450 CE

The Nazca people of Peru are famous for their painted pottery and the Nazca Lines – incredible carvings in the desert soil of the region. The pictures are so large, they are visible only from an aeroplane, so the artists could never have admired their work.

"Nazca Lines" monkey figure

Cerro Vicús

Sipán
Pacatnamú
Huaca del Brujo
Moche
Tornaval
Pañamarca
Chavín de Huántar
Shillacoto
Ancón
Garagay

Paracas
Pampa Ingenio
Cahuachi
Nazca
Tambo Viejo

PERU

Chavín culture, 1000 BCE–200 BCE

The Chavín culture of Peru may have evolved slowly from the earlier Norte Chico civilization, which built the first cities in the Americas. Chavín buildings had tenon heads – stone carvings of jaguar faces with long canine teeth – projecting from the tops of the walls.

KEY

Area of Olmec civilization	Olmec site
Area of Zapotec civilization	Zapotec site
Area of Maya civilization	Mayan site
Area of Chavín civilization	Chavín site
Area of Nazca civilization	Nazca site
Area of Moche civilization	Moche site

Alexander the Great

One of the greatest military leaders in history, Alexander the Great single-handedly united far-flung lands by conquering them and imposing on them Greek ideas, customs, and culture. In little more than a decade, the young king defeated the mighty Persian Empire and established a huge kingdom that stretched from India in the east to Egypt in the west.

EUROPE

Alexander the Great

Pella

MACEDONIA

GREECE

Athens

KEY

- ☐ Alexander's empire
- ▨ Dependent regions
- — Alexander's route
- ✕ Significant battles
- ◖ Mountain pass
- ○ Key town or city
- ① Key event
- 334 BCE Date of event

GRANICUS
334 BCE

ASIA MINOR

Sardis

Gordium

ISSUS
333 BCE

GAUGAMELA
331 BCE

Nine

Thapsacus

TYRE
332 BCE

Damascus

GAZA
332 BCE

Paraetonium

Alexandria

Heliopolis
Memphis

Siwa

EGYPT

2. Cities surrender
By spring 333 BCE, over 30 cities in Asia Minor had surrendered to Alexander.

3. Cutting the knot
Alexander reached Gordium where he cut the Gordian Knot (the impossible puzzle) with his sword. According to legend, it was a sign he would rule Asia.

1. Invasion
Alexander launched his invasion of the Persian Empire in 334 BCE.

4. Enemies meet
In November 333 BCE, Alexander met Persian emperor Darius III in battle for the first time. The Persian army was outmanoeuvred and suffered heavy losses. Darius fled.

8. Taking Babylon
The great city of Babylon surrendered in 331 BCE. Alexander entered the gates in triumph.

5. Siege of Gaza
In 332 BCE, Alexander was wounded by a catapult bolt during the Siege of Gaza.

6. Consulting the Oracle
Alexander visited the oracle of Ammon at Siwa. The oracle (a person thought to be able to predict the future) told him he was the son of Ammon-Zeus, the ruler of the Greek gods.

Changing the world

As Alexander the Great conquered empires, he took Greek language, customs, and culture with him. Greek-style portraiture has been found from Turkey in the east to central Asia in the west.

Greek-style coin from Bactria (in modern-day Afghanistan).

MANY OF THE COUNTRIES AND REGIONS THAT ALEXANDER CONQUERED

Battle of Gaugamela

Alexander III of Macedonia

Alexander spent his childhood watching his father, Philip II of Macedonia, unify Greece. Just 21 when he became king, he soon showed his qualities as a fearsome fighter and military genius who never lost a battle. However, he is also remembered as a leader who displayed great diplomacy and compassion to those he conquered.

"My son, you must find a kingdom big enough for your ambitions."

Philip II of Macedonia, Alexander's father, 346 BCE

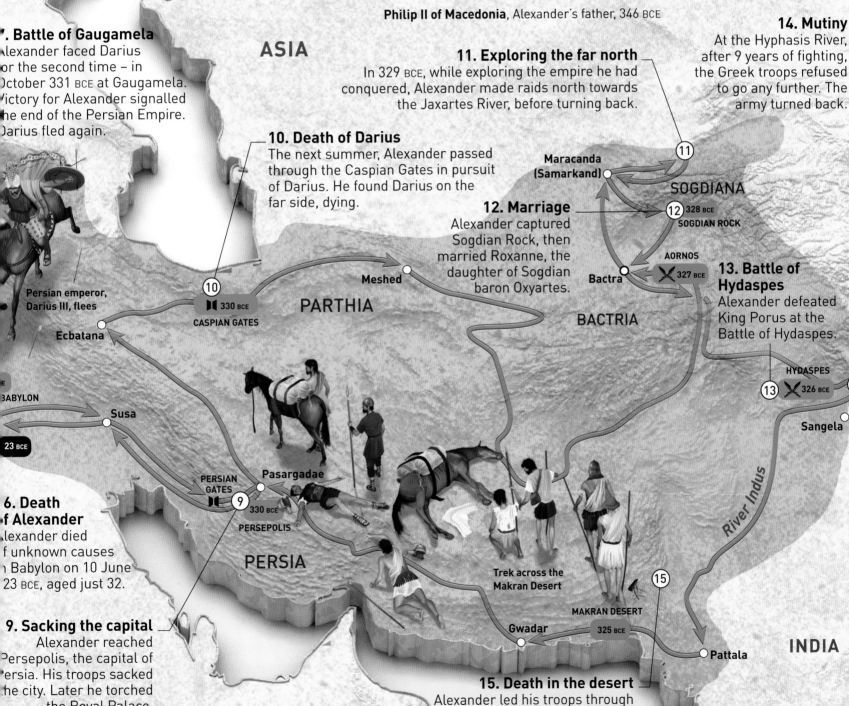

ASIA

. Battle of Gaugamela
Alexander faced Darius for the second time – in October 331 BCE at Gaugamela. Victory for Alexander signalled he end of the Persian Empire. Darius fled again.

11. Exploring the far north
In 329 BCE, while exploring the empire he had conquered, Alexander made raids north towards the Jaxartes River, before turning back.

14. Mutiny
At the Hyphasis River, after 9 years of fighting, the Greek troops refused to go any further. The army turned back.

10. Death of Darius
The next summer, Alexander passed through the Caspian Gates in pursuit of Darius. He found Darius on the far side, dying.

Maracanda (Samarkand)
11
SOGDIANA

12. Marriage
Alexander captured Sogdian Rock, then married Roxanne, the daughter of Sogdian baron Oxyartes.

12 328 BCE
SOGDIAN ROCK

AORNOS
Bactra
327 BCE

13. Battle of Hydaspes
Alexander defeated King Porus at the Battle of Hydaspes.

Meshed
PARTHIA
BACTRIA

Persian emperor, Darius III, flees

10 330 BCE
CASPIAN GATES

Ecbatana

HYDASPES
13
326 BCE
14

BABYLON

Susa

Sangela

23 BCE

PERSIAN GATES
Pasargadae
9
330 BCE
PERSEPOLIS

River Indus

6. Death of Alexander
Alexander died of unknown causes in Babylon on 10 June 23 BCE, aged just 32.

PERSIA

Trek across the Makran Desert

15

MAKRAN DESERT

9. Sacking the capital
Alexander reached Persepolis, the capital of Persia. His troops sacked the city. Later he torched the Royal Palace.

Gwadar
325 BCE

Pattala

INDIA

15. Death in the desert
Alexander led his troops through the Makran Desert. Many died.

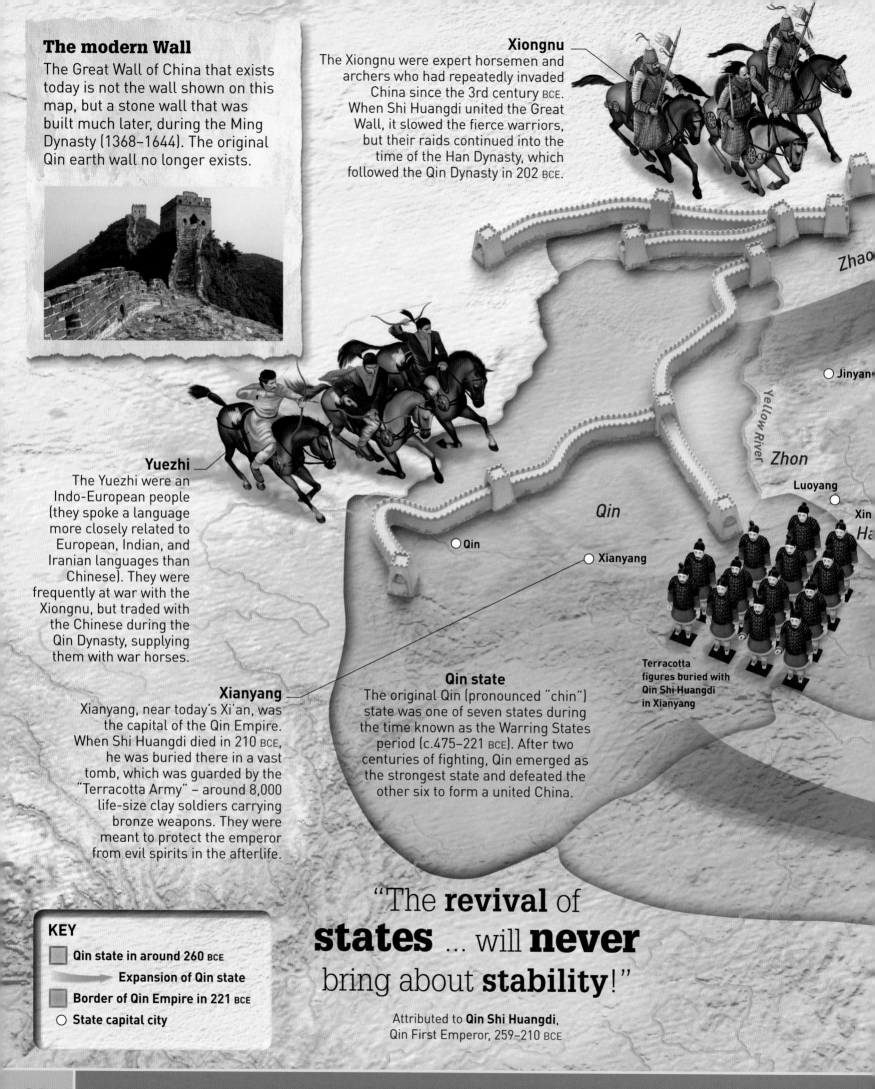

The modern Wall

The Great Wall of China that exists today is not the wall shown on this map, but a stone wall that was built much later, during the Ming Dynasty (1368–1644). The original Qin earth wall no longer exists.

Xiongnu

The Xiongnu were expert horsemen and archers who had repeatedly invaded China since the 3rd century BCE. When Shi Huangdi united the Great Wall, it slowed the fierce warriors, but their raids continued into the time of the Han Dynasty, which followed the Qin Dynasty in 202 BCE.

Yuezhi

The Yuezhi were an Indo-European people (they spoke a language more closely related to European, Indian, and Iranian languages than Chinese). They were frequently at war with the Xiongnu, but traded with the Chinese during the Qin Dynasty, supplying them with war horses.

Xianyang

Xianyang, near today's Xi'an, was the capital of the Qin Empire. When Shi Huangdi died in 210 BCE, he was buried there in a vast tomb, which was guarded by the "Terracotta Army" – around 8,000 life-size clay soldiers carrying bronze weapons. They were meant to protect the emperor from evil spirits in the afterlife.

Qin state

The original Qin (pronounced "chin") state was one of seven states during the time known as the Warring States period (c.475–221 BCE). After two centuries of fighting, Qin emerged as the strongest state and defeated the other six to form a united China.

Terracotta figures buried with Qin Shi Huangdi in Xianyang

Zhao

Jinyan

Yellow River

Zhon

Qin

Luoyang

Xin

Ha

Qin

Xianyang

"The **revival** of **states** ... will **never** bring about **stability**!"

Attributed to **Qin Shi Huangdi**, Qin First Emperor, 259–210 BCE

KEY

- Qin state in around 260 BCE
- Expansion of Qin state
- Border of Qin Empire in 221 BCE
- ○ State capital city

Beacon tower
There were beacon towers at intervals along the Great Wall. The original wall was built of rammed earth – earth that was poured into a wooden frame then compacted, layer by layer.

Zhongshan

Yan

Dong-hu
The Dong-hu, or "Eastern Barbarians", were the ancestors of the Mongols. They were conquered by the Xiongnu in 206 BCE, just before the start of the Han Dynasty.

○ Ji

Qi

Korea

Lu
○ Qufu

Linzi ●

CHINA

Yellow Sea

The northern wall
In 215 BCE, Shi Huangdi sent 300,000 citizens to build a wall across the north of the country. It was made by joining many smaller walls, which had been built previously by the Warring States. Many workers died during the construction.

ng

Song
○ Shangqin

Shouchun
○

Chu

Yangtze River

East China Sea

China's Great Wall
221– 206 BCE

The first parts of China's Great Wall were built when the country was split into many states, which were always at war with each other. Some of these states built walls to stop nomadic tribes invading from the north. In 221 BCE, Ying Zheng, king of Qin state, having conquered the other states and unified China, began joining up the shorter walls into one great wall. He renamed himself Qin Shi Huangdi (First Sovereign Emperor of Qin) and ruled over his empire until he died in 210 BCE.

8,850 TO 21,200 KM (5,500–13,170 MILES) AT ITS GREATEST EXTENT.

Roman land at the start of the Second Punic War

Carthaginian land at the start of the Second Punic War

Scipio's route

Hannibal's route

202 BCE Roman victory

202 BCE Carthaginian victory

○ Key town

● Capital city

① Key event

⑫ Key event in a capital city

1. River Ebro
In 226 BCE, Hannibal's brother-in-law, Hasdrubal the Fair, signed a treaty with Rome. It set down in writing that the River Ebro was the border between Carthaginian and Roman territory.

EUROPE

Gaul

Pyrenees

River Ebro

3. Carthago Nova
Determined to take the war to the heart of Italy, Hannibal and his forces departed from Carthago Nova (where he had withdrawn after the Siege of Saguntum) in the spring of 218 BCE.

Iberian Peninsula

Tarraco

SAGUNTUM

219 BCE

Carthago Nova ③

②

2. Saguntum
The people of Saguntum feared the Carthaginians, so they asked Rome to be their ally. In 219 BCE, in an attempt to provoke Rome, Hannibal laid siege to Saguntum. This led to the second Punic War between Rome and Carthage.

4. Pyrenees
After fighting his way through Roman-occupied land in what is now Spain, Hannibal led his army over the Pyrenees and entered Gaul.

AFRICA

219–202 BCE

Rome and Hannibal

In 219 BCE, Hannibal of Carthage renewed a war between Rome and its greatest rival, the Carthaginian Empire. The Romans called these conflicts the Punic Wars, after the *Punici*, their name for the Phoenician people who founded Carthage. Hannibal led his army over the mountains and on into central Italy, and inflicted a string of victories that came close to toppling the entire Roman Republic. The war finally ended when he was defeated near Carthage.

. River Rhône
Hannibal and
his forces (now
numbering 38,000
infantry, 8,000
cavalry, and 38 war
elephants) crossed
the River Rhône in
September 218 BCE.

5

Narbo
hodae

6. The Alps
In one of the most brilliant feats of
military strategy in history, Hannibal
led his massive army across the
Alps and into northern Italy. Few
of his war elephants, survived
the journey, however.

6

River Rhône

Alps

Hannibal
One of the great military
leaders of ancient times,
Hannibal of Carthage was
the most ingenious and
formidable opponent the
Romans ever faced. If he
had received the support
from Carthage he needed,
he would almost certainly
have defeated Rome.

9. Journey through Italy
Hannibal travelled through
central and southern Italy
in an attempt to stir up a
general revolt against
the Roman Republic.

Placentia

11. Metaurus
Hannibal's brother and
general, Hasdrubal
Barca, was defeated at
the battle of Metaurus
in 207 BCE. His head was
cut off and paraded
around Italy before
being thrown over the
wall of Hannibal's camp.

7. Trebia
In December 218 BCE, Hannibal
defeated Roman forces at
the battle of Trebia.

218 BCE
7 TREBIA

I swear, so
soon as age will
permit ... I will use **fire**
and **steel** to arrest
the destiny
of **Rome**."

Hannibal's oath to
his father, Hamilcar,
when he was a child

ITALY

9

LAKE TRASIMENE
8 217 BCE

Perusia

207 BCE
11
METAURUS

ROME

8. Lake Trasimene
In June 217 BCE,
Hannibal ambushed and
defeated the Romans on the
shores of Lake Trasimene.
He decided against attacking
Rome because he lacked
the equipment to do it.

10. Cannae
At the battle of
Cannae in 216
BCE, Hannibal's
army captured or
killed 50,000–70,000
Romans. It was one
of the worst defeats
the Romans ever
suffered.

Capua

10
216 BCE
CANNAE

Utica
12. Scipio
In 204 BCE, Roman forces
led by Scipio invaded Africa.

ZAMA
202 BCE
CARTHAGE **12**

Hadrumentum

Lilybaeum

Tarentum

Thurii

Agrigentium

Croton
13

Ecnomus

Rhegium

Messana

Syracuse

13. Croton
In 203 BCE, after nearly
15 years in Italy, Hannibal
returned to Carthage to face Roman
general Scipio. He left from Croton.

14. Zama
The Romans, under Scipio, defeated
Hannibal and the Carthaginians at the battle
of Zama on 19 October 202 BCE. Defeat for Carthage
marked the end of the Second Punic War.

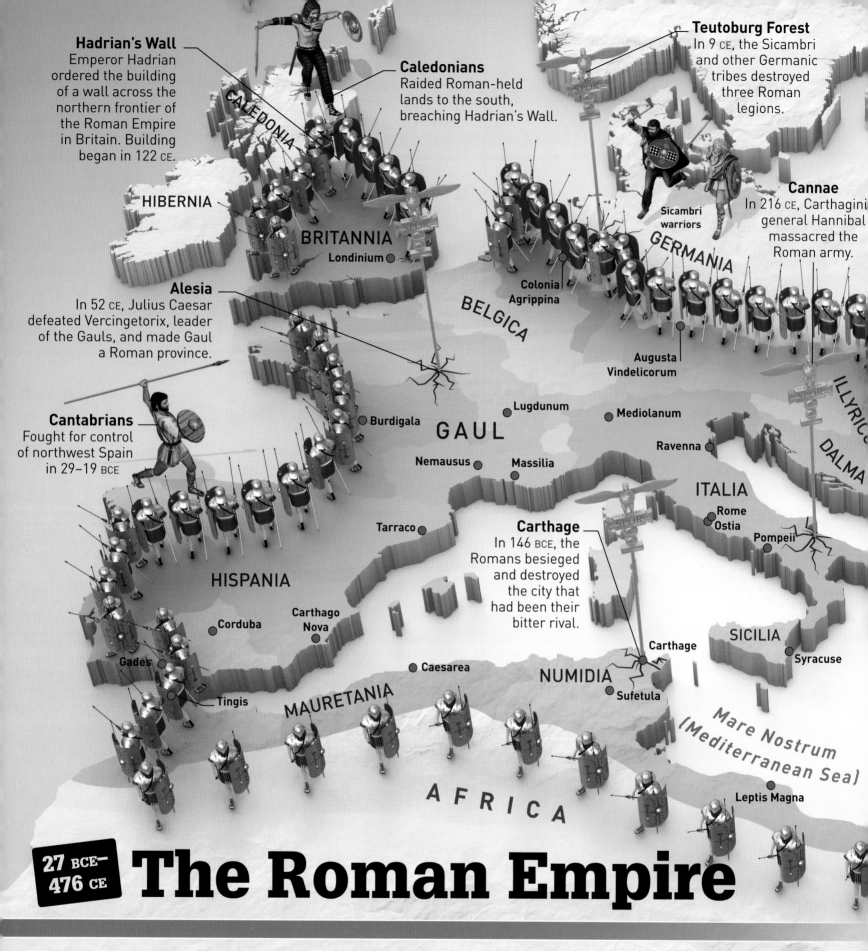

Hadrian's Wall
Emperor Hadrian ordered the building of a wall across the northern frontier of the Roman Empire in Britain. Building began in 122 CE.

Caledonians
Raided Roman-held lands to the south, breaching Hadrian's Wall.

Teutoburg Forest
In 9 CE, the Sicambri and other Germanic tribes destroyed three Roman legions.

Cannae
In 216 CE, Carthagini general Hannibal massacred the Roman army.

CALEDONIA

HIBERNIA

BRITANNIA
Londinium

Sicambri warriors

GERMANIA

Colonia Agrippina

BELGICA

Alesia
In 52 CE, Julius Caesar defeated Vercingetorix, leader of the Gauls, and made Gaul a Roman province.

Augusta Vindelicorum

ILLYRICO

DALMA

Cantabrians
Fought for control of northwest Spain in 29–19 BCE

Burdigala

GAUL

Lugdunum

Mediolanum

Nemausus

Massilia

Ravenna

ITALIA
Rome
Ostia

Tarraco

Carthage
In 146 BCE, the Romans besieged and destroyed the city that had been their bitter rival.

Pompeii

HISPANIA

Corduba

Carthago Nova

SICILIA

Carthage

Syracuse

Gades

Caesarea

NUMIDIA

Tingis

MAURETANIA

Sufetula

Mare Nostrum (Mediterranean Sea)

A F R I C A

Leptis Magna

27 BCE– 476 CE # The Roman Empire

At the end of the reign of Emperor Trajan in 117 CE, the Roman Empire was at its largest, stretching across Europe and North Africa, from Britain at its farthest north-west frontier to the Middle East in the far south east.

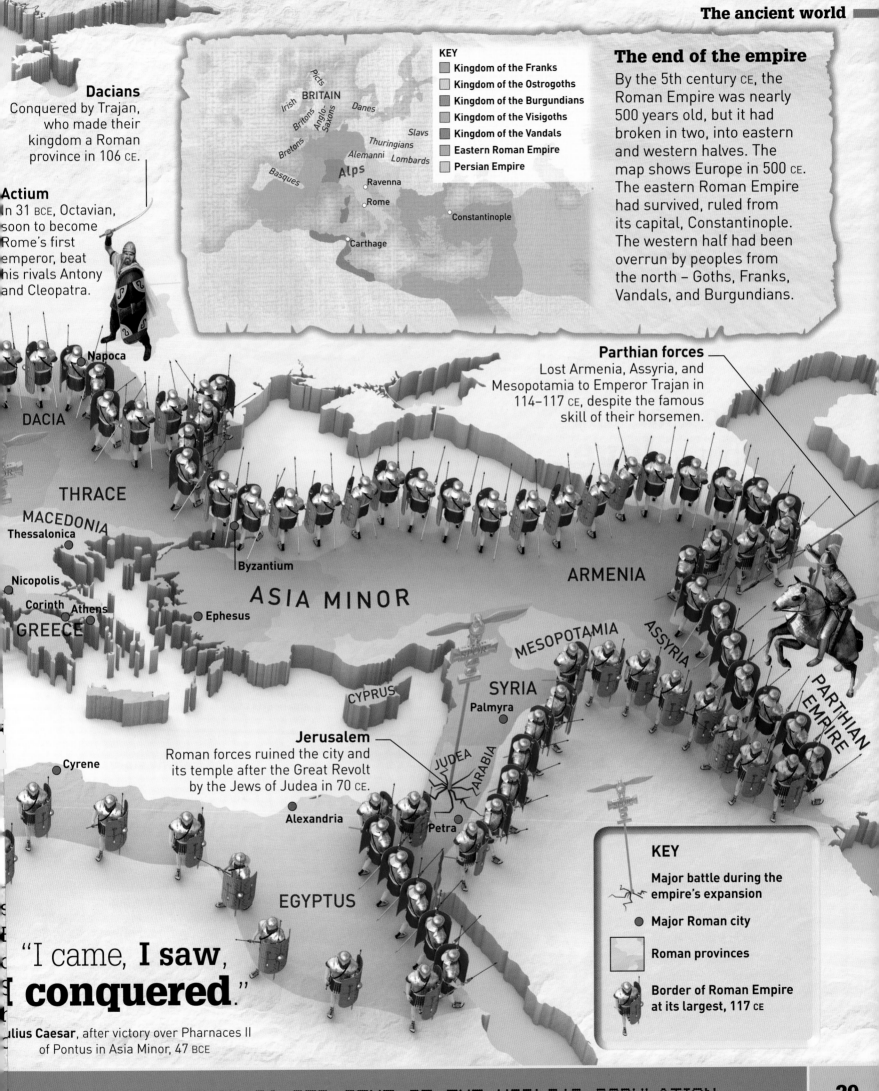

Dacians
Conquered by Trajan, who made their kingdom a Roman province in 106 CE.

Actium
In 31 BCE, Octavian, soon to become Rome's first emperor, beat his rivals Antony and Cleopatra.

KEY
- Kingdom of the Franks
- Kingdom of the Ostrogoths
- Kingdom of the Burgundians
- Kingdom of the Visigoths
- Kingdom of the Vandals
- Eastern Roman Empire
- Persian Empire

BRITAIN
Picts
Irish
Britons
Bretons
Anglo-Saxons
Danes
Slavs
Thuringians
Alemanni
Lombards
Basques
Alps
Ravenna
Rome
Constantinople
Carthage

The end of the empire
By the 5th century CE, the Roman Empire was nearly 500 years old, but it had broken in two, into eastern and western halves. The map shows Europe in 500 CE. The eastern Roman Empire had survived, ruled from its capital, Constantinople. The western half had been overrun by peoples from the north – Goths, Franks, Vandals, and Burgundians.

Napoca

DACIA

THRACE

MACEDONIA
Thessalonica

Nicopolis

Corinth
Athens

GREECE

Byzantium

ASIA MINOR

Ephesus

Parthian forces
Lost Armenia, Assyria, and Mesopotamia to Emperor Trajan in 114–117 CE, despite the famous skill of their horsemen.

ARMENIA

MESOPOTAMIA
ASSYRIA

SYRIA
Palmyra

CYPRUS

PARTHIAN EMPIRE

Jerusalem
Roman forces ruined the city and its temple after the Great Revolt by the Jews of Judea in 70 CE.

JUDEA
ARABIA

Cyrene

Alexandria

Petra

EGYPTUS

"I came, I saw, conquered."
Julius Caesar, after victory over Pharnaces II of Pontus in Asia Minor, 47 BCE

KEY
- Major battle during the empire's expansion
- Major Roman city
- Roman provinces
- Border of Roman Empire at its largest, 117 CE

KEY
The Pacific islands were settled in several waves of migration.

- :: Origin of the Pacific settlers
- 2000–1000 BCE
- 1000 BCE–1 CE
- 1–500 CE
- 1000–1400 CE

Departure, 2000 BCE
The people who settled the Pacific islands came from a group of islands now called the Bismarck Archipelago. The people belonged to a group known as the Lapita culture.

Settling of the Marshall Islands, 1–500 CE
Seafarers from Fiji or Samoa discovered the Marshall Islands.

Mariana Islands

Guam

Marshall Islands

Palau

Caroline Islands

Gilbert Islands

Indonesia

New Guinea

Bismarck Archipelago

Tuvalu

Solomon Islands

Samoa

Vanuatu

Australia

Coral Sea Islands

Fiji

New Caledonia

Tonga

"How shall we account for this nation **spreading itself** so far over this **vast ocean**?"

Captain James Cook, on arriving in Hawaii in 1778

Lapita migration, 2000–1000 BCE
The Lapita people spread as far east as Fiji, Samoa, and Tonga. We know this, because archaeologists have found distinctive Lapita pottery in these places.

Final landfall, 1000 CE
The islands of New Zealand were the last of the Pacific islands to be discovered, by Polynesian seafarers from either the Society Islands or the Cook Islands.

New Zealand

Innovative navigators
The Pacific settlers found amazing ways to navigate the vast Pacific Ocean. They watched the direction and size of ocean waves, studied the movement of stars and clouds, and followed the flight of birds that fished at sea. They then placed all this information, plus the location of islands, on a map made of sticks.

Stick map

Chatham Islands (New Zealand)

Discovery of Hawaii, 400 CE
Polynesian voyagers from the Marquesas Islands or the Cook Islands discovered Hawaii.

Hawaii

Exploration of eastern Polynesia, 200 BCE
Seafarers from Tonga and Samoa discovered and settled what we now know as eastern Polynesia – Tahiti (in the Society Islands), the Cook Islands, the Marquesas Islands, and the Tuamotus.

Line Islands

Phoenix Islands

Plants and animals
Pacific settlers took supplies with them to survive the journey and to help them establish settlements on the islands they found.

Taro
The taro plant, which has an edible tuber, was grown in freshwater marshes and manmade pits.

Tuber

Pig
The pigs of Polynesia were descendants of wild boars native to Eurasia.

Polynesian rat
Rats were not taken as supplies – they were stowaways. They settled in every island colonized by humans.

Marquesas Islands

PACIFIC
OCEAN

Society Islands

Cook Islands

Tuamotu Islands

Austral Islands

Gambier Islands

Rapa Nui

2,000 BCE –1400 CE

Pacific settlers

Arrival at humans' most distant outpost, 500 CE
Polynesians from the Tuamotus or the Gambier Islands discovered and settled Rapa Nui, or Easter Island – one of the most remote islands on Earth.

The discovery and settling of the Pacific islands is a dramatic story of human migration. Daring explorers, the world's first deep-sea sailors and navigators, crossed the vast Pacific Ocean in simple, double-hulled boats called "outriggers". They did so at a time when Europeans were still afraid to sail out of sight of dry land.

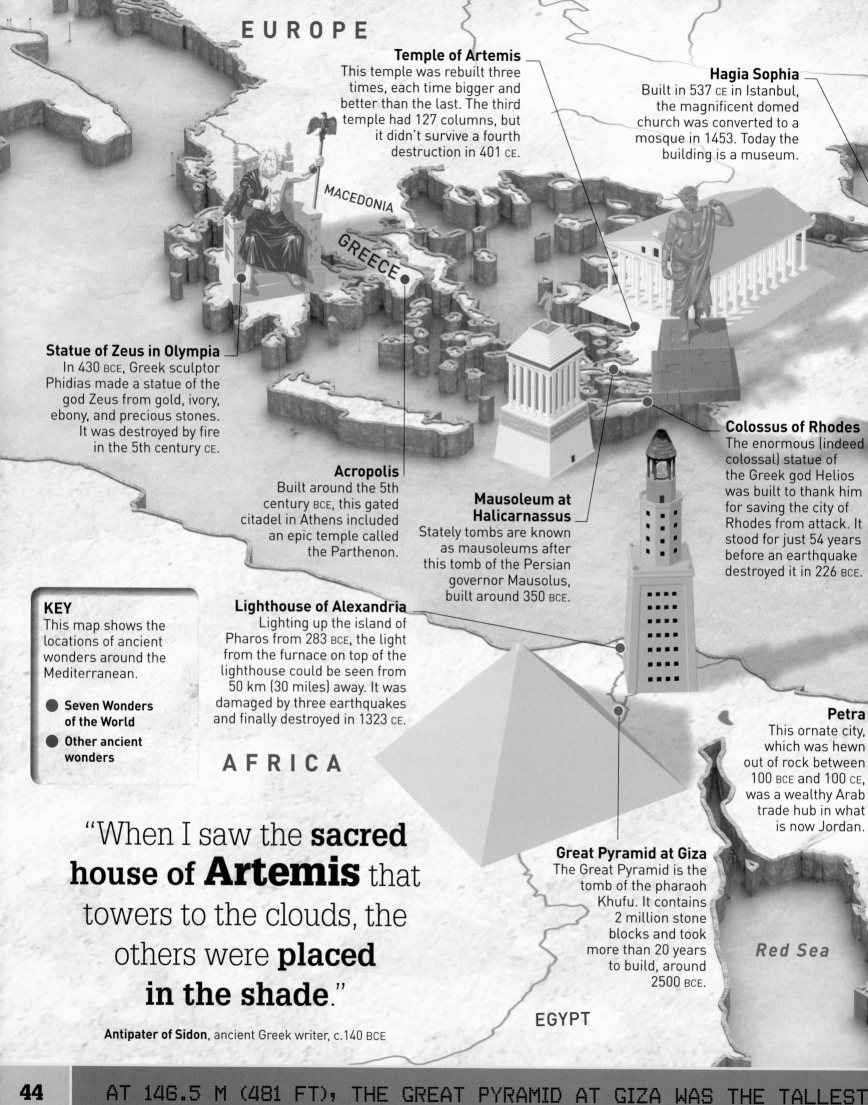

EUROPE

Temple of Artemis
This temple was rebuilt three times, each time bigger and better than the last. The third temple had 127 columns, but it didn't survive a fourth destruction in 401 CE.

Hagia Sophia
Built in 537 CE in Istanbul, the magnificent domed church was converted to a mosque in 1453. Today the building is a museum.

MACEDONIA

GREECE

Statue of Zeus in Olympia
In 430 BCE, Greek sculptor Phidias made a statue of the god Zeus from gold, ivory, ebony, and precious stones. It was destroyed by fire in the 5th century CE.

Colossus of Rhodes
The enormous (indeed colossal) statue of the Greek god Helios was built to thank him for saving the city of Rhodes from attack. It stood for just 54 years before an earthquake destroyed it in 226 BCE.

Acropolis
Built around the 5th century BCE, this gated citadel in Athens included an epic temple called the Parthenon.

Mausoleum at Halicarnassus
Stately tombs are known as mausoleums after this tomb of the Persian governor Mausolus, built around 350 BCE.

KEY
This map shows the locations of ancient wonders around the Mediterranean.

● Seven Wonders of the World
● Other ancient wonders

Lighthouse of Alexandria
Lighting up the island of Pharos from 283 BCE, the light from the furnace on top of the lighthouse could be seen from 50 km (30 miles) away. It was damaged by three earthquakes and finally destroyed in 1323 CE.

Petra
This ornate city, which was hewn out of rock between 100 BCE and 100 CE, was a wealthy Arab trade hub in what is now Jordan.

AFRICA

"When I saw the **sacred house of Artemis** that towers to the clouds, the others were **placed in the shade**."

Antipater of Sidon, ancient Greek writer, c.140 BCE

Great Pyramid at Giza
The Great Pyramid is the tomb of the pharaoh Khufu. It contains 2 million stone blocks and took more than 20 years to build, around 2500 BCE.

Red Sea

EGYPT

EUROPE

③

④
⑤

NORTH
AMERICA

**Area of
enlarged
map**

ASIA

⑧

⑨

Black Sea

①

⑥

ASIA ⑦

SOUTH
AMERICA

AFRICA

②

AUSTRALASIA

Worldwide wonders

Other marvels of engineering from ancient times can be found across the world today. Here are nine of them.

① Great Pyramid of Cholula Built in Mexico in 300 BCE, this is the largest pyramid in the world by volume.

② Nazca Lines These extraordinary carvings patterns, animals, and plants were etched into the desert in Peru in 350 BCE–650 CE.

③ Stonehenge The arches made of 4-tonne stones were erected in Britain in 3100–1600 BCE. No one knows what they were used for.

④ Pont-du-Gard This Roman aqueduct (water-carrying bridge) in France dates back to 19 BCE. It stands 50 m (165 ft) high.

⑤ Colosseum This 50,000-seater stadium in Italy was built in 80 CE, when crowds gathered to watch gladiators.

⑥ Temples of Abu Simbel Twin temples made of rock in 1264–44 BCE mark the reign of Pharaoh Ramesses II and his wife Nefertari.

⑦ Sigiriya This Sri Lankan palace was carved into a massive column of rock in 495 CE. It is guarded by a gateway shaped like a lion.

⑧ Terracotta Army An army of 8,000 life-sized clay warriors was buried with the first emperor of China in 210 BCE.

⑨ Daisen Kofun Built in the 5th century, this Japanese tomb is the world's largest burial mound. Seen from above, it has the shape of a keyhole.

ANATOLIA

Mediterranean Sea

ASIA

2500 BCE –650 CE Ancient wonders

Hanging Gardens of Babylon
In around 600 BCE, King Nebuchadnezzar built a series of beautiful stepped gardens for his wife, Amytis. They were destroyed in the 1st century CE and no evidence remains today.

There were some incredible feats of engineering in the ancient world. The "Seven Wonders of the World" were especially famous. The ancient Greeks considered this group of buildings and statues to be more spectacular than any other. All seven were located around the Mediterranean region, where the Greeks travelled. Only one – the Great Pyramid at Giza – survives today.

BABYLONIA

Musical instruments, 43,000–40,000 years ago
The oldest known musical instruments are flutes made of mammoth bone, found in the Swabian Alps, Germany.

EUROPE

Wheeled vehicle, 3200 BCE
The oldest known wheel used for transport was unearthed in Slovenia in 2002 and is believed to have belonged to a two-wheeled cart.

Aqueduct, 2000
Aqueducts were chann running along the grou underground, or above grou on bridges, that suppli fresh spring or river water wherever people needed Aqueducts were first bu in the ancient city Nineveh (Mos in Ira

Brick, 7500 BCE
The earliest known bricks were made of mud and straw. Experts believe they originated in Anatolia (Turkey).

Map, 13,000 years ago
A stone tablet found in Abauntz Cave, Spain, in 1993 contains the earliest known map, which is of the surrounding area.

Glass, 3500 BCE
Archaeologists believe that glass was first used in Mesopotamia (modern-day Iraq) more than 5,000 years ago to make ornamental beads.

Soap, 2800
Soap made of and salts was used in Babyl (modern-day to clean wool and cotton.

Coin, 610–600 BCE
The first coin was used in the ancient kingdom of Lydia, in modern-day Turkey. It was marked with a roaring lion.

Bronze, 3200 BCE
Archaeological findings suggest that bronze was first used in ancient Egypt to make tools and weapons.

Shadow clock, 1500 BCE
The ancient Egyptian shadow clock was a simple pillar. The length of the shadow it cast indicated the time of day.

Fire, 790,000 years ago
(See box below)

Potter's wheel, 3500 BCE
The potter's wheel allowed people to make perfectly round pots. Experts believe that it wa invented in Mesopotamia.

AFRICA

Mastery of fire

Archaeologists have found evidence in Israel of the earliest known use of fire – by ancestors of humans, such as *Homo erectus*. They discovered that burning happened in specific spots, which shows that hearths existed. The control of fire meant that *Homo erectus* was able to spread to colder regions, drive away dangerous predators, and cook food.

THE WHEEL WAS ACTUALLY INVENTED FOR USE IN MAKING POTTERY

90,000 years ago – 50 BCE

Ancient inventions

It is impossible to know the origin of most of the great inventions of the ancient world because they occurred before people recorded things in writing. Therefore, historians have had to rely on archaeological discoveries to trace the earliest known appearance of many of these inventions.

> "**Necessity** is the **mother** of invention."
>
> English proverb

Blast furnace, 100 BCE
Invented in China, blast furnaces were used to make cast iron – an important metal that was used for making tools and cooking pots.

ASIA

Plumbing, 2600 BCE
Remains of the earliest known drainage systems were found in the Indus Valley (modern-day Pakistan). They directed rainwater into drains and stopped the cities of Harappa and Mohenjo-Daro from flooding.

Paper, 1st century BCE
Paper was invented during China's Han Dynasty. It was cheap to produce and replaced more expensive writing materials, such as bamboo and silk.

Ink, 2600 BCE
Made of soot and glue, the first ink was used in China for shading artwork. It came in a solid block and needed wetting before use.

Stirrup, 500–200 BCE
Ancient sculptures suggest that stirrups were first used in India. The stirrup gave riders greater control of their horse, which helped them to fight on horseback.

Pottery, 18,000 BCE
In 2012, archaeologists found shards of the earliest known pots in Jiangxi, China.

AND WAS ONLY ADAPTED FOR TRANSPORT SOME 300 YEARS LATER.

The medieval world

Aztec calendar
One of the most advanced civilizations of medieval times, the Aztecs developed their own calendar. The "Sun Stone" represents this calendar and shows Tonatiuh, the Sun god, at the centre.

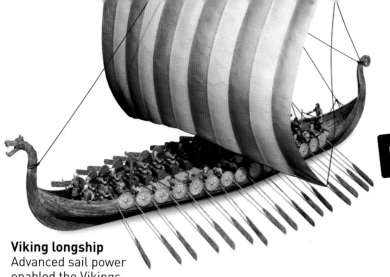

Viking longship
Advanced sail power enabled the Vikings to cross oceans to trade and settle in new lands.

BYZANTINE EMPIRE (555) The eastern Roman empire, known as the Byzantine Empire, reaches its greatest size.

TANG DYNASTY RULE CHINA (618–907) The Chinese empire expan west, meeting the Pers Empire. »pp56–57

500 CE

CLASSIC MAYA PERIOD (500s) The Maya civilization of Central America is at the height of its powers. »pp70–71

MOHAMMAD'S FLIGHT TO MEDINA (622) The Prophet Mohammad flees from Mecca and establishes the new religion of Islam in Medina, Saudi Arabia.

FOURTH TO EIGHTH CRUSADES (1202–70) Five more major Crusades take place. They are all attacks on non-Catholics. »pp60–61

THIRD CRUSADE (1189–92) Another attempt fails to claim Jerusalem for Christianity. »pp60–61

ETHIOPIAN EMPIRE (1137–1974) The Ethiopian Empire of east Africa begins under the rule of the Zagwe dynasty. »pp68–69

SILK ROAD (1200s) The trade route from China to India and Europe is at its busiest in the 13th century. »pp52–53

SECOND CRUSADE (1147–48) The Crusader armies are defeated in Anatolia (modern-day Turkey). »pp60–61

KINGDOM OF ZIMBABWE (1100s–1450) Zimbabwe controls trade in ivory and gold from the African coast to the interior. »pp68–69

Mongol warrior

MONGOLS UNITED (1206) Genghis Khan stops the Mongol tribes from fighting and unites them, forming the first Mongol khanate (empire). »pp62–63

PEAK OF THE MONGOL EMPIRE (1279) The Mongol Empire stretches from Ukraine to eastern China. »pp62–63

MONGOL KHANATES (1294) The Mongol Empire splits into four khanates under the authority of the Yuan dynasty in Beijing, China. »pp62–63

SPECTACLES (1286) The first glasses are invented in Italy. »pp72–73

Spectacles

OTTOMAN EMPIRE (1301–1922) Ruler Osman I founds the Ottoman state in Turkey. It later expands to become a major Islamic power in the eastern Mediterranean.

Medieval times

END OF THE BYZANTINES (1453) Ottoman sultan (ruler Mehmet II conquers Constantinople, endin the Byzantine Empire.

1500 CE

Ottoman Sultan Mehmet II

At the start of the Middle Ages in 500 CE, the Roman Empire was crumbling, but clung on in the eastern Mediterranean, becoming the Byzantine Empire. In the 600s, a new power – the Islamic Caliphate – spread quickly from the Middle East. Meanwhile, China was the world's most advanced and prosperous country.

SPREAD OF ISLAM
(632–750) Islam spreads quickly after the death of Mohammad. A Caliphate (Islamic state) stretches from Morocco to India. »pp68–69

MOORISH SPAIN
(711–1492) North African Moors invade and rule over Spain, bringing it under Islamic rule.

VIKINGS ARRIVE (793)
The first Viking raid outside Scandinavia destroys the abbey on the British island of Lindisfarne. »pp54–55

PAPER MONEY (900)
The world's first paper money is used in China. »pp72–73

WINDMILL (644)
Windmills are invented in Persia for grinding grain and pumping water. »pp72–73

HEAVY PLOUGH (c.650)
The invention of the heavy plough allows people to live and farm in places with dense, clay soil. »pp72–73

THE VIKING AGE (840s–900s)
Viking seafarers spread from Scandinavia into England, Ireland, Iceland, Greenland, and France. »pp54–55

Krak des Chevaliers castle, Syria, built by Crusaders in the 12th century

FIRST CRUSADE
(1096–99) After much slaughter, the Crusaders take Jerusalem, but lose it 50 years later. »pp60–61

END OF ANCIENT GHANA (1076) The west African kingdom of Ghana is conquered by Moroccan Berbers. »pp68–69

HEIGHT OF CASTLE BUILDING (1000s)
Fortified residences are built across Europe and the Middle East. »pp58–59

CRUSADER CALL (1095)
Pope Urban II calls for Christians across Europe to reclaim Jerusalem from Muslim rule. »pp60–61

COMPASS (1040–44)
The Chinese military is the first to use the magnetic compass for navigation. »pp72–73

FINDING AMERICA
(1001) Viking Leif Eriksson becomes the first European to land in the Americas. »pp54–55

SONG DYNASTY RULES CHINA (960–1279) Guns, rockets, and printing with movable type are invented in this period. »pp56–57

THE HUNDRED YEARS' WAR
(1337–1453) Battles between France and England – which last 116 years in total – are mostly won by the English.

BLACK DEATH
(1347–51) The plague sweeps across Europe, carried by rats from central Asia. »pp64–65

INCA EMPIRE (1400s–1531)
The largest empire in South America spreads from Peru throughout the Andes before being destroyed by Spanish Conquistadors. »pp70–71

HOURGLASS (1338)
Possibly invented for use at sea, the hourglass is the first accurate way of counting one hour. »pp72–73

END OF THE MONGOLS
(1368) The Mongol Yuan Dynasty of China is overthrown by the Chinese Ming Dynasty.

Machu Picchu
Built around 1450, this spectacular mountain-top Inca site was unknown to the Spanish conquerors and so escaped destruction.

END OF THE ROAD
(1450s) The Ottoman Empire stops trade along the Silk Road in protest against the West and the Crusades.

AZTEC EMPIRE (1428–1519)
The Aztec Empire rules the Valley of Mexico until it is conquered by Spaniard Hernán Cortés. »pp70–71

PRINTING PRESS
(1440) The invention of the printing press causes a revolution in communication in Europe. »pp72–73

ZHENG HE'S VOYAGES
(1405–33) Chinese admiral Zheng He sails to Africa to encourage trade with the West. »pp66–67

IS A COPY OF THE BUDDHIST DIAMOND SUTRA, PRODUCED IN 868.

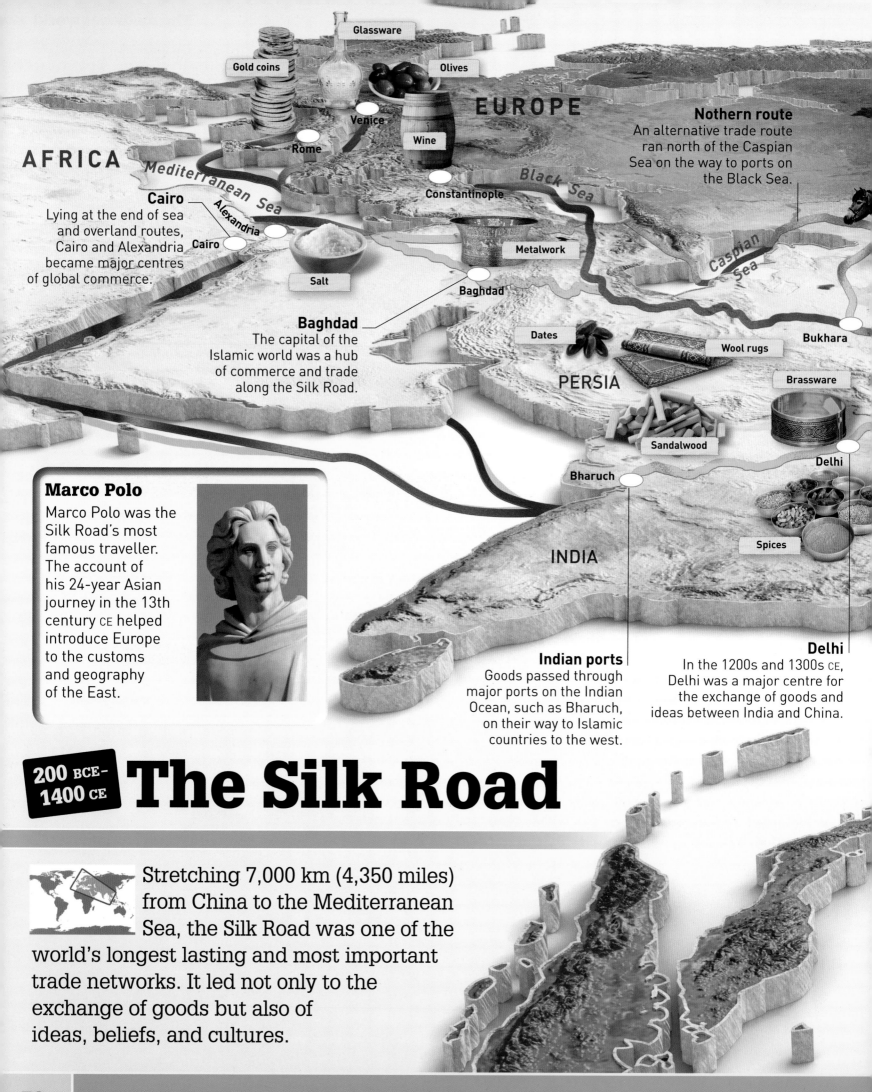

Glassware

Gold coins

Olives

EUROPE

Nothern route
An alternative trade route ran north of the Caspian Sea on the way to ports on the Black Sea.

Wine

Venice

Rome

AFRICA

Mediterranean Sea

Black Sea

Constantinople

Cairo
Lying at the end of sea and overland routes, Cairo and Alexandria became major centres of global commerce.

Alexandria

Cairo

Caspian Sea

Metalwork

Salt

Baghdad

Baghdad
The capital of the Islamic world was a hub of commerce and trade along the Silk Road.

Dates

Wool rugs

Bukhara

PERSIA

Brassware

Sandalwood

Delhi

Bharuch

Marco Polo

Marco Polo was the Silk Road's most famous traveller. The account of his 24-year Asian journey in the 13th century CE helped introduce Europe to the customs and geography of the East.

INDIA

Spices

Indian ports
Goods passed through major ports on the Indian Ocean, such as Bharuch, on their way to Islamic countries to the west.

Delhi
In the 1200s and 1300s CE, Delhi was a major centre for the exchange of goods and ideas between India and China.

The Silk Road

200 BCE– 1400 CE

Stretching 7,000 km (4,350 miles) from China to the Mediterranean Sea, the Silk Road was one of the world's longest lasting and most important trade networks. It led not only to the exchange of goods but also of ideas, beliefs, and cultures.

SO MUCH GOLD WAS SHIPPED OUT OF ROME IN EXCHANGE FOR SILK IN

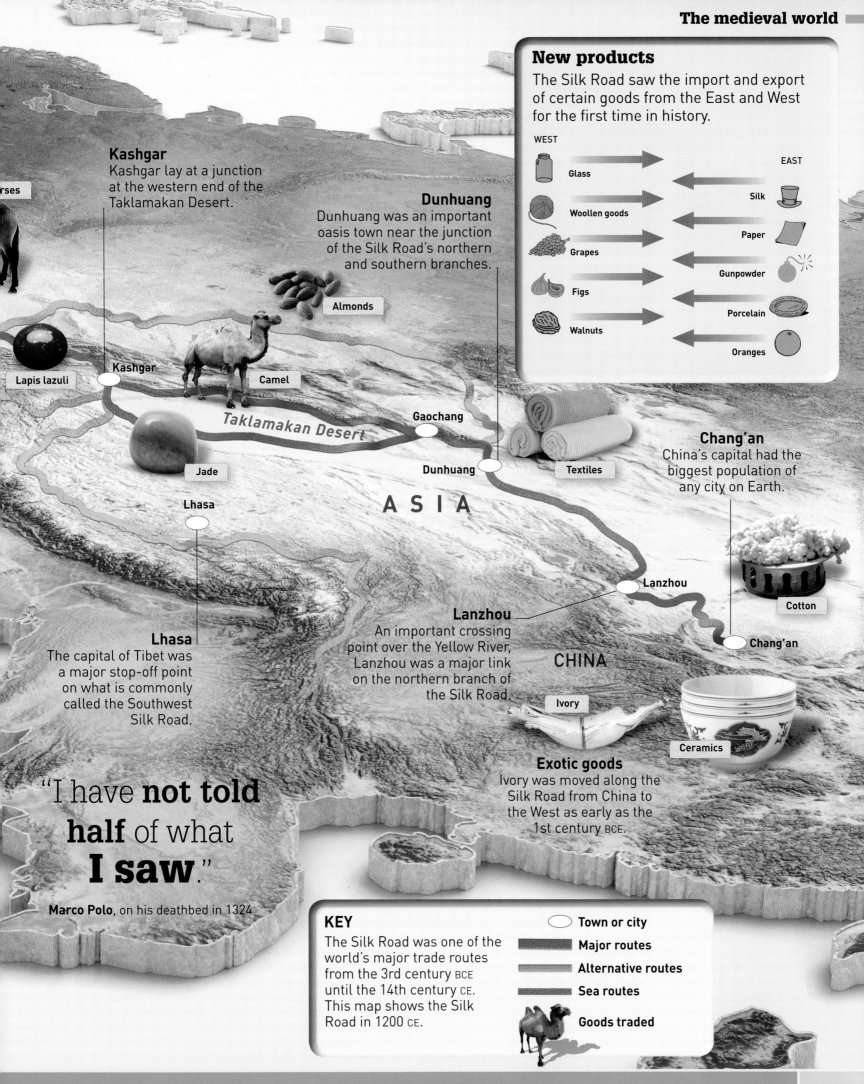

Kashgar
Kashgar lay at a junction at the western end of the Taklamakan Desert.

Lapis lazuli

Kashgar

Dunhuang
Dunhuang was an important oasis town near the junction of the Silk Road's northern and southern branches.

New products
The Silk Road saw the import and export of certain goods from the East and West for the first time in history.

WEST

EAST

Glass

Silk

Woollen goods

Paper

Grapes

Gunpowder

Figs

Porcelain

Walnuts

Oranges

Almonds

Camel

Gaochang

Taklamakan Desert

Dunhuang

Jade

Textiles

Chang'an
China's capital had the biggest population of any city on Earth.

Lhasa

A S I A

Lanzhou

Cotton

Lhasa
The capital of Tibet was a major stop-off point on what is commonly called the Southwest Silk Road.

Lanzhou
An important crossing point over the Yellow River, Lanzhou was a major link on the northern branch of the Silk Road.

CHINA

Chang'an

Ivory

Exotic goods
Ivory was moved along the Silk Road from China to the West as early as the 1st century BCE.

Ceramics

"I have **not told half** of what **I saw**."

Marco Polo, on his deathbed in 1324

KEY
The Silk Road was one of the world's major trade routes from the 3rd century BCE until the 14th century CE. This map shows the Silk Road in 1200 CE.

◯ Town or city

━━ Major routes

━━ Alternative routes

━━ Sea routes

🐫 Goods traded

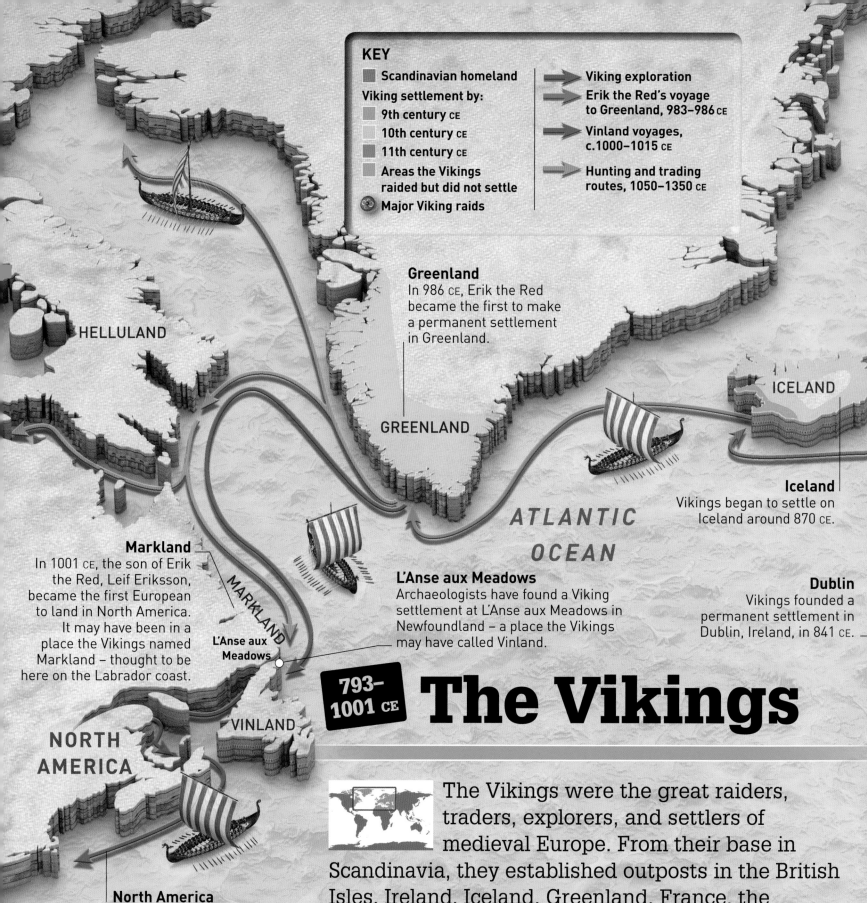

KEY
- ▢ Scandinavian homeland
- Viking settlement by:
- ▢ 9th century CE
- ▢ 10th century CE
- ▢ 11th century CE
- ▢ Areas the Vikings raided but did not settle
- ⦿ Major Viking raids
- ➤ Viking exploration
- ➤ Erik the Red's voyage to Greenland, 983–986 CE
- ➤ Vinland voyages, c.1000–1015 CE
- ➤ Hunting and trading routes, 1050–1350 CE

HELLULAND

Greenland
In 986 CE, Erik the Red became the first to make a permanent settlement in Greenland.

GREENLAND

ICELAND

ATLANTIC OCEAN

Iceland
Vikings began to settle on Iceland around 870 CE.

Markland
In 1001 CE, the son of Erik the Red, Leif Eriksson, became the first European to land in North America. It may have been in a place the Vikings named Markland – thought to be here on the Labrador coast.

MARKLAND

L'Anse aux Meadows

L'Anse aux Meadows
Archaeologists have found a Viking settlement at L'Anse aux Meadows in Newfoundland – a place the Vikings may have called Vinland.

Dublin
Vikings founded a permanent settlement in Dublin, Ireland, in 841 CE.

VINLAND

NORTH AMERICA

793–1001 CE

The Vikings

North America
The Greenland Vikings had no wood for building or fuel. Expeditions south along the North American coast were mainly to get timber.

The Vikings were the great raiders, traders, explorers, and settlers of medieval Europe. From their base in Scandinavia, they established outposts in the British Isles, Ireland, Iceland, Greenland, France, the Mediterranean, and Russia. They were probably also the first people from Europe to set foot in North America – almost 500 years before the arrival of Christopher Columbus.

"Never before has such terror appeared in Britain."

Alcuin of York, on the Viking raid on Lindisfarne, in a letter to King Ethelred of Northumberland (northeast England), 793 CE

Scandinavia
The Vikings came from Norway, Sweden, and Denmark in modern-day Scandinavia.

Viking longships
The Vikings used superbly designed boats called "longships" to raid and explore. Powered by oar or sail, these boats had shallow bottoms, and could be sailed far inland on rivers and lakes. They had the added advantage of being light enough to drag over land to another lake or river.

The medieval world

Lindisfarne
In 793 CE, Vikings raided the abbey at Lindisfarne, a centre of learning famous throughout Europe.

Faeroe Islands

Orkney Islands

Shetland Islands

Lindisfarne

SCANDINAVIA

Norwegians

Swedes

Danes

Novgorod
The Vikings expanded to the east and became rulers of Novgorod, in what is now Russia, in 862 CE.

Novgorod

Kievan Russia
A Scandinavian tribe known as "Rus" appeared for the first time in what is now Russia around 880 CE.

York

BRITAIN

EUROPE

KIEVAN RUSSIA

Normandy
France's Charles the Simple gave land in northern France to a band of Vikings led by Rollo. Rollo's great-great-great grandson was William the Conqueror, who became king of England in 1066 CE.

Kiev

FRANCE

CALIPHATE OF CORDOBA

Sicily

BYZANTINE EMPIRE

Constantinople

Constantinople
In 860 CE, the Vikings launched their first assault on Constantinople (which the Vikings called Miklegard). Further failed raids followed.

Noirmoutier
Vikings attacked a monastery on the French island of Noirmoutier in 799 CE. It was the first recorded attack on mainland Europe.

Mediterranean Sea

TRANSLATES AS "SOMEONE WHO GOES ON AN OVERSEAS EXPEDITION".

Windsor Castle
Built by William I of England in the 1070s as a fortress to control his new territory, it has been occupied ever since by English and British monarchs.

Prague Castle
The largest medieval castle in the world, this was the home of Czech royalty from the 9th century. Its fortifications have been renovated several times.

NORTH AMERICA

Chateau St Louis, Canada

San Juan de Ulúa, Mexico

Trim Castle, Ireland

Castle of São Jorge, Portugal

EUROPE

Europe
The earliest medieval castles were built in Europe. Rulers and local lords alike had to keep order, raise armies, and defend their homes against neighbours and invaders.

Alhambra, Spain

Aït Benhaddou, Morrocco

AFRICA

Ruins of Loropéni, Burkina Faso

Chan Chan, Peru

Sacsayhuaman, Peru

SOUTH AMERICA

Palace of Cortés
Conquistador Hernán Cortés built this castle in Mexico as his home in 1526, to protect him from the Aztec people he had conquered.

Krak des Chevaliers
This 11th-century castle in Syria was built as a fortress by Christian Crusaders who fought to conquer Jerusalem.

Harlech Castle
in Wales once withstood a **siege** lasting **7 years**.

Castle of Good Hope
Built in 1666–79 by the Dutch East India Company, this castle is the oldest surviving colonial building in South Africa.

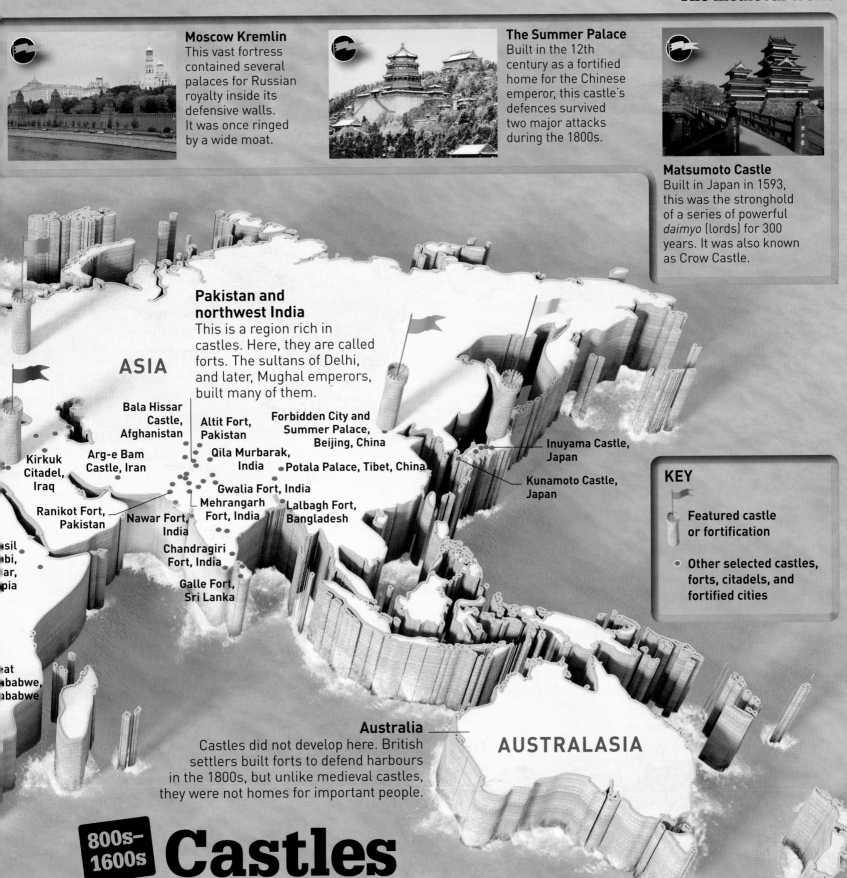

Moscow Kremlin
This vast fortress contained several palaces for Russian royalty inside its defensive walls. It was once ringed by a wide moat.

The Summer Palace
Built in the 12th century as a fortified home for the Chinese emperor, this castle's defences survived two major attacks during the 1800s.

Matsumoto Castle
Built in Japan in 1593, this was the stronghold of a series of powerful *daimyo* (lords) for 300 years. It was also known as Crow Castle.

ASIA

Pakistan and northwest India
This is a region rich in castles. Here, they are called forts. The sultans of Delhi, and later, Mughal emperors, built many of them.

Bala Hissar Castle, Afghanistan

Altit Fort, Pakistan

Forbidden City and Summer Palace, Beijing, China

Kirkuk Citadel, Iraq

Arg-e Bam Castle, Iran

Qila Murbarak, India

Potala Palace, Tibet, China

Inuyama Castle, Japan

Kunamoto Castle, Japan

Ranikot Fort, Pakistan

Nawar Fort, India

Gwalia Fort, India

Mehrangarh Fort, India

Lalbagh Fort, Bangladesh

Chandragiri Fort, India

Galle Fort, Sri Lanka

sil
bi,
ar,
pia

at
babwe,
babwe

KEY

Featured castle or fortification

• Other selected castles, forts, citadels, and fortified cities

Australia
Castles did not develop here. British settlers built forts to defend harbours in the 1800s, but unlike medieval castles, they were not homes for important people.

AUSTRALASIA

800s–1600s Castles

The Middle Ages were the highpoint of castle building. There were frequent breakdowns in law and order, which led rulers, nobles, and other rich and powerful people to build their homes as impregnable fortresses, in order to keep raiders at bay.

CASTLE COVERS AN AREA LARGER THAN SEVEN FOOTBALL FIELDS.

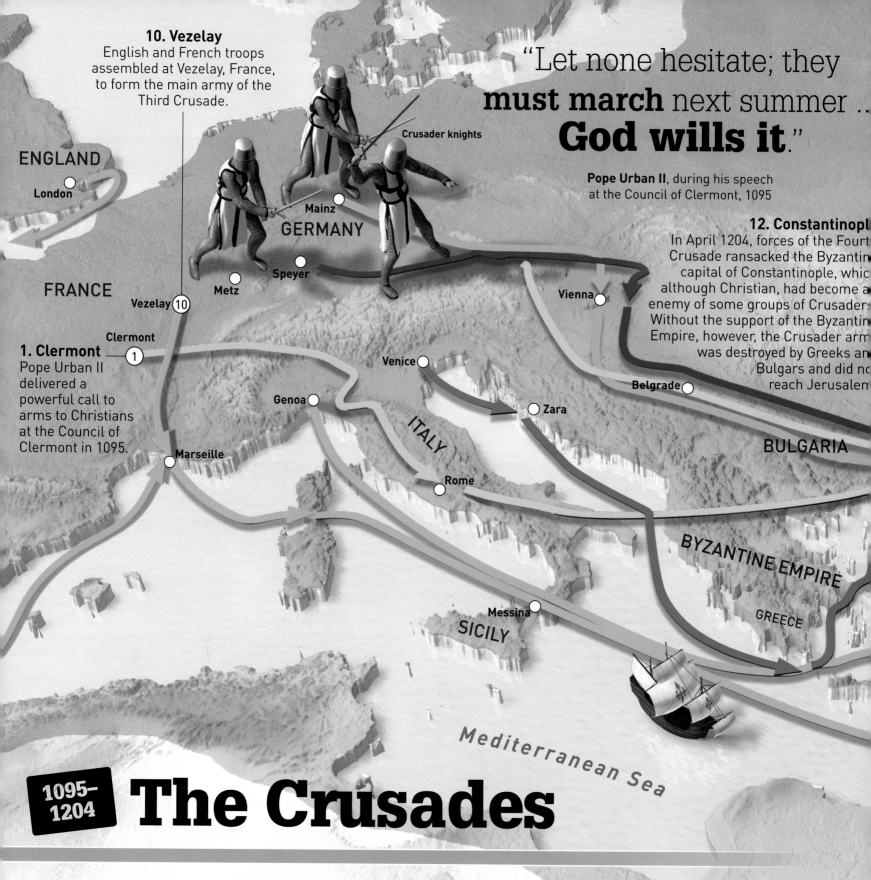

10. Vezelay
English and French troops assembled at Vezelay, France, to form the main army of the Third Crusade.

Crusader knights

ENGLAND

London

"Let none hesitate; they **must march** next summer ... **God wills it**."

Pope Urban II, during his speech at the Council of Clermont, 1095

Mainz

GERMANY

12. Constantinopl
In April 1204, forces of the Fourt Crusade ransacked the Byzantin capital of Constantinople, whic although Christian, had become a enemy of some groups of Crusader Without the support of the Byzantin Empire, however, the Crusader arm was destroyed by Greeks an Bulgars and did n reach Jerusalem

FRANCE

Speyer

Metz

Vienna

Vezelay ⑩

1. Clermont
Clermont
① Pope Urban II delivered a powerful call to arms to Christians at the Council of Clermont in 1095.

Venice

Genoa

Belgrade

Zara

Marseille

ITALY

BULGARIA

Rome

BYZANTINE EMPIRE

Messina

SICILY

GREECE

Mediterranean Sea

The Crusades

In 1095, at the Council of Clermont in France, Pope Urban II delivered one of the most influential speeches of the Middle Ages. In it, he urged French barons and knights to take up arms to recapture the holy city of Jerusalem, which had been in Muslim hands since 673 CE. What followed was a series of wars between Christians and Muslims that lasted for over 200 years. Together, these wars are known as the Crusades.

AFTER MUSLIM LEADER SALADIN'S VICTORY IN BATTLE IN 1187, HE

1206–1294

Korea in the

Knightly virtues

Chivalry is a code of conduct followed by knights. The Crusades introduced a golden age of chivalry, in which Crusaders, such as King Richard the Lionheart of England (right), and his rival Saladin, sultan of Egypt and Syria, were thought of as the perfect knights, living their lives according to honour, courage, valour, and pride.

2. Nicaea
The first official Crusaders attacked the important fortress city of Nicaea in May 1097. The city surrendered in June.

7. Dorylaeum
At the start of the Second Crusade in October 1147, Muslims crushed King Conrad of Germany's forces at the battle of Dorylaeum.

3. Antioch
The Crusaders defeated Muslim forces following the 8-month siege of Antioch (1097–98).

5. Crusader States
Following the end of the First Crusade, the Crusaders established four Crusader States: the County of Edessa; the County of Tripoli; the Principality of Antioch; and the Kingdom of Jerusalem.

6. Edessa
Muslims retook Edessa in 1144, leading to the loss of one of the Crusader States. Pope Eugenius III called for the Second Crusade.

8. Second Crusade
The Second Crusade ended in humiliation in July 1148, after Crusader forces under Louis VII of France failed to take Damascus.

11. Jaffa
King Richard I of England (Richard the Lionheart) and Saladin signed a peace treaty on 2 September 1192. The Crusader States were preserved, but, because the Third Crusade did not retake Jerusalem, it was a failure.

9. Battle of Hattin
United under a new leader, Saladin, Muslim forces defeated the Christians at the battle of Hattin in 1187 and retook Jerusalem. This sparked the Third Crusade.

4. Jerusalem
In 1099, Jerusalem fell to the Crusaders. Thousands of Muslims and Jews were massacred. This marked the end of the First Crusade.

Karakorum ...enghis ...tablished ...ongol ...adquarters ...Karakorum ...1220.

KARA KHITAI EMPIRE

Saracen horsemen

KEY
- ▦ Muslim lands in 1096, apart from those that became Crusader States
- ▦ Christian lands in 1096
- ✕ Major battles
- ▦ Crusader States in 1135 (these were Muslim in 1096)
- ⟶ First Crusade, 1095–99
- ⟶ Second Crusade, 1147–49
- ⟶ Third Crusade, 1187–92
- ⟶ Fourth Crusade, 1202–04
- ① Key location
- ○ Key town

Nicaea, Dorylaeum, Antioch, Tripoli, Damascus, Tyre, Jaffa, Edessa, Jerusalem

9. Li
The Mongols d
a combined
Poles, Templa
Teutonic Kni
Liegnitz i

10. Pe
Following th
victory at Lieg
the Mongols sack
Pest in modern-
Hungary later t
same ye

T
t
Dy

The Mamlu
the Mongo
in 1260
M

Genghis

Revered in
feared amc
Genghis Kh
leader and
was respor
deaths, but
to a vast er
8,000 km (5

Kutchin
The Kutchin were hunter-gatherers who lived in Alaska and did not make contact with Europeans until 1789.

Chinook
The Chinook lived in permanent villages in the Pacific Northwest region. Peoples of the region carved totem poles, but all those carved before 1800 have since rotted away.

Inuit
The Inuit adapted to the extreme Arctic climate, where they lived, in many ways, such as fishing through holes in the ice.

Inuit

Dogrib

Kutchin

Chinook

Blackfeet

Crow

Shoshone

Sioux

Cheyenne

Navajo

Apac

Hopi

Comanc

"We do not inherit the Earth from our ancestors; we borrow it from our children."

American Indian proverb

NORTH

AMERICA

Sioux
The Sioux were great bison hunters and warriors who lived in the North American Plains, or prairies.

1400s **15th-century Americas**

Before Christopher Columbus's arrival in 1492, the American continents had been settled for thousands of years. In the North, the American Indians were a mix of hunter-gatherers, who were nomadic, and farmers, some of whom lived in large settlements. The largest settlments, however, were in Central and South America, where developed some of the greatest empires of the time.

Aztec Empire
Originally desert people, the Aztecs took control of the Valley of Mexico in the early 14th century. At their peak, they controlled an empire of roughly 10 million people. Their capital, Tenochtitlan (artist's reconstruction, right), was one of the largest cities in the world, with a population of roughly 300,000 people.

206–1294 The age of the Mongols

During the 13th century, the Mongols were the most feared warriors on Earth. United under Genghis Khan in 1206, they terrorized people from Russia and Poland in the west to China and Korea in the east, and established the largest empire the world had ever seen.

1. Mongolia
Temujin completed his conquest of rival Mongol tribes in 1206 and received the title Genghis Khan, meaning "universal ruler".

Buryats

Mongols *Tatars*

Karakorum
Genghis established Mongol headquarters at Karakorum in 1220.

Merkits Karakorum

Naimans

KARA KHITAI EMPIRE

3. Zhongdu
In 1215, Genghis starved the city of Zhongdu into submission. The city was sacked and burned.

JIN EMPIRE

Zhongdu

XIA EMPIRE
Ningxia

2. Ningxia
During the siege of Ningxia, in his first campaign against the Xia Empire in 1210, Genghis dammed the Yellow River.

Feng

Yellow River

Ningbo

KOREA
Kaesong

14. Japan
The Mongols made two attempts to invade Japan (in 1274 and 1281). Both failed due to bad weather. These were the only attacks on Japan in its history, until World War II.

JAPAN

8. Xianyang
General Meng of the Southern Song Dynasty (the remnants of China's Song Dynasty) retook Xianyang in 1239. The Mongols had captured the city 3 years earlier.

Xianyang

Hangzhou

SOUTHERN SONG DYNASTY OF CHINA

15. Hangzhou
The Mongols marched into Hangzhou in 1276 and replaced the Chinese Song Dynasty with the Mongol-led Yuan Dynasty.

Daluo
ANNAM

16. Annam
In 1288, the Mongol's 4-year campaign against Annam was halted by a combination of guerilla warfare, heat, and disease.

"The Mongol army **swarmed** in like **ants and locusts** from all directions."

Rashid-ad-Din, Persian politician and historian, on the Mongol attack on Baghdad in 1258

The Black Death

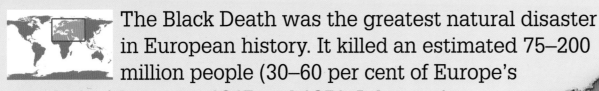

The Black Death was the greatest natural disaster in European history. It killed an estimated 75–200 million people (30–60 per cent of Europe's population) between 1347 and 1351. It began in central Asia, was carried along the Silk Road by fleas living on rats, and was then passed from person to person.

4. Weymouth, England
A ship from Gascony, France, carrying infected sailors docked in Weymouth, England, on 7 July 1348. The Black Death spread across the British Isles in a year.

Weymouth **4**
Gascony
Genoa
3
Messina

EUROPE

KEY

Area reached by the Black Death by 1351

 Major outbreaks of Black Death

① Key location in the story of the spread of the Black Death

Percentage of population known to have died in major cities:

◆ **Bremen, Germany: 60%**

◆ **Hamburg, Germany: 60%**

◆ **Venice, Italy: 60%**

◆ **Florence, Italy: 55%**

◇ **Paris, France: 50%**

◇ **Avignon, France: 50%**

◆ **Cairo, Egypt: 40%**

◆ **London, England: 40%**

◆ **Damascus, Syria: 38%**

◆ **Baghdad, Iraq: 33%**

◇ **Isfahan, Iran: 33%**

○ Other key town

3. Messina, Italy
Galleys from Caffa carrying the plague arrived in Messina, Sicily, in October 1347. The Black Death soon spread into mainland Italy.

"And so many **died** that all believed it was the **end of the world**."

Agnolo di Tura, in *The Plague in Siena: An Italian Chronicle*, 1351

AFRICA

THE BLACK DEATH KILLED NUMEROUS ROYALS, BUT KING ALFONSO XI OF

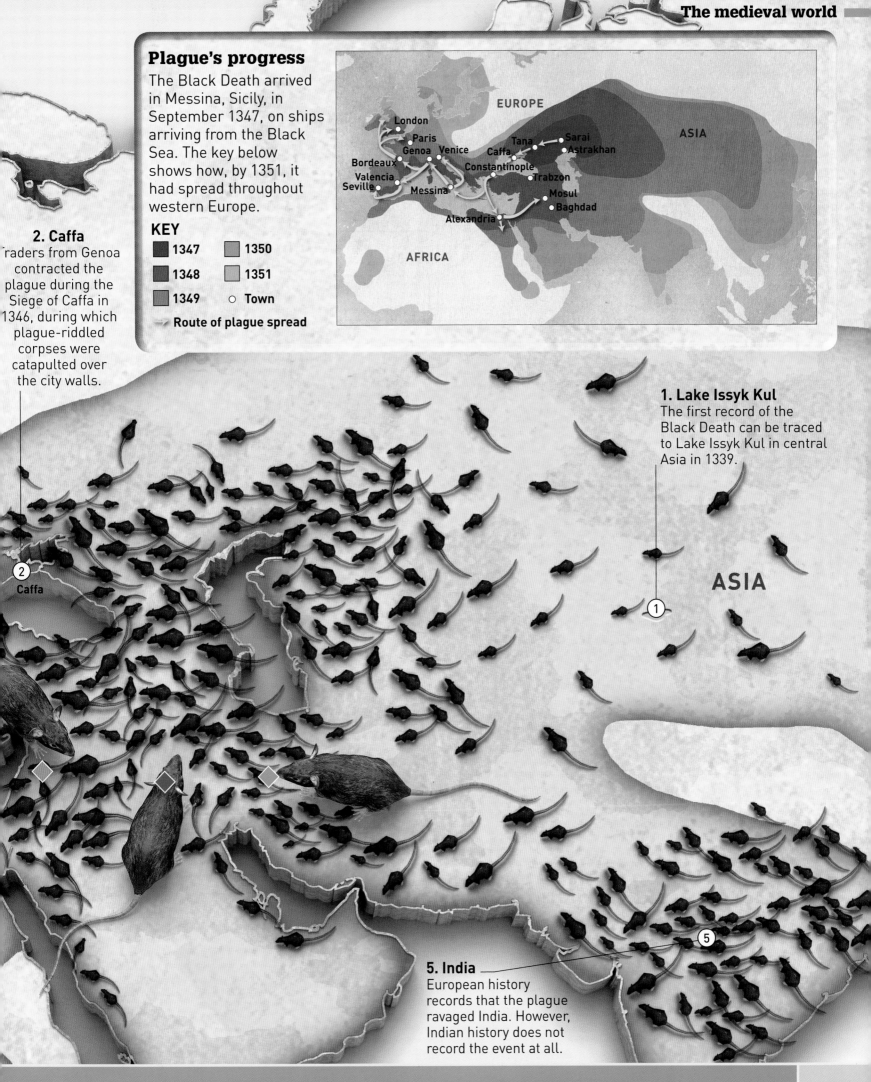

Plague's progress

The Black Death arrived in Messina, Sicily, in September 1347, on ships arriving from the Black Sea. The key below shows how, by 1351, it had spread throughout western Europe.

KEY

■	1347	■	1350
■	1348	■	1351
■	1349	○	Town

↗ Route of plague spread

EUROPE
ASIA
AFRICA

London
Paris
Genoa Venice
Bordeaux
Valencia
Seville Messina
Tana Sarai
Caffa Astrakhan
Constantinople
Trabzon
Mosul
Baghdad
Alexandria

2. Caffa

Traders from Genoa contracted the plague during the Siege of Caffa in 1346, during which plague-riddled corpses were catapulted over the city walls.

1. Lake Issyk Kul

The first record of the Black Death can be traced to Lake Issyk Kul in central Asia in 1339.

ASIA

Caffa

5. India

European history records that the plague ravaged India. However, Indian history does not record the event at all.

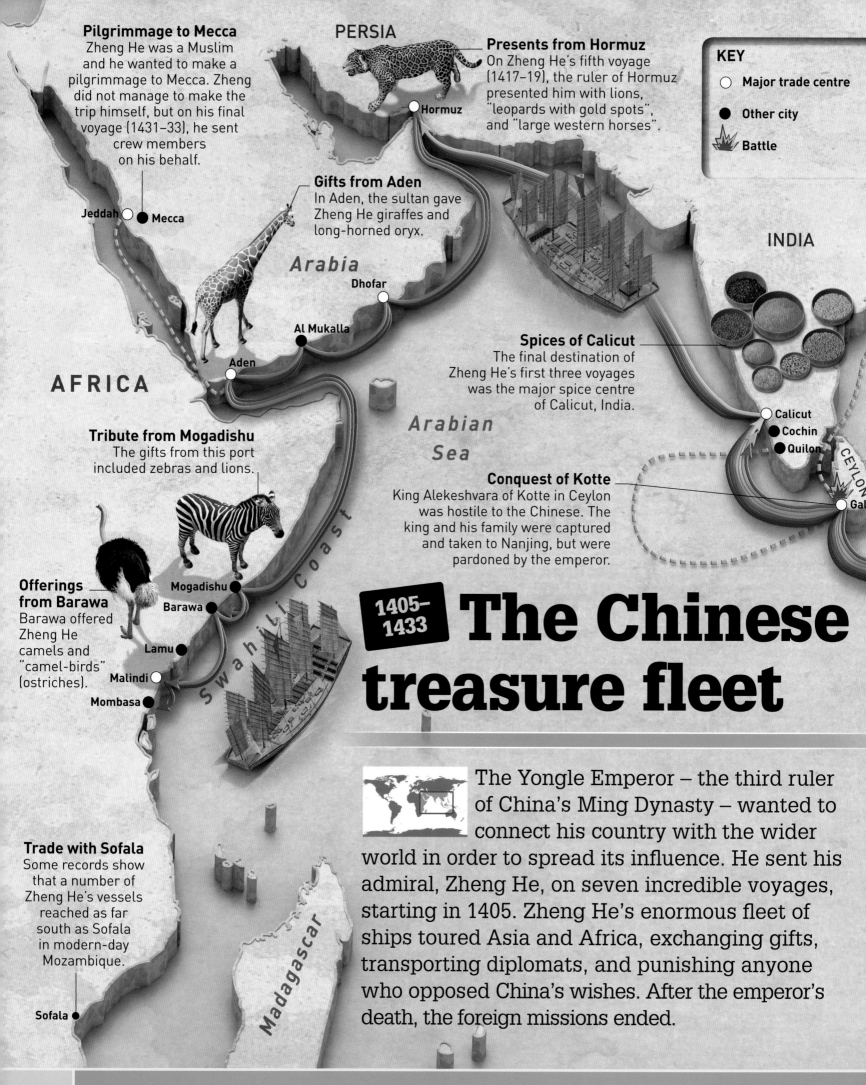

Pilgrimmage to Mecca
Zheng He was a Muslim and he wanted to make a pilgrimmage to Mecca. Zheng did not manage to make the trip himself, but on his final voyage (1431–33), he sent crew members on his behalf.

Gifts from Aden
In Aden, the sultan gave Zheng He giraffes and long-horned oryx.

PERSIA

Presents from Hormuz
On Zheng He's fifth voyage (1417–19), the ruler of Hormuz presented him with lions, "leopards with gold spots", and "large western horses".

Hormuz

Arabia

Dhofar

Al Mukalla

Aden

Jeddah ● Mecca

AFRICA

INDIA

Spices of Calicut
The final destination of Zheng He's first three voyages was the major spice centre of Calicut, India.

*Arabian
Sea*

● Calicut
● Cochin
● Quilon

CEYLON

Tribute from Mogadishu
The gifts from this port included zebras and lions.

Conquest of Kotte
King Alekeshvara of Kotte in Ceylon was hostile to the Chinese. The king and his family were captured and taken to Nanjing, but were pardoned by the emperor.

Gal

Mogadishu

Barawa

Offerings from Barawa
Barawa offered Zheng He camels and "camel-birds" (ostriches).

Lamu

Malindi

Mombasa

Swahili Coast

1405–1433 The Chinese treasure fleet

Trade with Sofala
Some records show that a number of Zheng He's vessels reached as far south as Sofala in modern-day Mozambique.

Madagascar

Sofala ●

The Yongle Emperor – the third ruler of China's Ming Dynasty – wanted to connect his country with the wider world in order to spread its influence. He sent his admiral, Zheng He, on seven incredible voyages, starting in 1405. Zheng He's enormous fleet of ships toured Asia and Africa, exchanging gifts, transporting diplomats, and punishing anyone who opposed China's wishes. After the emperor's death, the foreign missions ended.

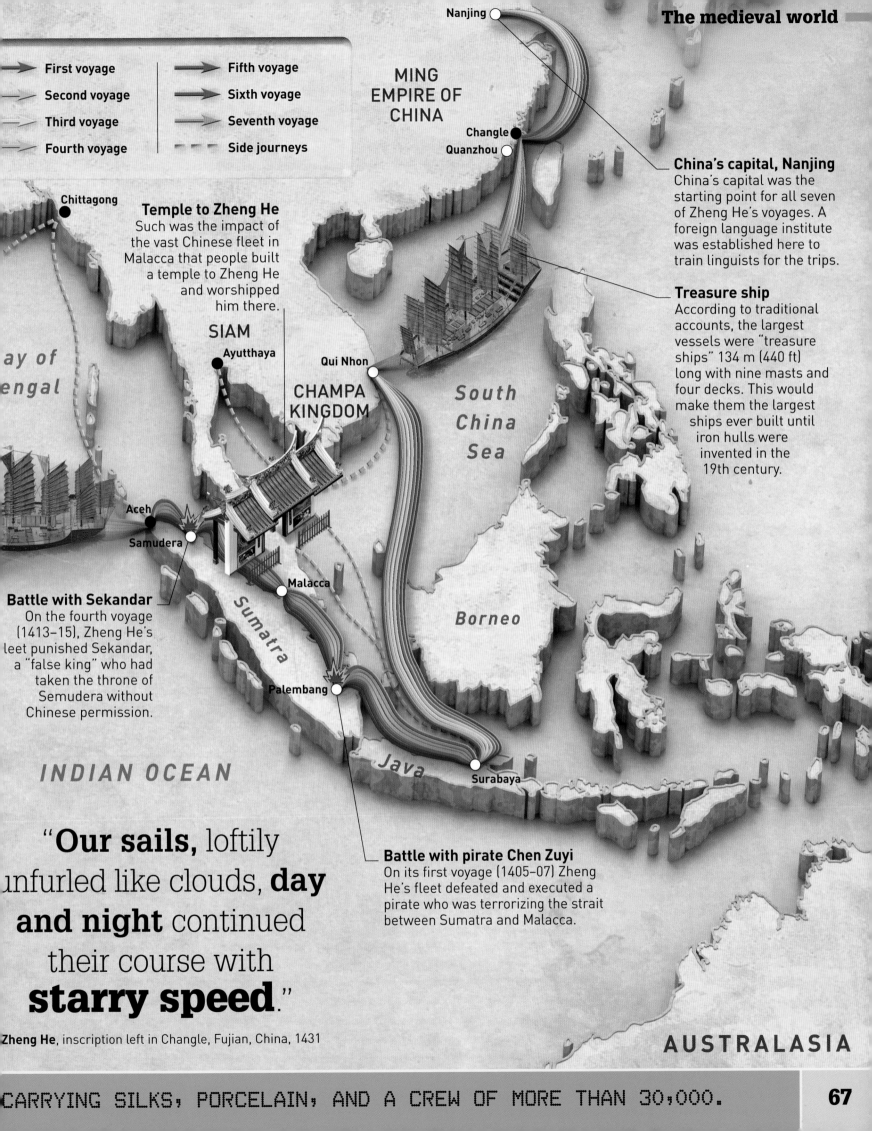

First voyage
Second voyage
Third voyage
Fourth voyage
Fifth voyage
Sixth voyage
Seventh voyage
Side journeys

MING EMPIRE OF CHINA

Nanjing

Changle
Quanzhou

China's capital, Nanjing
China's capital was the starting point for all seven of Zheng He's voyages. A foreign language institute was established here to train linguists for the trips.

Chittagong

Temple to Zheng He
Such was the impact of the vast Chinese fleet in Malacca that people built a temple to Zheng He and worshipped him there.

SIAM

Ayutthaya

Qui Nhon

CHAMPA KINGDOM

South China Sea

Treasure ship
According to traditional accounts, the largest vessels were "treasure ships" 134 m (440 ft) long with nine masts and four decks. This would make them the largest ships ever built until iron hulls were invented in the 19th century.

ay of
engal

Aceh
Samudera

Battle with Sekandar
On the fourth voyage (1413–15), Zheng He's fleet punished Sekandar, a "false king" who had taken the throne of Semudera without Chinese permission.

Malacca

Sumatra

Borneo

Palembang

INDIAN OCEAN

Java

Surabaya

"Our sails, loftily unfurled like clouds, **day and night** continued their course with **starry speed."**

Zheng He, inscription left in Changle, Fujian, China, 1431

Battle with pirate Chen Zuyi
On its first voyage (1405–07) Zheng He's fleet defeated and executed a pirate who was terrorizing the strait between Sumatra and Malacca.

AUSTRALASIA

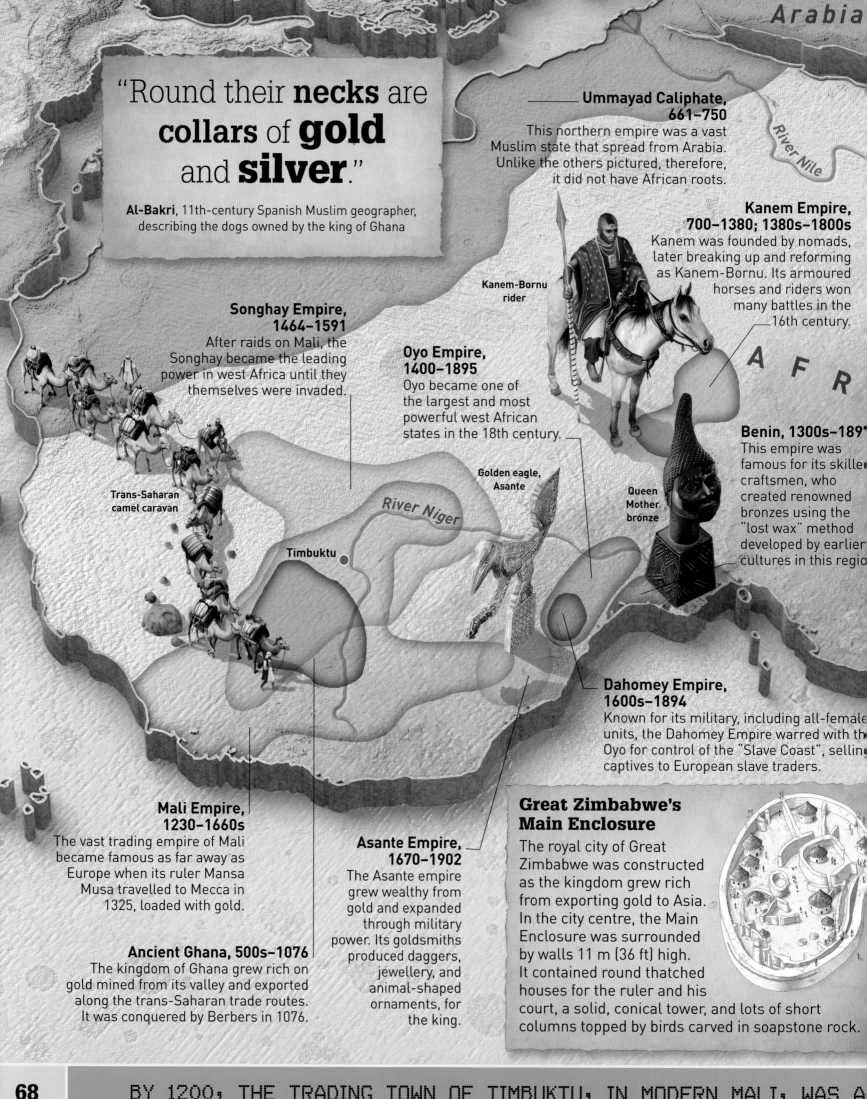

"Round their **necks** are collars of **gold** and **silver**."

Al-Bakri, 11th-century Spanish Muslim geographer, describing the dogs owned by the king of Ghana

Ummayad Caliphate, 661–750
This northern empire was a vast Muslim state that spread from Arabia. Unlike the others pictured, therefore, it did not have African roots.

Kanem Empire, 700–1380; 1380s–1800s
Kanem was founded by nomads, later breaking up and reforming as Kanem-Bornu. Its armoured horses and riders won many battles in the 16th century.

Kanem-Bornu rider

Songhay Empire, 1464–1591
After raids on Mali, the Songhay became the leading power in west Africa until they themselves were invaded.

Oyo Empire, 1400–1895
Oyo became one of the largest and most powerful west African states in the 18th century.

Trans-Saharan camel caravan

Golden eagle, Asante

River Niger

Timbuktu

Queen Mother bronze

Benin, 1300s–189
This empire was famous for its skille craftsmen, who created renowned bronzes using the "lost wax" method developed by earlier cultures in this regio

Dahomey Empire, 1600s–1894
Known for its military, including all-female units, the Dahomey Empire warred with th Oyo for control of the "Slave Coast", sellin captives to European slave traders.

Mali Empire, 1230–1660s
The vast trading empire of Mali became famous as far away as Europe when its ruler Mansa Musa travelled to Mecca in 1325, loaded with gold.

Asante Empire, 1670–1902
The Asante empire grew wealthy from gold and expanded through military power. Its goldsmiths produced daggers, jewellery, and animal-shaped ornaments, for the king.

Great Zimbabwe's Main Enclosure
The royal city of Great Zimbabwe was constructed as the kingdom grew rich from exporting gold to Asia. In the city centre, the Main Enclosure was surrounded by walls 11 m (36 ft) high. It contained round thatched houses for the ruler and his court, a solid, conical tower, and lots of short columns topped by birds carved in soapstone rock.

Ancient Ghana, 500s–1076
The kingdom of Ghana grew rich on gold mined from its valley and exported along the trans-Saharan trade routes. It was conquered by Berbers in 1076.

Great African kingdoms

100 BCE–1902 CE

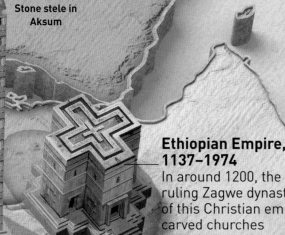

Stone stele in Aksum

Church in Lalibela

Ethiopian Empire, 1137–1974
In around 1200, the ruling Zagwe dynasty of this Christian empire carved churches straight into the rocky ground in the town of Lalibela.

Kingdom of Aksum, 100 BCE–600s CE
This trading kingdom is best known for building tall stone stelae (columns), which were probably used as burial markers.

The lost kingdoms and empires of Africa acquired power through trade and natural resources. They were also known for their crafts, created to honour rulers and gods. Some kingdoms lasted hundreds of years, but none survive to the present day. The later ones were swallowed up in the colonization of Africa by European powers in the late 19th and early 20th centuries.

Carved wooden headrest

King João Nzinga

Luba Kingdom, 1580s–1889
Luba was ruled by kings who claimed to be descended from a mythical hunter. Carved wooden objects celebrated their divine status.

Soapstone bird carving

Lunda Kingdom, 1660s–1884
This kingdom conquered its neighbours through its military might, expanding significantly in the 1740s.

Great Zimbabwe

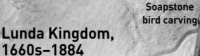
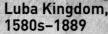
River Zambezi

Zulu shield and spears

Ndongo, 1500s–1671
Ndongo broke away from Kongo in the 1560s. It sold people as slaves to Portugal, but in 1623 the Portuguese took some slaves by force and refused to return them, leading to war with Ndongo.

Kingdom of Zimbabwe, 1100s–1450
Medieval Zimbabwe grew wealthy over hundreds of years by trading cattle and gold, reaching its peak in the early 15th century.

Kingdom of Kongo, 1390–1857
Kongo was the centre of a trade network in cloth and pottery when the Portuguese first arrived in 1483. Their king was baptized as João Nzinga, and the kingdom kept good relations with Portugal for hundreds of years.

Zulu Kingdom, 1816–97
Warrior chief Shaka founded what was the most powerful nation in South Africa – until the British took over at the end of the 19th century.

Kutchin
The Kutchin were hunter-gatherers who lived in Alaska and did not make contact with Europeans until 1789.

Chinook
The Chinook lived in permanent villages in the Pacific Northwest region. Peoples of the region carved totem poles, but all those carved before 1800 have since rotted away.

Inuit
The Inuit adapted to the extreme Arctic climate, where they lived, in many ways, such as fishing through holes in the ice.

Inuit

Dogrib

Kutchin

Chinook

Blackfeet

Crow

Shoshone

Sioux

Cheyenne

Navajo   Apach

Hopi   Comanch

NORTH

AMERICA

"We do not **inherit the Earth** from our ancestors; we **borrow it** from our **children**."

American Indian proverb

Sioux
The Sioux were great bison hunters and warriors who lived in the North American Plains, or prairies.

 **1400s**

15th-century Americas

 Before Christopher Columbus's arrival in 1492, the American continents had been settled for thousands of years. In the North, the American Indians were a mix of hunter-gatherers, who were nomadic, and farmers, some of whom lived in large settlements. The largest settlments, however, were in Central and South America, where developed some of the greatest empires of the time.

Aztec Empire
Originally desert people, the Aztecs took control of the Valley of Mexico in the early 14th century. At their peak, they controlled an empire of roughly 10 million people. Their capital, Tenochtitlan (artist's reconstruction, right), was one of the largest cities in the world, with a population of roughly 300,000 people.

Inuit hunting
Like Inuit in Canada and Alaska, the Inuit of Greenland hunted seals by kayak.

KEY
Experts group the peoples of the Americas according to the climate and terrain (shown by the different colours on the map). These varied environments affected the peoples' culture and lifestyle. For example, nomadic, tepee-dwelling bison hunters lived on the Plains, while farming villages dominated the Southeast.

- Arctic
- Subarctic
- Northeast woods
- Southeast
- Plains
- Great Basin
- Plateau
- Pacific Northwest
- California
- Southwest
- Mesoamerican
- Caribbean
- Andean
- Amazonian
- Cono/Southern

Montagnais

Abenaki

Iroquois

Shawnee

Maya
By 1492, the Maya people lived in rival cities in what is now south-eastern Mexico, Guatemala, Belize, and Honduras.

Mundurucú
After European contact, these warriors of the Amazon raided Portuguese villages along the river.

Rainforest hunters
Many varied groups of people lived in the Amazonian rainforest. Some used blowpipes to kill animals for food.

Maya

Arawak

Teremembé

Mundurucú

...htitlan

Central America

Aztec
The Aztecs dominated large parts of Central America between the 14th and 16th centuries.

Inca   Macchu Pichu
          Cuzco

Tupinambá

Chiquito

Qulla   *Guaraní*

Inca
By 1492, the Inca Empire stretched from what is now Colombia to Chile and northwest Argentina, and the population could have been as high as 15 million.

Atacama

SOUTH AMERICA

Charrúa

Northern Tehuelche

...nca Empire
...he Inca Empire was ...e largest empire in the ...mericas in 1492. It arose ...om the highlands of Peru ... the 13th century, and by ...e 15th century, controlled ... area almost as large ...s the Roman Empire. The ...erritory was connected ...ith a road system that was ...9,000 km (18,000 miles) long.

Mapuche

Mapuche
The Mapuche, whose name means "Earth People", inhabited a vast territory in what is now Chile and Argentina.

Southern Tehuelche

Ona

Printing press

Printing press, 1440 CE
Invented by Johannes Gutenberg in Germany, the printing press could print text quickly, unlike block printing, which had to be done by hand.

Keeping time
The first mechanical clock was invented by China's Su Sung. It was powered by the energy of falling water and the bucket collecting the water had to be emptied regularly. The first clock to use a clockwork mechanism (powered by a wound-up spring), appeared in Europe more than 200 years later.

Horseshoe, 400–450 CE
Metal shoes, nailed to horses' hooves, appeared in western Europe by about 450 CE.

Longbow, 1200 CE
The English longbow was much more powerful than the ordinary bow and helped the English win many battles against the French. Despite its name, it originated in Wales.

Artesian well, 1126 CE
An Artesian well allowed access to underground water without the need for it to be pumped. The earliest known well was dug in Artois, France.

Stern-mounted rudder, 1180 CE
The rudder enabled ships to steer through water more easily. The earliest known evidence of a rudder was found in Belgian art.

EUROPE

Spectacles, 1286 CE
In 1286, Italian monk Giordano da Pisa wrote a description of eyeglasses – the first mention of them anywhere in the world.

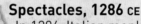

Spectacles

Hourglass, 1338 CE
Invented by the Venetians, the hourglass was ideal at sea because its accuracy was unaffected by bobbing waves.

Heavy plough, 650
The heavy plough allowed farmers to farm on dense clay soil, which helped to increase food production throughout northern Europe

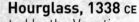

Plough

SOUTH AMERICA

Rope bridge, 600 CE
The earliest known rope bridge was built in Peru. The design has since inspired some of the world's largest suspension bridges.

"The greatest **inventions** were **produced** in the times of ignorance."

Jonathan Swift, British author, in *Thoughts on Various Subjects*, 1727

CHINESE ALCHEMISTS (EXPERIMENTERS) DISCOVERED GUNPOWDER B

450–1500 CE Medieval inventions

The medieval era – between around 450 and 1500 CE – was a time of great technological advancements across Europe and the Far East. During this period, European explorers also swapped many ideas with people from the Islamic world and China.

ASIA

Gunpowder, 850 CE
Gunpowder was first used by the Chinese to scare away what they believed were evil spirits. Later, it became a key part of explosives and flamethrowers.

Spinning wheel

Compass, 1040–44 CE
The Chinese military was the first to employ the magnetic compass for navigation. Chinese sailors had adapted it for sea use by 1117 CE.

Windmill

Windmill, 644 CE
The first windmills appeared in Persia and were used to grind grain and pump water.

Horse collar, 470–500 CE
The horse collar enabled a horse to pull three times more weight. Evidence of its earliest known use has been found in the Mogao Caves in China.

Wood block printing, 650 CE
Invented in China during the Tang Dynasty, block printing allowed scrolls and books to be produced quickly.

Spinning wheel, 1150 CE
Invented in China, the spinning wheel was used to turn animal or plant fibre into threads for making clothes.

Mechanical clock, 1088 CE
(See box on opposite page).

AFRICA

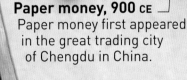

Paper money

Paper money, 900 CE
Paper money first appeared in the great trading city of Chengdu in China.

ACCIDENT WHEN THEY WERE LOOKING FOR A POTION FOR IMMORTALITY!

73

The modern world

Modern technology
Isambard Kingdom Brunel, one of the greatest engineers of the 1800s, oversees the building of his steamship *Great Eastern* in 1857. Able to sail from Britain to Australia without refuelling, it represents an era of exploration and technology.

Sextant at sea

The sextant, invented around 1730, could tell sailors where they were at sea. It measured the angle of the Sun, Moon, or stars above the horizon.

1488

AGE OF EXPLORATION (1488–1597) European explorers discover new trade routes and countries across the Atlantic. »pp78–79

VASCO DA GAMA (1497) The Portuguese explorer creates a new direct trade route from Europe to Asia. »pp78–79

REFORMATION (1517) Martin Luther begins the Protestant movement with his complaints against the Catholic Church. »pp84–85

NEW WORLD DISCOVERY (1492) Italian explorer Christopher Columbus sails from Spain to find a trade route to Asia, but instead discovers the Americas. »pp78–79

ATLANTIC SLAVE TRADE (1500s–1800s) More than 12.5 million Africans are enslaved and transported to the Americas. »pp90–91

END OF THE AZTECS (1521) Spanish Conquistador Hernán Cortés conquers the Aztec Empire of Central America. »pp80–81

FRENCH REVOLUTION (1789–94) With the motto "liberty, equality, fraternity", protestors revolt against the monarchy and church. »pp96–97

AMERICAN WAR OF INDEPENDENCE (1775–81) The US becomes an independent country with 13 states, free from British control. »pp92–93

RUBBER (1735) French explorer Charles-Marie de la Condamine brings rubber to Europe from Ecuador. »pp120–21

CONVICTS IN AUSTRALIA (1788) Britain transports 1,500 convicts to Botany Bay, Australia, and sets up a penal colony at Port Jackson (modern-day Sydney). »pp94–95

THE INDUSTRIAL REVOLUTION (1770s–1870s) Machines begin to do the jobs previously done by people, making and transporting goods quickly and efficiently. »pp104–05

BLACKBEARD (1716–18) Pirate Edward Teach, known as Blackbeard, terrorizes the Caribbean and southeast American coast. »pp86–87

HMS *Sirius*, flagship of the first transportation to Australia

NAPOLEONIC WARS (1792–1815) French leader Napoleon Bonaparte extends his control across Europe before being defeated at Waterloo. »pp98–99

FIRST FREE SETTLERS IN AUSTRALIA (1793) The first voluntary immigrants from Britain move to Australia. »pp94–95

SOUTH AMERICAN REVOLUTIONS (1808–26) After 300 years of European rule, most colonies in South America become independent. »pp100–0

VACCINE (1796) Edward Jenner invents the vaccine – a way of triggering the human body to fight smallpox. »pp120–21

STEAM RAILWAYS (1825) The world's first public steam railway opens, in northern England. »pp116–17

Modern times

TRANS-SIBERIAN RAILWAY (1891–1916) The world's longest railway is built across Russia. »pp116–17

1900

The end of the 15th century signalled the start of the age of exploration. Europeans possessed new technology to sail and navigate long distances and wanted to find new trade routes. Christopher Columbus's discovery of the Americas – the New World – brought goods to trade, new foods, wealth, and gold. However, it also led to the colonization of New World countries, piracy, and slavery.

SOUTH AFRICAN GOLD RUSH (1886) Johannesburg becomes a large and wealthy city following a gold rush in Witwatersrand. »pp110–11

THE WORLD'S POPULATION REACHED 1 BILLION IN 1804. TODAY,

SULEIMAN THE MAGNIFICENT (1520–66)
Suleiman expands the Ottoman Empire through Europe. »pp118–19

END OF THE INCAS (1531)
On his third expedition to Peru, Conquistador Francisco Pizarro conquers the Inca Empire. »pp80–81

PRIVATEERING (1560–86)
The English privateer Sir Francis Drake carries out sea raids all over the Caribbean. »pp78–79; 86–87

COLONIZING AMERICA (1585) The Spanish establish the first European colony in what is now the US. »pp88–89

AROUND THE WORLD (1521–22) Ferdinand Magellan's ship completes the first circumnavigation of the globe. »pp78–79

CARIBBEAN PIRATES (1550–1720) British, French, and Dutch ships try to sieze gold being exported from the Americas by the Spanish. »pp86–87

NEW FOOD (1565)
Potatoes first arrive in Europe, brought from Mexico by Spanish ships. »pp82–83

FIRST GOLD RUSH (1693)
Gold is discovered at Mina Gerais, Brazil. By 1720, 400,000 Portuguese prospectors have moved to Brazil. »pp110–11

Gold nugget

EDO PERIOD, JAPAN (1615–1868) A military leader called a shogun rules Japan. No foreigners are allowed into the country. »pp114–15

FRENCH QUÉBEC (1608)
The first French colony in the Americas is set up in Québec – now in Canada. »pp88–89

QING DYNASTY, CHINA (1644–1912) Manchu people from the north of China replace China's Ming ruler and begin the Qing Dynasty. »pp118–19

NEW AMSTERDAM (1614) The Dutch West India Company establishes a new city in North America. In 1665, the English claim it and rename it New York. »pp88–89

JAMESTOWN, VIRGINIA (1607) Settlers arrive to set up the first successful English colony in North America. »pp88–89

DARWIN'S VOYAGE (1831–36) Charles Darwin develops his theory of evolution while travelling the world. »pp102–03

REVOLUTION! (1848)
People take to the streets across Europe to fight for better working conditions and voting rights. »pp106–07

JAPAN BEGINS TRADING (1853) Japan is forced by the US into its first trade agreement with a foreign country. »pp114–15

Steam locomotive
The first steam-powered railway engine ran in 1804 and steam engines continued to pull trains well into the 1900s. The *King Edward II* was built in 1930.

CALIFORNIAN GOLD RUSH (1848–55) More than 300,000 people flock to California to search for gold. »pp110–11

European protestors in 1848

BRITISH RAJ (1858–1947)
The British take direct control of India after the Indian Rebellion of 1857. British rule was called the Raj. »pp118–19

SCRAMBLE FOR AFRICA (1880s–1914) European powers enter Africa to end the slave trade, but invade and colonize countries as they do so. »pp118–19

MEIJI RESTORATION (1868)
Forces opposing Japan's shogun restore the emperor to power, beginning the Meiji Period. »pp114–15

ELECTRIC LIGHT (1879)
Thomas Edison invents a light bulb that is safe for use in people's houses. »pp120–21

BATTLE OF LITTLE BIGHORN (1876)
American Indians defeat the US Army in a territory war. »pp108–09

AMERICAN CIVIL WAR (1861–65) The deadliest war in US history leads to the abolition of slavery. »pp112–13

6023

THERE ARE MORE THAN 7 BILLION PEOPLE IN THE WORLD.

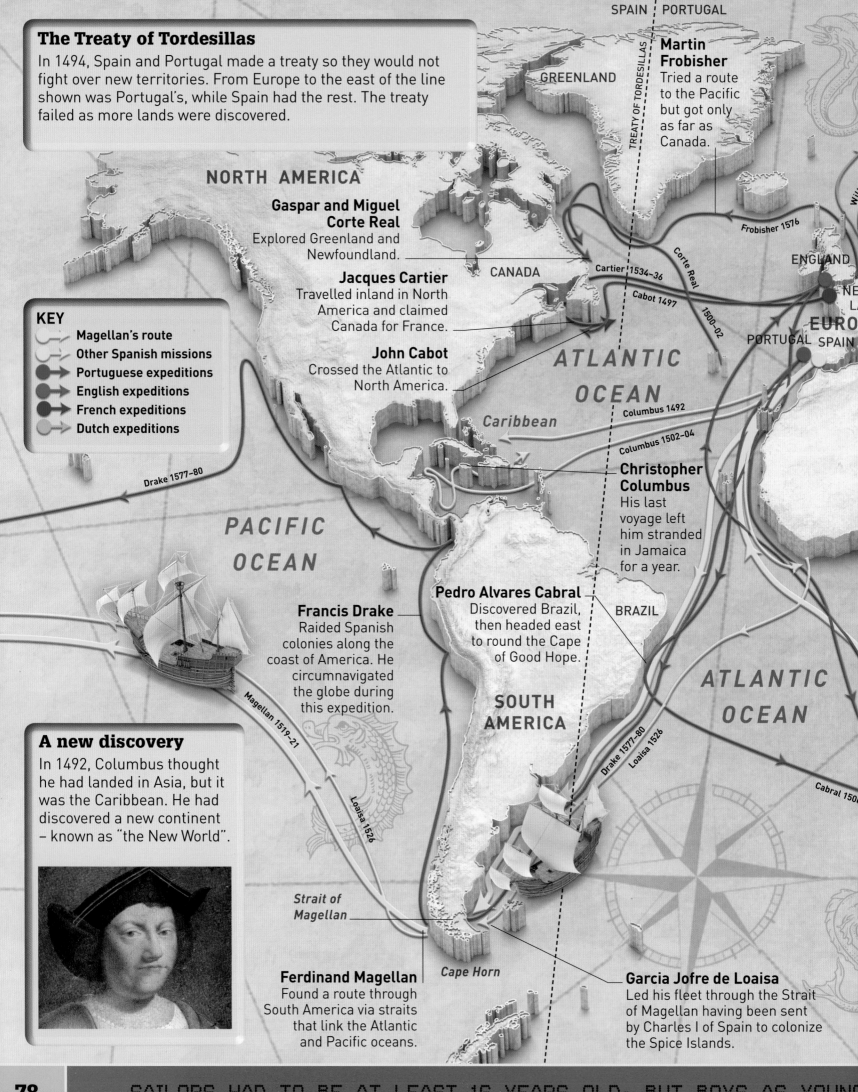

The Treaty of Tordesillas

In 1494, Spain and Portugal made a treaty so they would not fight over new territories. From Europe to the east of the line shown was Portugal's, while Spain had the rest. The treaty failed as more lands were discovered.

Martin Frobisher
Tried a route to the Pacific but got only as far as Canada.

GREENLAND

NORTH AMERICA

Gaspar and Miguel Corte Real
Explored Greenland and Newfoundland.

Jacques Cartier
Travelled inland in North America and claimed Canada for France.

CANADA

John Cabot
Crossed the Atlantic to North America.

Frobisher 1576

ENGLAND

Cartier 1534–36

Corte Real

Cabot 1497

1500–02

NE
L A

EURO

PORTUGAL SPAIN

KEY

- Magellan's route
- Other Spanish missions
- Portuguese expeditions
- English expeditions
- French expeditions
- Dutch expeditions

ATLANTIC OCEAN

Columbus 1492

Caribbean

Columbus 1502–04

Christopher Columbus
His last voyage left him stranded in Jamaica for a year.

Drake 1577–80

PACIFIC OCEAN

Francis Drake
Raided Spanish colonies along the coast of America. He circumnavigated the globe during this expedition.

Pedro Alvares Cabral
Discovered Brazil, then headed east to round the Cape of Good Hope.

BRAZIL

ATLANTIC OCEAN

Magellan 1519–21

A new discovery

In 1492, Columbus thought he had landed in Asia, but it was the Caribbean. He had discovered a new continent – known as "the New World".

SOUTH AMERICA

Drake 1577–80

Loaisa 1526

Cabral 150

Loaisa 1526

Strait of Magellan

Ferdinand Magellan
Found a route through South America via straits that link the Atlantic and Pacific oceans.

Cape Horn

Garcia Jofre de Loaisa
Led his fleet through the Strait of Magellan having been sent by Charles I of Spain to colonize the Spice Islands.

SAILORS HAD TO BE AT LEAST 16 YEARS OLD, BUT BOYS AS YOUNG

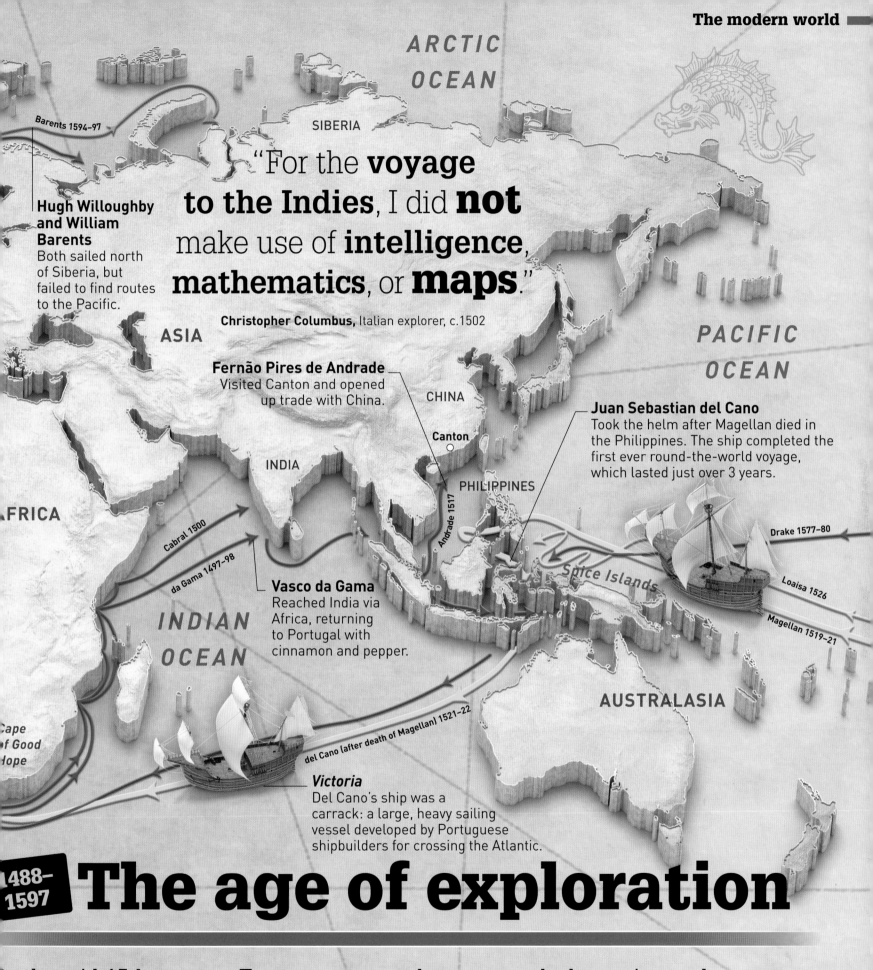

ARCTIC
OCEAN

SIBERIA

Barents 1594–97

Hugh Willoughby and William Barents
Both sailed north of Siberia, but failed to find routes to the Pacific.

"For the **voyage to the Indies**, I did **not** make use of **intelligence**, mathematics, or **maps**."

Christopher Columbus, Italian explorer, c.1502

ASIA

PACIFIC OCEAN

Fernão Pires de Andrade
Visited Canton and opened up trade with China.

CHINA

Canton

INDIA

PHILIPPINES

Andrade 1517

Juan Sebastian del Cano
Took the helm after Magellan died in the Philippines. The ship completed the first ever round-the-world voyage, which lasted just over 3 years.

AFRICA

Cabral 1500

da Gama 1497–98

Drake 1577–80

Spice Islands

Loaisa 1526

Vasco da Gama
Reached India via Africa, returning to Portugal with cinnamon and pepper.

Magellan 1519–21

INDIAN OCEAN

del Cano (after death of Magellan) 1521–22

AUSTRALASIA

Cape of Good Hope

Victoria
Del Cano's ship was a carrack: a large, heavy sailing vessel developed by Portuguese shipbuilders for crossing the Atlantic.

488–1597

The age of exploration

By the mid-15th century, European powers began to seek alternative trade routes from the West to the East, as the main routes were under the control of various Muslim rulers. This led them to explore parts of the world they had never seen before.

AS SEVEN OR EIGHT COULD BE FOUND WORKING ON THE BOATS.

Conquest of the Aztecs

In 1519, Hernán Cortés built a huge army made of native people who wanted to rebel against the Aztecs. They seized the Aztec capital, Tenochtitlan, but the Aztecs re-captured it while Cortés was diverted at the coast, confronting a rival Conquistador, Pánfilo de Narváez. On Cortés's return in 1521, the city surrendered.

Page from an Aztec book, or codex, made in 1552–85 to tell the story of the conquest

Francisco Vásquez de Coronado, 1540

Led an expedition into modern-day Arizona, New Mexico, Texas, Oklahoma, and Kansas. One scouting party of de Coronado's became the first Europeans to see the Colorado River and the Grand Canyon.

Hernando de Soto, 1539–42

Head of the first European trek deep into the territory of the modern-day United States. Historians believe that he was the first European to cross the Mississippi River.

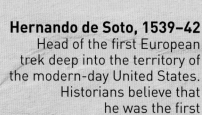

VICEROYALTY OF NEW SPAIN

Tenochtitlan ○

Alvar Núñez Cabeza de Vaca, 1528

A member of the disastrous 1528 Navárez expedition to colonize Florida, in which only 4 of 600 men survived. He tried to find a land-based route back to New Mexico, but American Indians captured him and held him for 8 years. He wrote the first European book on the customs of American Indian life.

Hernán Cortés, 1519

Mounted an expedition to mainland Central America. He amassed a vast army, marched on the Aztec capital, Tenochtitlan, and conquered the Aztec Empire.

Francisco de Montejo, 1527

Tried to conquer the east of the Yucatán Peninsula in 1527, but was driven back by the Maya. His son, also called Francisco, completed the conquest in 1545.

1513–1570 Conquistadors

Columbus's discovery of the New World in 1492 brought a wave of ambitious Spaniards, known as Conquistadors, in his wake. All were seeking fame and fortune, but while some triumphed, conquering empires and amassing great personal wealth, others failed and sometimes died in the process.

← Francisco Vásquez de Coronado
← Juan Ponce de León
← Hernán Cortés
← Pedro de Alvarado
← Francisco de Montejo
← Vasco Núñez de Balboa
← Hernando de Soto
← Francisco Pizarro
← Alvar Núñez Cabeza de Va

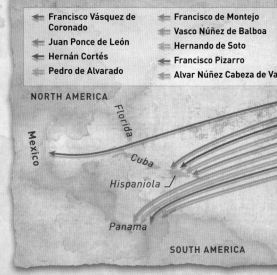

NORTH AMERICA

Mexico
Florida
Cuba
Hispaniola
Panama

SOUTH AMERICA

A CENTURY AFTER THE CONQUISTADORS ARRIVED, 90 PER CENT OF THE

KEY
○ Key city
☐ Area under Spanish control by 1570

ATLANTIC OCEAN

The last Inca emperor
Francisco Pizarro and his 180 men arrived in the Inca Empire in 1531. They met the Inca leader, Atahualpa, and his army at a camp in northern Peru. Pizarro kidnapped Atahualpa and demanded a huge ransom for his release. Pizarro received the ransom, but executed Atahualpa anyway, to please his troops. Two years later, the mighty Inca Empire had fallen.

Modern illustration of Pizarro and Atahualpa

Juan Ponce de León, 1513
Explored lands north of the island of Hispaniola. On 2 April 1513, he sighted what he thought was an island and named it Florida.

Vasco Núñez de Balboa, 1513–14
Best known for leading an expedition across Panama. During the journey, he became the first European to reach the Pacific Ocean from the New World.

Puerto Rico

Cuba

Hispaniola

Jamaica

Panama

Santa Mariá la Antigua del Darién

SOUTH AMERICA

Quito

"I and **my companions suffer** from a **disease of the heart** that only **gold** can **cure**."

Hernán Cortés, in an appeal to the Aztec emperor, 1519

Pedro de Alvarado, 1522
A member of Cortés's victorious expedition against the Aztecs. He earned fame as the most brutal of the Conquistadors by enslaving and killing native people. He went on to sieze more of Central America for the Spanish.

EUROPE

Where did they come from?
The Conquistadors were the hundreds of ambitious men who left Spain to seek fame and fortune in the New World. This map shows how the principal Conquistadors crossed the Atlantic Ocean from Spain and where they first made landfall in the New World.

Spain

AFRICA

ATLANTIC OCEAN

Cuzco

VICEROYALTY OF PERU

Francisco Pizarro, 1524–33
Tantalized by reports of Peru's riches, led two failed expeditions there in 1524 and 1526. He returned and conquered the Inca Empire in 1531.

AMERICAS' NATIVE POPULATION HAD DIED, MANY FROM NEW DISEASES.

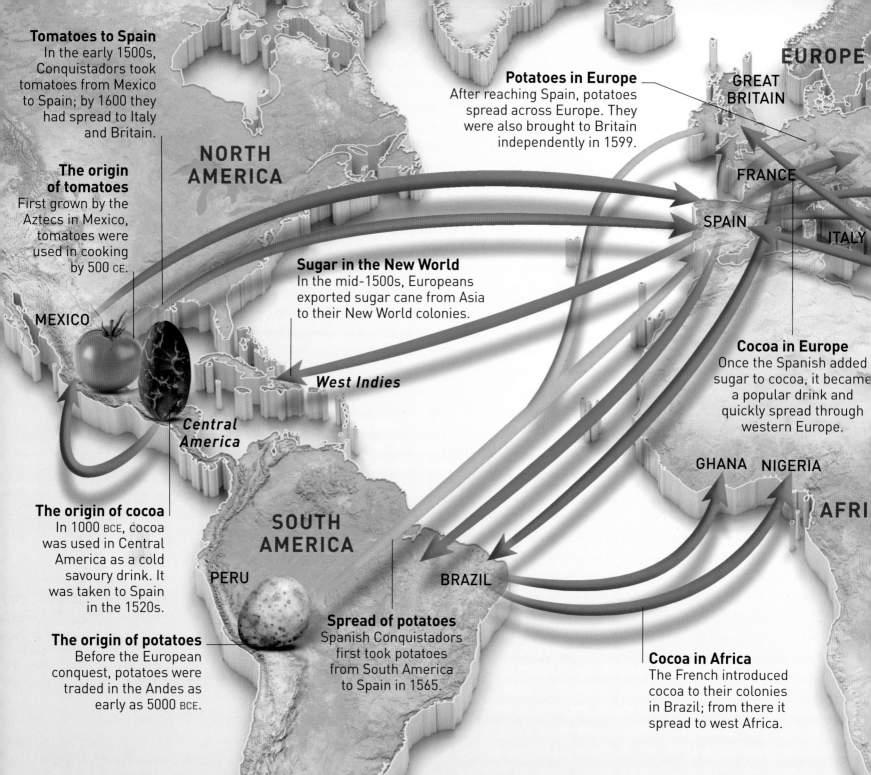

Tomatoes to Spain
In the early 1500s, Conquistadors took tomatoes from Mexico to Spain; by 1600 they had spread to Italy and Britain.

The origin of tomatoes
First grown by the Aztecs in Mexico, tomatoes were used in cooking by 500 CE.

NORTH AMERICA

MEXICO

Potatoes in Europe
After reaching Spain, potatoes spread across Europe. They were also brought to Britain independently in 1599.

EUROPE

GREAT BRITAIN

FRANCE

SPAIN

ITALY

Sugar in the New World
In the mid-1500s, Europeans exported sugar cane from Asia to their New World colonies.

West Indies

Central America

Cocoa in Europe
Once the Spanish added sugar to cocoa, it became a popular drink and quickly spread through western Europe.

GHANA **NIGERIA**

AFRI

The origin of cocoa
In 1000 BCE, cocoa was used in Central America as a cold savoury drink. It was taken to Spain in the 1520s.

SOUTH AMERICA

PERU

BRAZIL

The origin of potatoes
Before the European conquest, potatoes were traded in the Andes as early as 5000 BCE.

Spread of potatoes
Spanish Conquistadors first took potatoes from South America to Spain in 1565.

Cocoa in Africa
The French introduced cocoa to their colonies in Brazil; from there it spread to west Africa.

The Columbian Exchange

When the Old and New worlds met in 1492–1600, they exchanged fruit, grain, vegetables, and livestock. This event is called the Columbian Exchange. Disease-causing organisms (germs) were also transferred by accident. Some of these killed huge numbers of Native Americans.

New World (The Americas)
Fruit, vegetables, and seeds, including avocados, beans, chilli peppers, cocoa, peanuts, pineapples, potatoes, sweet potatoes, squashes, tomatoes, and vanilla; grains, such as corn (maize); livestock, for instance, turkeys; non-edible plants, such as tobacco; diseases, including syphilis.

Old World (Europe, Africa, and Asia)
Fruit, vegetables, and seeds, including bananas, citrus fruit, coffee, olives, onions, peaches, pears, and sugar cane; grains, such as barley, oats, rice, and wheat; livestock, including chickens, cows, and sheep; diseases, such as chickenpox, smallpox, and malaria.

IN THE 1600S, COCOA WAS VERY POPULAR IN EUROPE AND CLASSED

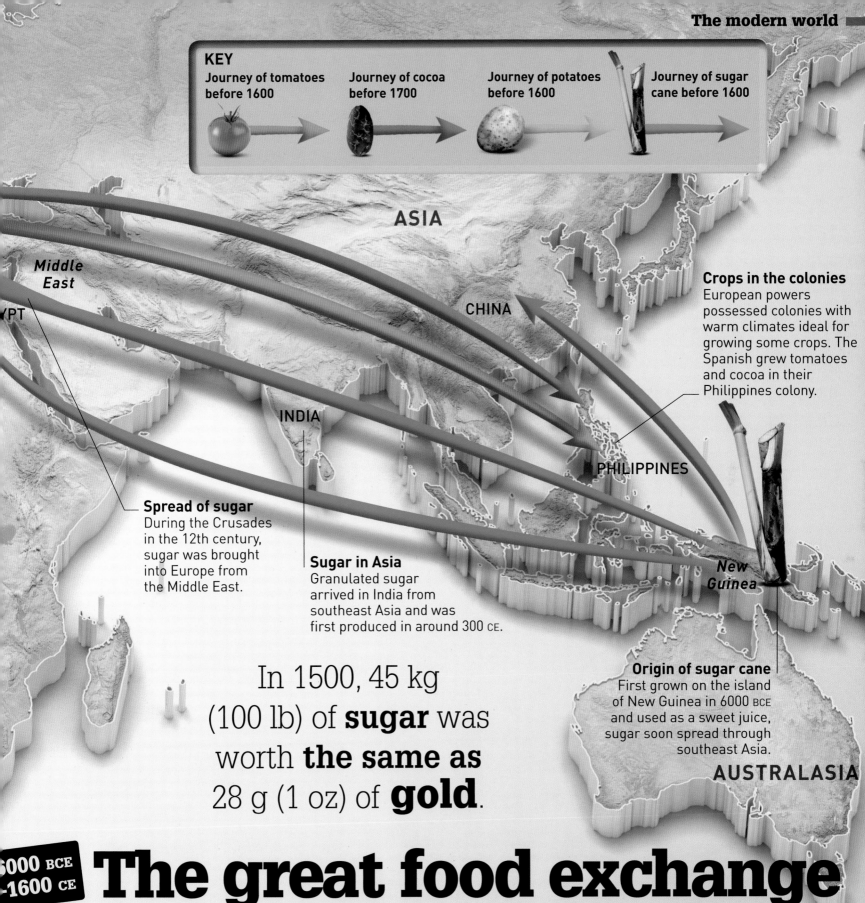

KEY

Journey of tomatoes before 1600

Journey of cocoa before 1700

Journey of potatoes before 1600

Journey of sugar cane before 1600

ASIA

Middle East

YPT

CHINA

Crops in the colonies
European powers possessed colonies with warm climates ideal for growing some crops. The Spanish grew tomatoes and cocoa in their Philippines colony.

INDIA

PHILIPPINES

Spread of sugar
During the Crusades in the 12th century, sugar was brought into Europe from the Middle East.

Sugar in Asia
Granulated sugar arrived in India from southeast Asia and was first produced in around 300 CE.

New Guinea

Origin of sugar cane
First grown on the island of New Guinea in 6000 BCE and used as a sweet juice, sugar soon spread through southeast Asia.

In 1500, 45 kg (100 lb) of **sugar** was worth **the same as** 28 g (1 oz) of **gold**.

AUSTRALASIA

6000 BCE –1600 CE # The great food exchange

When cultures meet, they discover new foods by trading with each other. Possibly the greatest ever meeting of cultures happened when Europeans explored the New World (the Americas) for the first time in the 16th century. People on both sides of the Atlantic discovered a vast range of previously unknown food plants.

AS A LUXURY FOOD — IT WAS MORE EXPENSIVE THAN THE BEST WINE.

The Reformation

The Catholic Church had been in religious control of western Europe for 1,000 years when in 1517, a monk named Martin Luther nailed a list of 95 complaints against the Church (called "theses") to a church door in Wittenberg, Germany. Luther's ideas sparked 130 years of wars and persecution, but they changed, or reformed, the Church and gave birth to a new branch of Christianity called Protestantism.

England's church founded
Henry VIII of England broke from the Catholic Church because the pope would not le[t] him divorce his wife. In 1534, he founded a new Protestant church, the Church of England with himself in charge.

Religious war breaks out
At the end of the 80 Years War in 1648, the Netherlands was split into a Catholic south (modern Belgium) and a Protestant north (modern Netherlands).

Huguenots massacred
Leading Protestants (known as Huguenots in France) were killed in Paris, in 1572, in what became known as the St Bartholomew's Day Massacre. The killing of Protestants was widespread during the French Wars of Religion (1562–98).

Protestants burnt
Protestants were persecuted in Spain. Many were put on trial and burnt to death. The first to suffer were those in Seville and Valladolid in 1558–62. Protestantism virtually disappeared from the country.

Martin Luther
Luther wanted to reform the Catholic Church rather than break away from it, but when he was excluded from the Church in 1520, he became a revolutionary leader.

"**Everything tha[t] is done** in the worl[d] is done by **hope**.[**"**]

Martin Luther, published in a collection of his sayings in 1566

SWEDEN

NORWAY

Church assets seized
In 1527, Gustav Vasa, ruler of Sweden, seized church lands and reformed the state church according to Luther's ideas.

● Stockholm

KEY
This map shows Europe in 1600, by which stage the Reformation had mainly settled the pattern of Catholic and Protestant areas.

☐ **Mainly Catholic**
☐ **Mainly Protestant**

DENMARK
Copenhagen ●

Luther posts his list
On 31 October 1517, Martin Luther posted his *95 Theses* on the door of a church in Wittenberg, in modern-day Germany.

● Riga

● Hamburg

PRUSSIA

mperor makes peace
1555 in Augsburg, after years of religious war, the Catholic Emperor Charles V allowed utheranism in German states whose rulers were Lutheran.

SMALL
GERMAN
STATES

● Berlin
Wittenberg ●

John Calvin
After becoming Protestant, John Calvin settled in Geneva, Switzerland, in 1536. He developed his own strand of the new religion, which became known as Calvinism. Calvin sent missionaries who helped to establish Protestant churches in Scotland, France, and the Netherlands.

POLAND–LITHUANIA

Prague ●

AUSTRIA

● Augsburg

● Cracow

● Zurich

HUNGARY

TZERLAND

● Trent

● Buda

Debrecen ●

lan ●

VENICE
Venice ●

TRANSYLVANIA

MALL ITALIAN
STATES

noa
ENOA

OTTOMAN EMPIRE

● Florence
TUSCANY

Belgrade ●

WALLACHIA

PAPAL STATES

Council of Trent meets
The Catholic Church, knowing it had to stop people flocking to the new Protestant churches, met three times at Trento in 1545–62. It decided to change itself to draw people back. The changes are known as the Counter-Reformation.

● Rome

NAPLES

● Naples

● Adrianople

Salonica ●

● Istanbul

SICILY

OTTOMAN EMPIRE

Caribbean pirates

In the 16th century, galleons left the Spanish Main (parts of the American mainland under Spanish control) loaded with plundered gold. They attracted privateers, who were licensed by other countries to take Spanish ships as prizes, and pirates, or buccaneers, whose robbery was against the law. The age of pirates and privateers ended in the 1800s when better-equipped navies restored order.

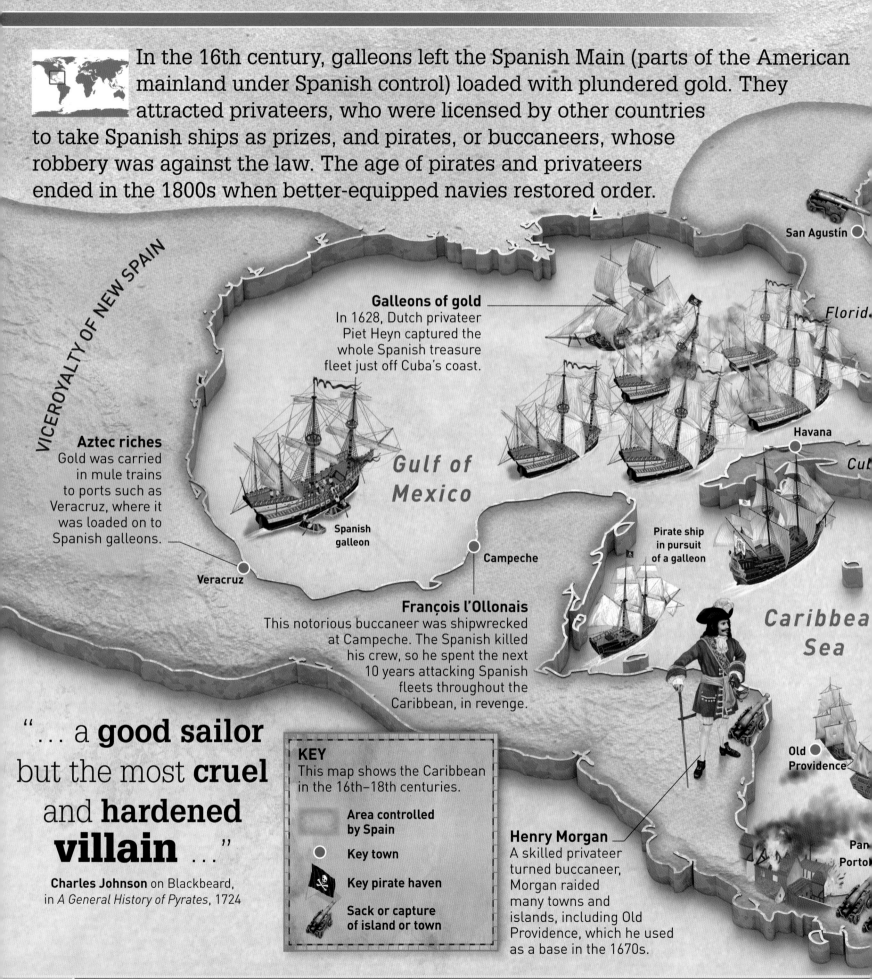

VICEROYALTY OF NEW SPAIN

San Agustín

Florid

Galleons of gold
In 1628, Dutch privateer Piet Heyn captured the whole Spanish treasure fleet just off Cuba's coast.

Havana

Aztec riches
Gold was carried in mule trains to ports such as Veracruz, where it was loaded on to Spanish galleons.

Gulf of Mexico

Cu

Spanish galleon

Pirate ship in pursuit of a galleon

Campeche

Veracruz

Caribbea Sea

François l'Ollonais
This notorious buccaneer was shipwrecked at Campeche. The Spanish killed his crew, so he spent the next 10 years attacking Spanish fleets throughout the Caribbean, in revenge.

"… a **good sailor** but the most **cruel** and **hardened villain** …"

Charles Johnson on Blackbeard, in *A General History of Pyrates*, 1724

KEY
This map shows the Caribbean in the 16th–18th centuries.

- Area controlled by Spain
- Key town
- Key pirate haven
- Sack or capture of island or town

Old Providence

Henry Morgan
A skilled privateer turned buccaneer, Morgan raided many towns and islands, including Old Providence, which he used as a base in the 1670s.

Pan
Porto

SAILORS FROM SHIPS CAPTURED BY PIRATES OFTEN JOINED THE CREW

Ocracoke Island
A great place to hide out while waiting for ships to seize, Ocracoke was Blackbeard's haven until he was killed in a battle here in 1718.

Ocracoke

ATLANTIC OCEAN

Blackbeard
In 1718, Blackbeard blockaded the port of Charleston and ransomed the inhabitants. He was a fearsome sight, and people said that he would set his hat alight with fuses, so that it would smoke as he attacked.

ston

Mary Read
In 1720, Mary joined pirate Anne Bonny to sail with Captain Calico Jack, based in New Providence. Both women, who dressed as men, were said to be braver and better pirates than their captain.

Providence

Bahamas

Santa María del Puerto del Príncipe

ti-itus

Jamaica

Pirate haven
From the 1630s, the island of Tortuga off Hispaniola became a hideout for buccaneers. This motley crew of ex-privateers, convicts, and escaped slaves started to take over the seas once privateering was outlawed.

Buccaneer

Tortuga

Hispaniola

Santo Domingo

Puerto Rico

Port Royal
From 1655, pirates came to this safe haven. It gained a reputation for wild partying until anti-piracy laws were passed in 1687.

os attacking astal towns

Pirate ship
Pirates often sailed small, fast ships that could overtake heavy Spanish galleons. In 1720, Black Bart captured 15 ships in three days.

re s

Cartagena

Maracaibo

Coast raids
Coastal towns were repeatedly raided as gold was held there, ready to be shipped. Maracaibo had 16 cannon on the coast to repel attacks.

Gibraltar

Privateer or buccaneer?
The first pirates were privateers, sent by their countries to raid enemy ships in times of war. The Netherlands, England, and France used them against Spain. They often seized ships for gold and slaves, but remained respected. Buccaneers were pirates who robbed solely for their own benefit and often came to a sticky end.

Queen Elizabeth I of England knighting Francis Drake for his privateering services, 1581

Privateer's prize
Francis Drake seized a Spanish galleon off Puerto Rico in 1571. He gained loot from later voyages too, including a spree in 1585–86, during which he sacked towns from Cartagena to San Agustín.

Land grab
The islands not taken by Spain often changed hands as they were fought over by the Dutch, French, and English.

Borburata
Caracas

The Queen's man
Sailing with Queen Elizabeth I's blessing in 1564, John Hawkins made a profit selling seized slaves in towns along the South American coast.

OF THEIR PIRATE CAPTORS, HOPING TO GET RICHES AND MORE FREEDOM.

87

The Pilgrim Fathers

The Pilgrim Fathers were not the first European settlers to arrive in North America, but they have become the most well-known. A party of 102 men, women, and children left England on 16 September 1620, on a ship called the *Mayflower*. They landed at Plymouth Rock on 21 December.

Hudson Bay

European traders made the most of the fur trade routes established by the Native Americans. In the 1670s, the British Hudson Bay Company set up factories on the coast of Hudson Bay.

Hudson Bay

NORTH AMERICA

NEW FRANCE

KEY

This map shows British, French, and Spanish possessions in North America in 1733.

- British possession
- French possession
- Spanish possession
- Disputed territory
- ⚒ Fur trading post

Mai[ne]

Conflicts betwe[en] settlers and Nati[ve] Americans – such [as] King Philip's War, focussed [on] Maine (1675–76) – were [a] constant problem for t[he] early colonize[rs].

New Amsterdam

The British claimed New Amsterdam in 1665 (first settled by the Dutch in 1614), and renamed it New York.

Jamestown

The first successful British colony, Jamestown, was established in 1607.

Santa Fe

The Spanish explored the southwest United States from Mexico in the 16th century onwards and founded a capital at Santa Fe in 1609.

NEW MEXICO ○ Santa Fe LOUISIANA

1500–1733 Colonial America

Colonization (or settlement) of North America started in the 16th century as European countries tried to claim these newly discovered lands. At first, life for the colonizers was extremely tough, with many people dying. Within a few years of their founding, however, many settlements began to flourish.

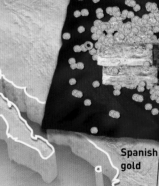

Spanish gold

VICEROYALTY OF NEW SPAIN

New Orlea[ns]

New Spain

In 1500–1650, the Spanish focussed their attention on New Spain, from which they exported 164 tonnes of gold and 15,400 tonnes of silver.

New Orleans

Some 7,000 immigrants arrived in New Orleans from France in 1718 to start the growth of French Louisiana.

"Ay, call it **holy ground**, The soil where first **they trod**"

Felicia Dorothea Hemans,
The Landing of the Pilgrim Fathers, 1825

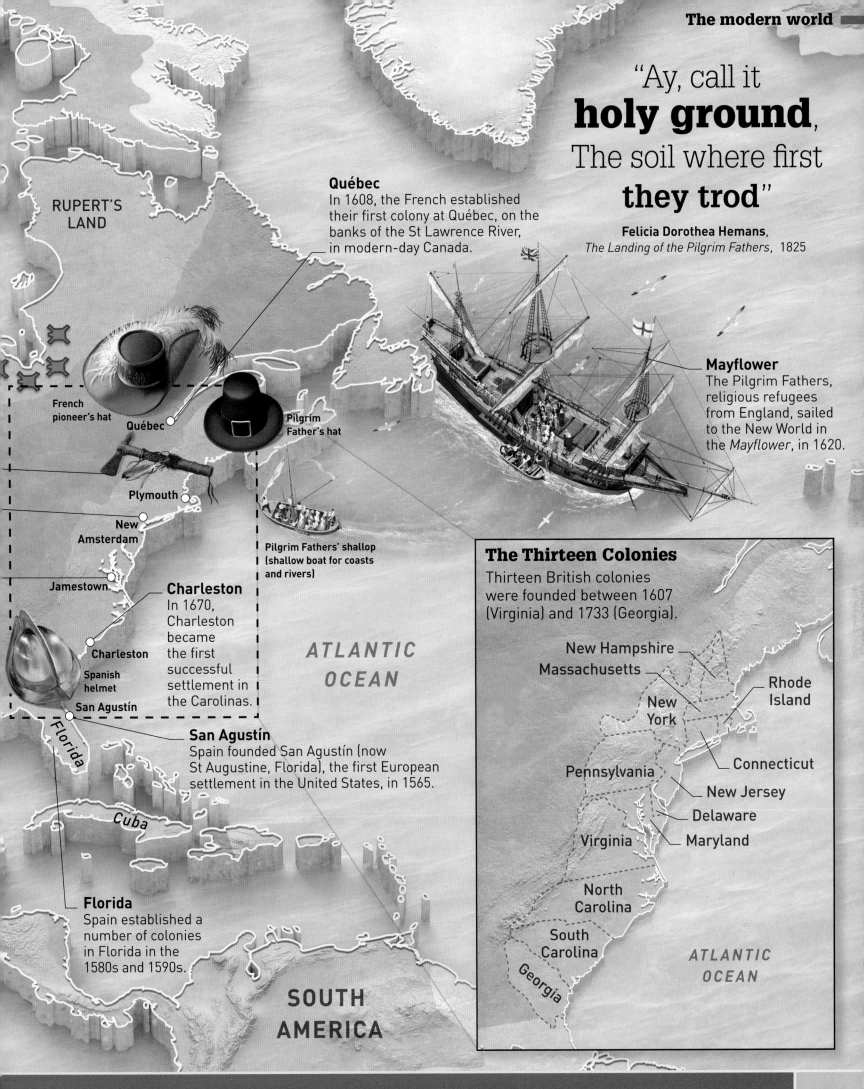

RUPERT'S LAND

Québec
In 1608, the French established their first colony at Québec, on the banks of the St Lawrence River, in modern-day Canada.

French pioneer's hat

Québec

Pilgrim Father's hat

Plymouth

New Amsterdam

Jamestown

Charleston

Spanish helmet

San Agustín

Mayflower
The Pilgrim Fathers, religious refugees from England, sailed to the New World in the *Mayflower*, in 1620.

Pilgrim Fathers' shallop (shallow boat for coasts and rivers)

Charleston
In 1670, Charleston became the first successful settlement in the Carolinas.

ATLANTIC OCEAN

San Agustín
Spain founded San Agustín (now St Augustine, Florida), the first European settlement in the United States, in 1565.

Florida

Cuba

Florida
Spain established a number of colonies in Florida in the 1580s and 1590s.

SOUTH AMERICA

The Thirteen Colonies
Thirteen British colonies were founded between 1607 (Virginia) and 1733 (Georgia).

New Hampshire
Massachusetts
New York
Rhode Island
Connecticut
Pennsylvania
New Jersey
Delaware
Virginia
Maryland
North Carolina
South Carolina
Georgia

ATLANTIC OCEAN

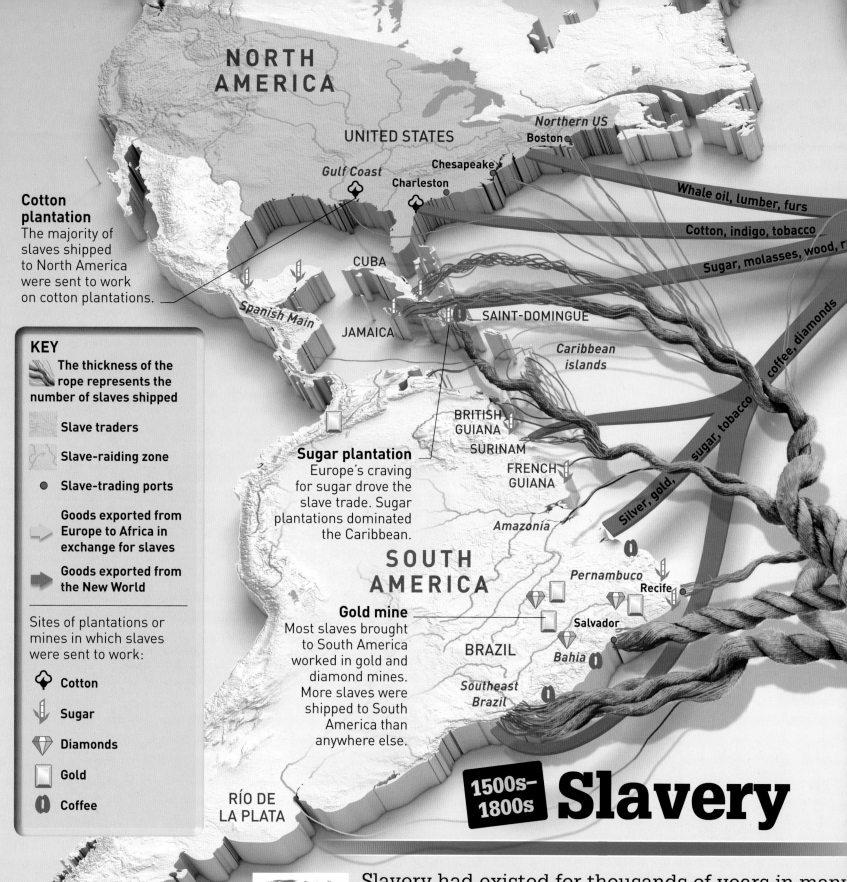

NORTH AMERICA

UNITED STATES

Northern US
Boston

Gulf Coast

Chesapeake

Charleston

Whale oil, lumber, furs

Cotton, indigo, tobacco

Sugar, molasses, wood, r...

Cotton plantation
The majority of slaves shipped to North America were sent to work on cotton plantations.

CUBA

Spanish Main

JAMAICA

SAINT-DOMINGUE

Caribbean islands

BRITISH GUIANA

SURINAM

FRENCH GUIANA

Sugar plantation
Europe's craving for sugar drove the slave trade. Sugar plantations dominated the Caribbean.

Amazonia

coffee, diamonds

sugar, tobacco

Silver, gold,

SOUTH AMERICA

Gold mine
Most slaves brought to South America worked in gold and diamond mines. More slaves were shipped to South America than anywhere else.

Pernambuco

Recife

Salvador

BRAZIL

Bahia

Southeast Brazil

RÍO DE LA PLATA

1500s–1800s **Slavery**

Slavery had existed for thousands of years in many parts of the world, but its most infamous episode came with the Atlantic Slave Trade. Between the 16th and 19th centuries, slave traders took an estimated 12 million Africans by force and shipped them across the Atlantic in dreadful conditions to work as slaves on the plantations or in the mines of the Americas.

Slave-trading port
By the 17th century, one in four ships leaving Liverpool was a slave-trading ship.

Liverpool

DENMARK

BRITAIN

NETHERLANDS

Nantes
FRANCE

EUROPE

PORTUGAL SPAIN

Lisbon

, cloth, iron, beer, rum

Arguin

AFRICA

Senegambia

Slave-raiding zones
Slaves were captured in large areas of Africa and were then sent to camps, which were known as "slave factories", on the coast.

Sierra Leone

Windward Coast *Gold Coast* *Bight of Benin*

Bight of Biafra

West Central Africa

Middle Passage
The journey across the Atlantic Ocean was known as the "Middle Passage".

Southeast Africa

Madagascar

Human cargo
Conditions for slaves on board slave ships were horrendous. Some 350–600 people were crammed into the ship's hold, chained together for months at a time, with disease a constant threat.

The slave traders
The Portuguese and British were the major participants in the slave trade. Three-quarters of all slaves were shipped across the Atlantic in ships originating from those two countries.

Portugal – 48%
Great Britain – 26%
France – 11%
Spain – 8%
Netherlands – 4%
United States – 2%
Denmark – 1%

"The **shrieks** and **groans** rendered the whole a scene of **horror** almost unimaginable."

Former slave **Olaudah Equiano**, on the conditions on the slave ship, 1789

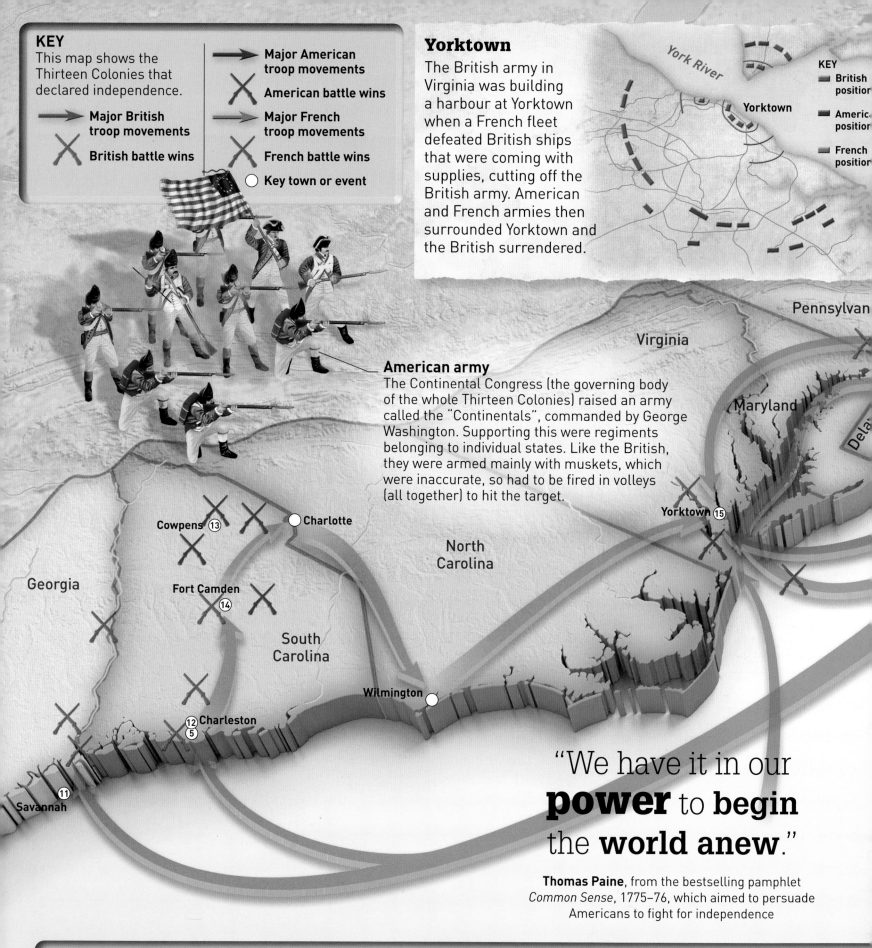

KEY
This map shows the Thirteen Colonies that declared independence.

→ Major British troop movements

✕ British battle wins

KEY
This map shows the Thirteen Colonies that declared independence.

→ Major British troop movements

✕ British battle wins

→ Major American troop movements

✕ American battle wins

→ Major French troop movements

✕ French battle wins

○ Key town or event

Yorktown

The British army in Virginia was building a harbour at Yorktown when a French fleet defeated British ships that were coming with supplies, cutting off the British army. American and French armies then surrounded Yorktown and the British surrendered.

York River

Yorktown

KEY
■ British position

■ Americ position

■ French position

Pennsylvan

Virginia

Maryland

Dela

American army

The Continental Congress (the governing body of the whole Thirteen Colonies) raised an army called the "Continentals", commanded by George Washington. Supporting this were regiments belonging to individual states. Like the British, they were armed mainly with muskets, which were inaccurate, so had to be fired in volleys (all together) to hit the target.

Cowpens ⑬

○ Charlotte

Yorktown ⑮

North Carolina

Georgia

Fort Camden
⑭

South Carolina

Wilmington ○

⑫ Charleston
⑤

Savannah
⑪

"We have it in our **power** to begin the **world anew**."

Thomas Paine, from the bestselling pamphlet *Common Sense*, 1775–76, which aimed to persuade Americans to fight for independence

① **16 December 1773**
A band of American patriots dressed as Mohawks dumped tea into Boston Harbor in a response to British tea tax.

② **19 April 1775**
Local people had an armed conflict with British forces at Lexington. The first shots of the war were fired.

③ **17 June 1775**
The British suffered huge casualties in winning the battle of Bunker Hill, outside Boston.

④ **17 March 1776**
British forces left Boston, destroying all military supplies in the city as they evacuated.

⑤ **28 June 1776**
A British attempt to take Charleston from the Americans ended in failure at the battle of Sullivan's Island.

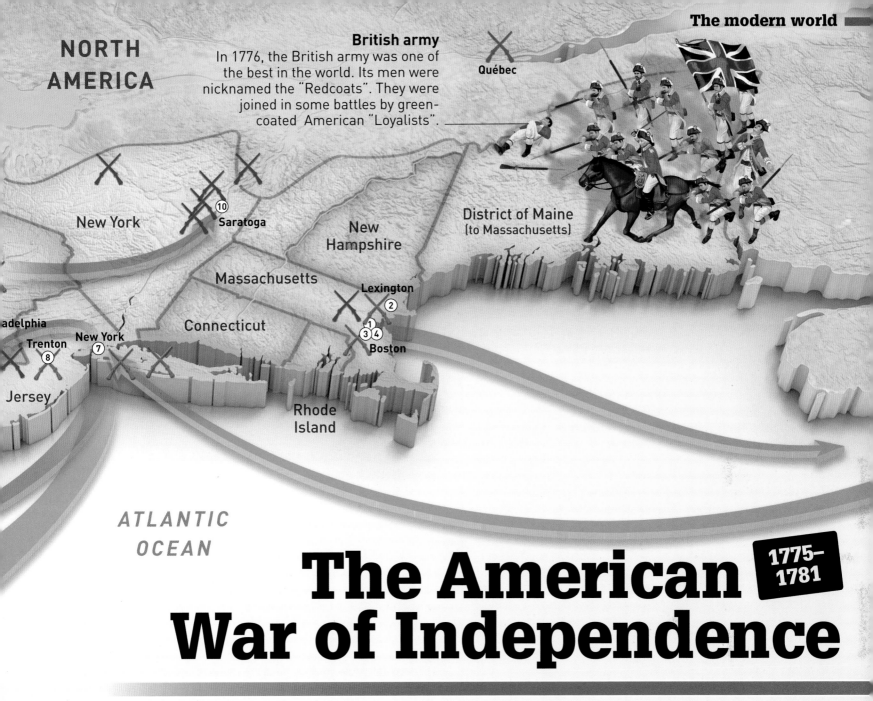

NORTH AMERICA

British army
In 1776, the British army was one of the best in the world. Its men were nicknamed the "Redcoats". They were joined in some battles by green-coated American "Loyalists".

Québec

Saratoga ⑩

New York

New Hampshire

District of Maine (to Massachusetts)

Massachusetts

Lexington ②

① ④
③

Boston

...adelphia

Trenton ⑧

New York ⑦

Connecticut

...Jersey

Rhode Island

ATLANTIC OCEAN

The American War of Independence

1775–1781

After years of tension over Britain's growing control, the American colonies declared themselves independent states. War was inevitable, and Britain and the United States fought for six years, with neither side winning a decisive victory, until the British were finally trapped, and surrendered in 1781.

4 July 1776
...he Thirteen Colonies ...pproved Thomas ...efferson's Declaration ...Independence in ...hiladelphia.

⑦ August 1776
The British won a series of skirmishes against George Washington's army and took control of New York.

⑧ 26 December 1776
The Americans won their first significant victory of the war at the battle of Trenton, New Jersey.

⑨ 26 September 1777
The British entered Philadelphia under General Howe, but they abandoned the city in 1778 and retreated to New York.

⑩ 17 October 1777
British general Burgoyne surrendered to the Americans at Saratoga. The American victory persuaded the French to enter the war on their side.

29 December 1778
...he British defeated ...e Americans in ...avannah. The rest of ...eorgia soon fell under ...ritish control.

⑫ 12 May 1780
The Americans, under Benjamin Lincoln, surrendered to the British after a month-long siege of Charleston.

⑬ 17 January 1781
The Americans, headed by Daniel Morgan, defeated the British at Cowpens, South Carolina.

⑭ 25 April 1781
The British defeated American forces at Fort Camden, but suffered heavy losses and were forced to retreat.

⑮ 17 October 1781
Lord Cornwallis surrendered to a combined French-American force after being cut off at Yorktown. Defeat for the British signalled the end of the war.

Exiled to Australia

INDIAN OCEAN

KEY
- Areas ex-convicts settled
- ○ Penal colonies
- ● Other important sites
- ➤ Route of the First Fleet, 1788

On 18 January 1788, the first of 11 ships carrying 1,500 people arrived at Botany Bay, Australia. Most passengers were British convicts sentenced to "transportation", or exile, for crimes ranging from minor theft to murder. From 1793, free settlers, who chose to emigrate, also began to arrive in Australia. All this had a devastating impact on the 300,000 Aboriginal people who lived there. Thousands died from disease or violence, and their land was taken over by the immigrants.

Aboriginal land
Aboriginal people were the original inhabitants of Australia, and there were clear boundaries around each group's territory. The Europeans did not see this and claimed the land for themselves, with no regard for either Aboriginal rights or heritage.

A U S T

Aboriginal population
Aboriginal people had been in Australia for more than 40,000 years when the Europeans arrived. Ravaged by conflict and disease, there were fewer than 100,000 Aboriginal people by 1920. However, they kept their culture alive, passing down traditions such as dance and body art to today's generation.

Swan River colony
The first colony in Western Australia was established on the Swan River, Perth, in 1828. It was a free colony, but penal colonies were set up in Western Australia, in 1850, when immigrants wanted convicts to help them farm the tough land.

> "We found ourselves in a **port superior** ... to **all** we had **seen before**."
>
> **Captain Lieutenant Watkin Tench**, on Port Jackson (modern-day Sydney), 26 January, 1788

Fremantle
The last convict ship arrived in Fremantle port in 1868. It brought the last of more than 9,000 convicts into Western Australia.

Perth ○
Fremantle ●
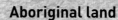

Albany ○

HMS *Siri...*
The flagship of the First Fle... (the first 11 ships that left England) was... Royal Navy armed escort ship. It left Englar... with fleet commander Captain Arthur Phill... aboard. On reaching Botany Bay, he becam... Governor in Chief and decided to mo... the settlement to Port Jackso...

Crossing the world

The First Fleet left Portsmouth, England, on 13 May 1787. It took 8 months to reach Botany Bay, with stops at Tenerife, Rio de Janeiro, and Cape Town to restock supplies and collect plants, seeds, and livestock (horses, sheep, and goats) to take to the new land.

NORTH AMERICA
Portsmouth
EUROPE
ASIA
Tenerife
AFRICA
SOUTH AMERICA
Rio de Janeiro
Cape Town
AUSTRALASIA
Botany Bay

Moreton Bay

Some convicts from Port Jackson who committed further crimes in Australia were sent to this penal colony. Conditions were particularly harsh and many convicts tried to escape, but were unsuccessful.

Myall Creek

In 1838, 28 Aboriginal people were murdered by white settlers at Myall Creek. There were many clashes between the Europeans and the Aboriginal people, started by both sides, but this case was unusual, because the European perpetrators were brought to justice. Seven of the 11 guilty men were hanged.

Castle Hill

In March 1804, a group of rebel convicts escaped from a farm in Castle Hill. It resulted in a battle between the rebels and the military. The military won and the rebels were put to death.

Liberty Plains

The first free immigrant settlers arrived in 1793. They were given land grants by the British government, plus convict labour to work the land. They were also given 2 years' food rations and 1 year's clothing.

Port Jackson

Australia's first penal colony (area for convicts) was established in Port Jackson, where the land was more fertile than in Botany Bay. The area later became Sydney.

Botany Bay

The First Fleet arrived in Botany Bay on 18–20 January 1788. The area had poor soil and little fresh water, so was not suitable for settlement.

Risdon Cove

In 1803, a penal colony was set up in Risdon Cove, after a party of British were sent from Sydney to Tasmania to prevent the French from claiming the island.

Port Arthur

From 1832, convicts who had broken the law while in their penal colonies were sent to Port Arthur. It had some of the strictest security and harshest punishments of any penal colony.

New Guinea

ALIA

Myall Creek
Moreton Bay
Port Macquarie
Port Stephens
Newcastle
Wellington
Castle Hill
Port Jackson
Botany Bay
Liberty Plains
Melbourne
Port Philip
Western Port
Port Dalrymple
Tasmania
Maria Island
Risdon Cove
Macquarie Harbour
Sullivan's Cove
Port Arthur

CONVICTS — MOSTLY THIEVES — IN 806 SHIPS TO AUSTRALIA.

Events in Paris

Many of the key events of the revolution took place around Paris.

14 July 1789 An angry mob demolished the Bastille – a fortress-prison that was a symbol of kingship. The Storming of the Bastille was the symbolic start of the revolution.

26 August 1789 The new National Assembly passed the *Declaration of the Rights of Man and Citizen*. This stated that all men and women are born equal, and so the nobility had no right to rule over the commoners. This was the start of French democracy.

10 August 1792 An angry mob stormed the Tuileries Palace, where King Louis XVI had been held under guard since trying to flee the country in 1791. The king was sent to prison.

22 September 1792 A new government proclaimed that France was a republic.

21 January 1793 King Louis XVI was executed.

31 May 1793 The Jacobin party, led by Maximilien Robespierre, took power and gave itself unlimited authority. The Jacobins accused many people of being anti-Republic, executing 40,000 of them during their "Reign of Terror".

August 1793 The Republic called for French troops to fight the Revolutionary Wars.

16 October 1793 The French queen, Marie Antoinette, was executed.

31 July 1794 The Jacobins were overthrown and their leader, Robespierre, was executed.

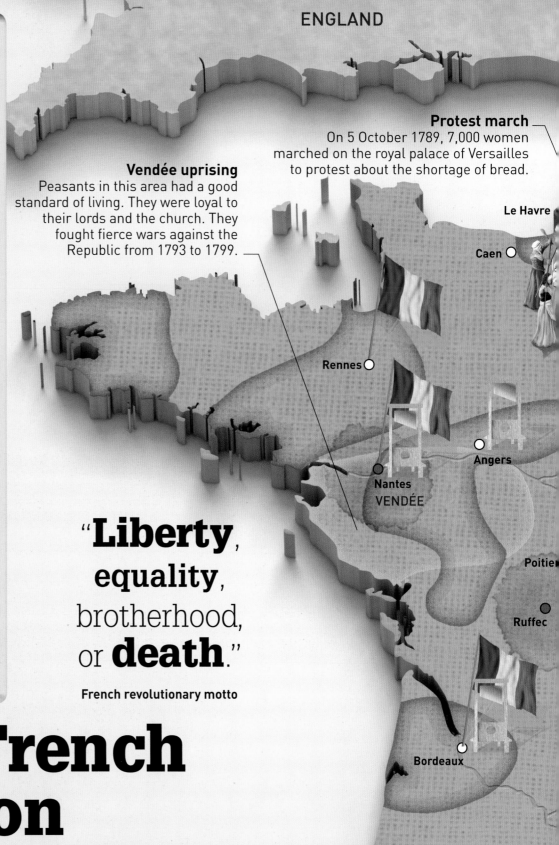

ENGLAND

Protest march
On 5 October 1789, 7,000 women marched on the royal palace of Versailles to protest about the shortage of bread.

Vendée uprising
Peasants in this area had a good standard of living. They were loyal to their lords and the church. They fought fierce wars against the Republic from 1793 to 1799.

Le Havre

Caen

Rennes

Angers

Nantes
VENDÉE

Poitie

Ruffec

Bordeaux

"**Liberty**, equality, brotherhood, or **death**."

French revolutionary motto

SPAIN

1789–1794

The French Revolution

In 1789, France was in turmoil. It was nearly bankrupt from wars it had fought, there was a bad harvest, and the king was demanding taxes from the poor while the nobility lived in luxury. The people rose up, overthrew the monarchy, and declared a republic in a revolution that caused a lot of bloodshed.

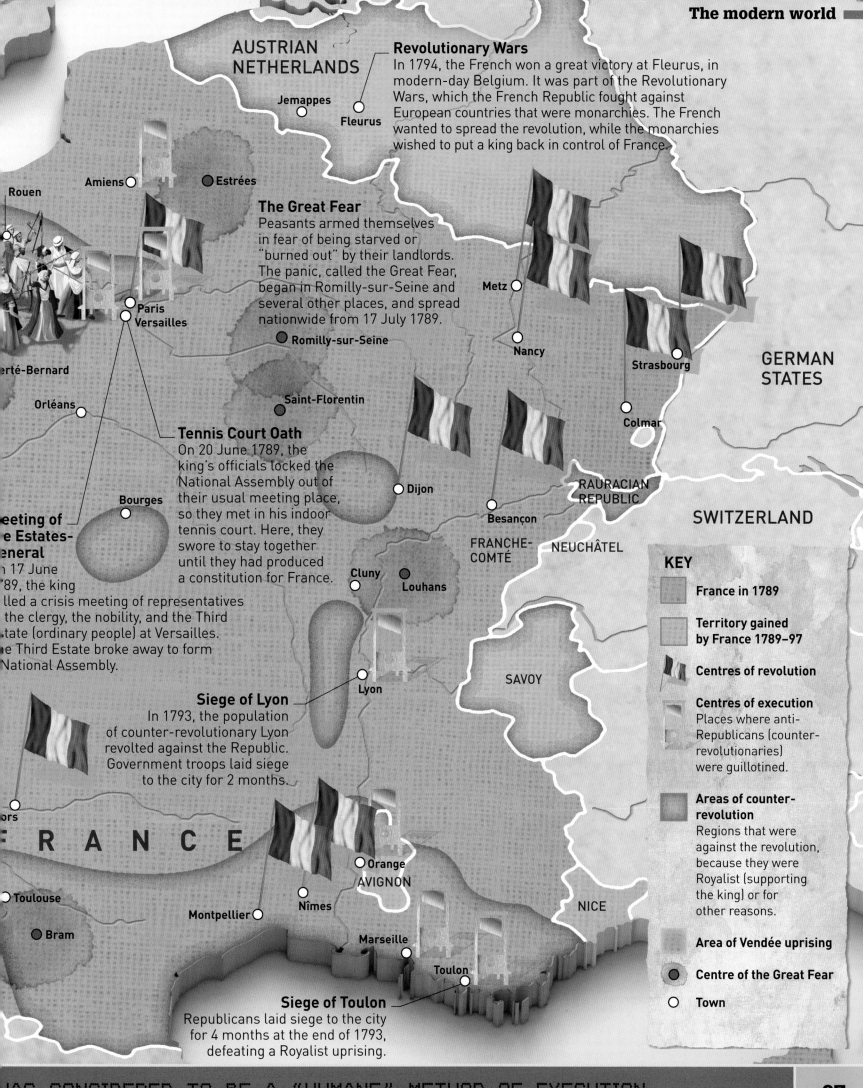

AUSTRIAN
NETHERLANDS

Revolutionary Wars
In 1794, the French won a great victory at Fleurus, in modern-day Belgium. It was part of the Revolutionary Wars, which the French Republic fought against European countries that were monarchies. The French wanted to spread the revolution, while the monarchies wished to put a king back in control of France.

Jemappes

Fleurus

Rouen

Amiens

Estrées

The Great Fear
Peasants armed themselves in fear of being starved or "burned out" by their landlords. The panic, called the Great Fear, began in Romilly-sur-Seine and several other places, and spread nationwide from 17 July 1789.

Metz

Paris
Versailles

Romilly-sur-Seine

Nancy

Strasbourg

GERMAN
STATES

erté-Bernard

Saint-Florentin

Orléans

Colmar

Tennis Court Oath
On 20 June 1789, the king's officials locked the National Assembly out of their usual meeting place, so they met in his indoor tennis court. Here, they swore to stay together until they had produced a constitution for France.

Bourges

Dijon

RAURACIAN
REPUBLIC

Besançon

SWITZERLAND

eeting of
e Estates-
eneral
17 June
89, the king
lled a crisis meeting of representatives
the clergy, the nobility, and the Third
tate (ordinary people) at Versailles.
e Third Estate broke away to form
National Assembly.

FRANCHE-
COMTÉ

NEUCHÂTEL

Cluny

Louhans

KEY

France in 1789

Territory gained
by France 1789–97

Centres of revolution

SAVOY

Lyon

Siege of Lyon
In 1793, the population of counter-revolutionary Lyon revolted against the Republic. Government troops laid siege to the city for 2 months.

Centres of execution
Places where anti-Republicans (counter-revolutionaries) were guillotined.

ors

Areas of counter-revolution
Regions that were against the revolution, because they were Royalist (supporting the king) or for other reasons.

R A N C E

Orange

AVIGNON

NICE

Toulouse

Nîmes

Montpellier

Area of Vendée uprising

Bram

Centre of the Great Fear

Marseille

Town

Toulon

Siege of Toulon
Republicans laid siege to the city for 4 months at the end of 1793, defeating a Royalist uprising.

KEY

This map shows Europe in 1812, when Napoleon controlled an empire, across which he imposed a legal code and the metric system of measures. The territories outside this empire fiercely rejected French influence.

- Napoleon's empire
- Dependent states and allies
- ✕ Key battle
- ① Key event

Russian campaign, 1812

➡ Advance into Russia

⬅ Return from Russia

10. Battle of Waterloo, 1815
This was Napoleon's last battle, as he was defeated by British and Prussian armies. He was then exiled to St Helena – a remote island in the middle of the Atlantic.

GREAT BRITAIN

KINGD SWE

KINGDOM OF DENMARK

Lübeck, 1806

⑧

Leipzig

CONFEDERATION OF THE RHINE

⑩ Waterloo

Jena, 1806

② Paris

2. Coronation, 1804
Napoleon had himself crowned emperor here in Paris.

Ulm, 1805

SWITZERLAND

KINGDOM OF ITALY

ILL PROV

4. Battle of Salamanca, 1812
This was a key battle in the Peninsular war, which French forces fought against a British and Portuguese army and anti-French Spanish forces.

ATLANTIC OCEAN

Corunna, 1805

FRENCH EMPIRE

Marengo, 1800

Mantua, 1796

⑨

KINGDOM OF SPAIN

KINGDOM OF PORTUGAL

④ Salamanca

9. Exile on Elba, 1814
Napoleon was exiled here in 1814, but escaped for one last campaign against the British.

KINGDOM OF SARDINIA

KING OF NA

3. Battle of Trafalgar, 1805
The French and Spanish fleets were destroyed by British ships commanded by Horatio Nelson. This stopped Napoleon invading Britain.

③ Trafalgar

Mediterranean Sea

KINGDOM OF SICILY

1796–1815 Napoleon

Napoleon Bonaparte was one of the most brilliant military commanders of all time. In 1796, he was given command of the French army in Italy; three years later, he was ruling France. Over the next decade, he led France in a series of wars that left him controlling most of Europe. However, his attempt to conquer the immense Russian Empire ended in disaster.

NAPOLEON WAS ALLOWED TO CONSCRIPT, OR RECRUIT BY FORCE, VAST

6. Arrival in Moscow, September 1812
Having chased the Russian army all the way to Moscow, Napoleon's forces found the city abandoned and burnt. The Russians refused to accept defeat. The French retreated as winter set in.

5. Advance into Russia, June 1812
Napoleon marched into Russia with an army of 400,000 men from several nations, including large numbers of Germans, Poles, and Italians, as well as French.

7. Retreat from Russia, November 1812
Freezing, starving, and under constant attacks from Russian forces, Napoleon's army retreated to Polish land, reduced to 27,000 men.

KINGDOM OF PRUSSIA

GRAND DUCHY OF WARSAW (POLAND)

8. Battle of Leipzig, 1813
The so called "Battle of Nations" was the biggest battle in Europe until World War I. Armies from Russia, Prussia, Austria, and Sweden defeated Napoleon's army.

usterlitz, 1805

agram, 1809

AUSTRIAN EMPIRE

Moscow

Maloyaroslavets, 1812

RUSSIAN EMPIRE

The fall of Napoleon

Under Napoleon, the French fought nearly every other European power of the time. These enemy powers teamed up in a series of coalitions. Napoleon couldn't defeat Britain, so he tried to cripple its economy with a trade blockade. To do so, he had to force Portugal, Spain, and Russia to join in, and he fought them all at the same time – at both ends of Europe. This was beyond even Napoleon, and in 1815, he was defeated and exiled.

OTTOMAN EMPIRE

Black Sea

A cartoon of the time shows Napoleon trying to stretch to control both ends of Europe.

"**You** say it is **impossible**. That word is **not French**."

Napoleon Bonaparte, in a letter demanding supplies for his exhausted army, 1813

Battle of the Nile, 1798

EGYPT

Battle of the Pyramids, 1798

1. Egyptian campaign, 1798–1801
Napoleon knew that if he controlled Egypt, he could threaten British dominance in India. As he occupied Egypt, he brought along scientists to survey the ancient ruins, leading to a craze in Europe for all things Egyptian. But, although Napoleon won land battles, the British navy forced the French to leave.

ARMIES. AROUND 1 MILLION SOLDIERS DIED IN BUILDING HIS EMPIRE.

99

Haiti helps Bolívar, 1816
Haiti had become independent in 1804, after slaves rebelled against France and took control. Haiti's president, Alexandre Pétion, gave Bolívar arms and support to re-invade the mainland – as long as Bolívar agreed to free the slaves there.

Bolívar's "Admirable Campaign", 1813
Simón Bolívar was a rebel leader who travelled across what is now Venezuela, winning victories against the ruling Spanish Royalists. Although he entered Caracas victoriously, he soon had to flee to Jamaica.

Letter from Jamaica, 1815
While in exile in Jamaica, Bolívar wrote a famous letter about his vision of a free South America.

Battle of Boyacá, 1◄
This battle betw◄ Bolívar's Independent and the Spanish wo◄ soon liberate G◄ Colombia (now Pana◄ Ecuador, Venezu◄ and Colom◄ from Sp◄

Bolívar meets San Martín, 1822
Bolívar and San Martín met to plan the final conquest of Peru. San Martín handed this task to Bolívar.

CUBA

JAMAICA

HAITI

Caracas

GRAN COLOMBIA

Admirable Campaign

Bogotá

Guayaquil

FRENCH GUIANA

SURINAM

BRITISH GUIANA

PERU

Lima

1808–1826 Free South America

In 1807–08, French leader Napoleon invaded Portugal and occupied Spain, and weakened both countries' hold on their empires in South America. Revolutionaries in South America, such as Simón Bolívar, took the chance to free their nations from 300 years of colonial rule. By 1826, all of Spain's colonies except Cuba and Puerto Rico had slipped out of its hands, and Portugal had lost Brazil.

KEY
Many revolutionary leaders, known as *Libertadores*, helped to free South America, but the the most famous were Simón Bolívar and José de San Martín.

➡ **Simón Bolívar's route**
➡ **José de San Martín's route**
● **Key town**

ATLANTIC OCEAN

BRAZIL

Brazil becomes an empire, 1822
The Portuguese royal family was in exile in Rio de Janeiro following Napoleon's invasion of Portugal. John, the Prince Regent, eventually returned and left his son, Pedro, in charge of Brazil. However, Pedro declared Brazil independent and became its first emperor, Dom Pedro I.

Paraguay freed, 1811
Spain had never had a strong hold over Paraguay. When Spain imposed a tax on Paraguay's main crop, *yerba mate*, a kind of tea, making it too expensive for locals to afford, the Paraguayans lost patience and declared independence.

Peru freed, 1824
Antonio José de Sucre, Simón Bolívar's lieutenant, won the Battle of Ayacucho and the defeated Spanish commander-in-chief signed the final surrender of the Royalist army in South America.

Rio de Janeiro

Río de la Plata freed, 1810
The Spanish government in these parts, then called the United Provinces of the Río de la Plata, was ousted in 1810. José de San Martín then joined the independence cause and, in 1814, marched on Upper Peru (then part of the same state) to complete the liberation.

Bolivia freed, 1825
Sucre stamped out Royalist resistance in Upper Peru and renamed the region Bolivia in honour of the *Libertador*.

UPPER PERU (BOLIVIA)

PARAGUAY

cucho

Potosí

URUGUAY

Buenos Aires

UNITED PROVINCES OF THE RÍO DE LA PLATA

PACIFIC OCEAN

The crossing of the Andes, 1818
José de San Martín decided to approach Peru via Chile. He took Chilean independence leaders, including Bernado O'Higgins, with him. Together, they led an army on a daring, dangerous crossing of the high Andes mountains.

Valparaiso

Santiago

"The **bonds** that united us to **Spain** ave been **severed**."

Simón Bolívar, *The Letter from Jamaica*, 1815

CHILE

Chile freed, 1818
San Martín and O'Higgins liberated Chile after only a few short battles, since no one had expected an army to attack from the mountains.

Darwin's voyage

While exploring South America, British scientist Charles Darwin studied rocks, plants, and animals that helped him develop his theory of evolution. This idea was one of the biggest leaps forward in the history of science.

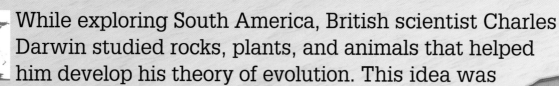

SOUTH AMERICA

Capybara
These huge rodents were a common sight for Darwin when on overland treks.

Andes

Lima

Around the world
To return to Britain, the *Beagle* had to cross the Pacific and complete a round-the-world voyage via Australia and South Africa.

NORTH AMERICA
ATLANTIC OCEAN
EUROPE
ASIA
PACIFIC OCEAN
AFRICA
SOUTH AMERICA
PACIFIC OCEAN
INDIAN OCEAN
AUSTRALASIA

KEY
← Route of HMS *Beagle*

The Galápagos
This island chain has such unusual wildlife that it started Darwin thinking about how such variety of life comes about.

PACIFIC OCEAN

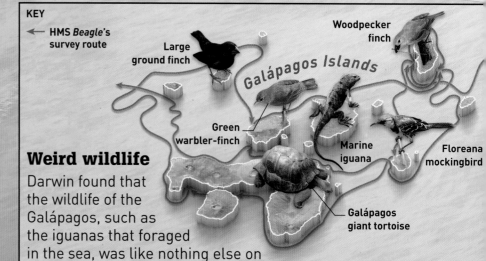

KEY
← HMS *Beagle*'s survey route

Large ground finch
Woodpecker finch
Galápagos Islands
Green warbler-finch
Marine iguana
Floreana mockingbird
Galápagos giant tortoise

Weird wildlife
Darwin found that the wildlife of the Galápagos, such as the iguanas that foraged in the sea, was like nothing else on Earth. Some islands had their own types of mockingbirds, finches, and giant tortoises. He thought that a few types of creatures must have reached the islands, before evolving in many new directions.

THE BEAGLE'S MISSION WAS ORIGINALLY PLANNED AS A TWO-YEAR TRIP,

HMS _Beagle_
A British survey vessel called HMS _Beagle_ sailed from Plymouth, England, in 1831, on a mission to chart the coast of South America. Darwin was taken along, aged 22, as ship's naturalist.

Evolution revolution
Darwin's discoveries seemed to confirm that the Earth was much older than people had thought. He formed a theory of how life forms change over millions of years. It was such a new idea that Darwin spent 20 years collecting specimens and other evidence to support it. When he published his theory in 1859, it caused a revolution in science.

Part of Darwin's beetle collection

ATLANTIC OCEAN

Salvador

Gaucho
For weeks, Darwin lived as a gaucho (a cowboy of the pampas grasslands).

Rio de Janeiro

Giant ground sloth
In Uruguay, Darwin found the fossil skeleton of this giant extinct sloth, called _Megatherium_.

Montevideo

" ...a **little world within itself**; its inhabitants being found **nowhere else**."

Charles Darwin, on the Galápagos Islands, 1835

Buenos Aires

Guanaco
This relative of the camel was often hunted by the crew for food.

Coquimbo

Valparaiso

ossilized forest
ome 1,800 m (6,000 ft) up in e Andes, Darwin found trees rned to stone on top of rocks at he realised had once been sea bed. These made him onder at the immense me needed for such anges to happen.

Valdivia

Darwin's rhea
Darwin discovered this smaller, southerly species of the giant flightless rhea. It is now named after him. He realised he had a specimen only after he and his party had eaten most of the bird.

Kissing bug
Darwin allowed this blood-sucking insect to drink from his arm, then kept it to see how long it could live on one blood meal.

Darwin's frog
Darwin discovered this bizarre frog in the forests of Chile. The tadpoles hatch and develop inside the male's throat.

Storms off the cape
The Beagle was caught for weeks in storms off Cape Horn.

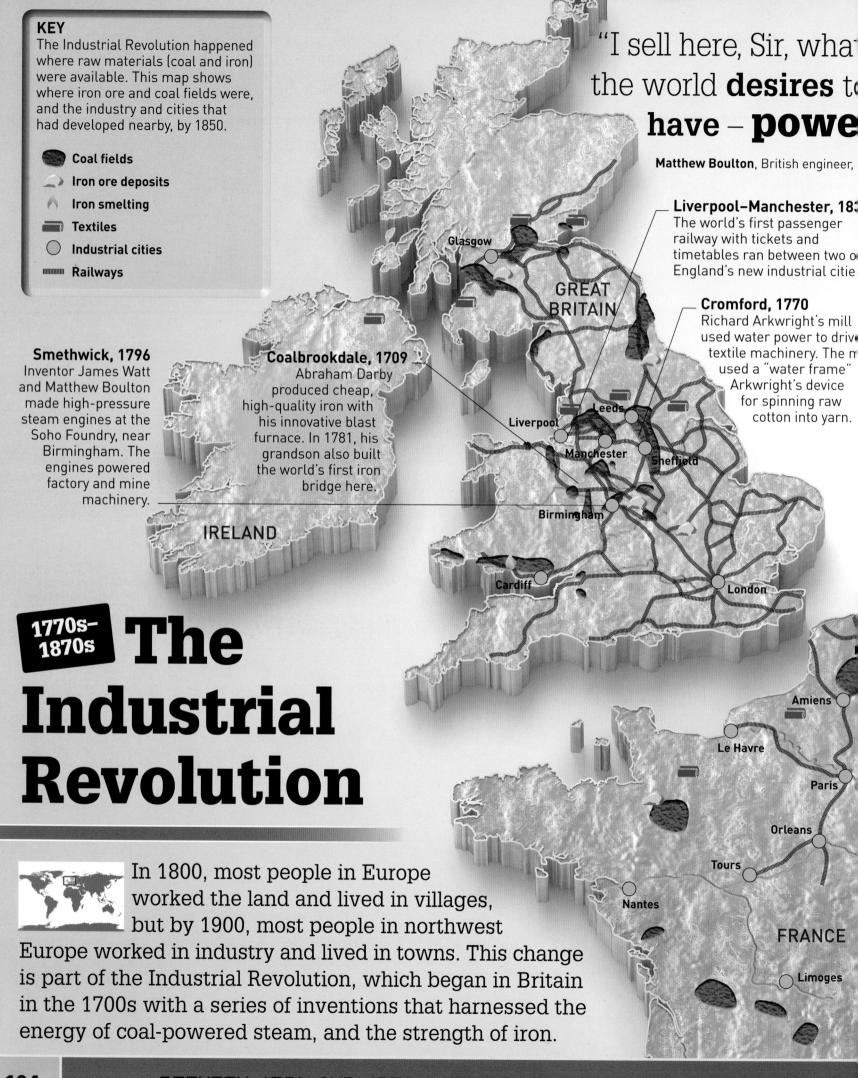

KEY

The Industrial Revolution happened where raw materials (coal and iron) were available. This map shows where iron ore and coal fields were, and the industry and cities that had developed nearby, by 1850.

- Coal fields
- Iron ore deposits
- Iron smelting
- Textiles
- Industrial cities
- Railways

"I sell here, Sir, what the world **desires** to have – **powe**

Matthew Boulton, British engineer,

Liverpool–Manchester, 183
The world's first passenger railway with tickets and timetables ran between two o England's new industrial citie

Cromford, 1770
Richard Arkwright's mill used water power to driv textile machinery. The m used a "water frame" Arkwright's device for spinning raw cotton into yarn.

Smethwick, 1796
Inventor James Watt and Matthew Boulton made high-pressure steam engines at the Soho Foundry, near Birmingham. The engines powered factory and mine machinery.

Coalbrookdale, 1709
Abraham Darby produced cheap, high-quality iron with his innovative blast furnace. In 1781, his grandson also built the world's first iron bridge here.

GREAT BRITAIN

Glasgow

Leeds

Liverpool

Manchester

Sheffield

Birmingham

Cardiff

London

IRELAND

Amiens

Le Havre

Paris

Orleans

Tours

Nantes

Limoges

FRANCE

The Industrial Revolution

1770s–1870s

In 1800, most people in Europe worked the land and lived in villages, but by 1900, most people in northwest Europe worked in industry and lived in towns. This change is part of the Industrial Revolution, which began in Britain in the 1700s with a series of inventions that harnessed the energy of coal-powered steam, and the strength of iron.

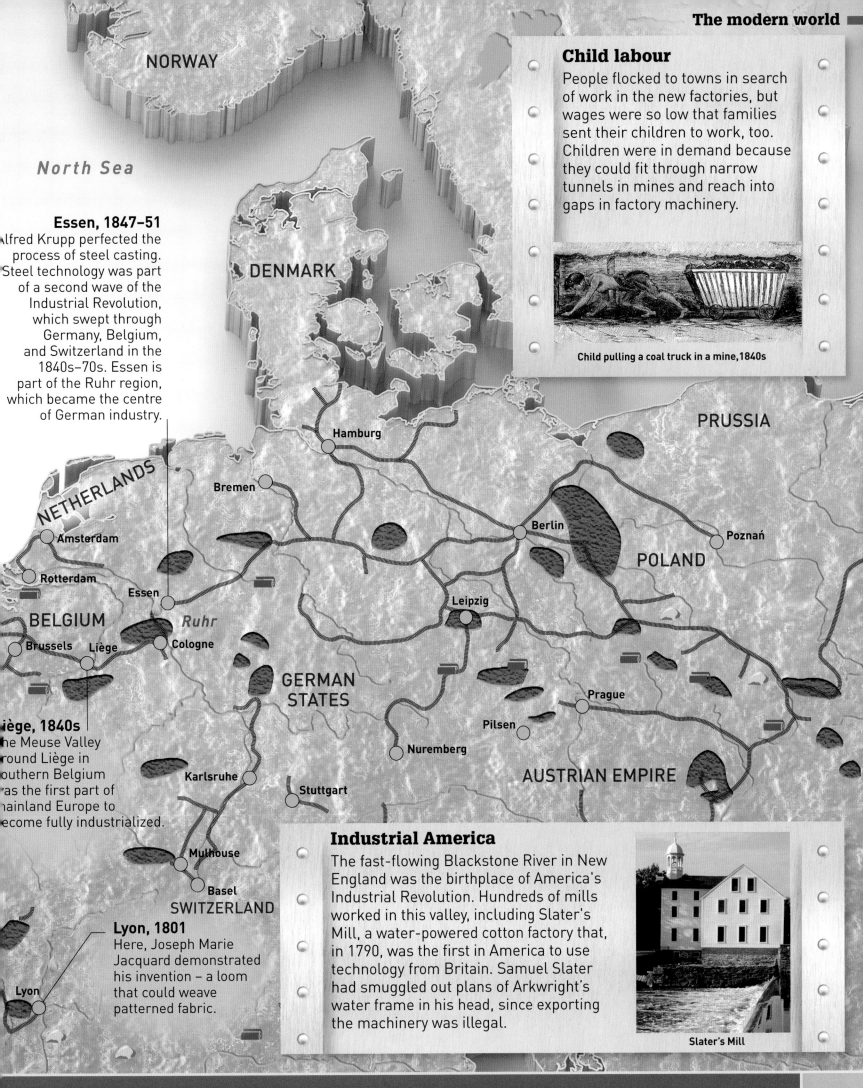

NORWAY

North Sea

DENMARK

PRUSSIA

Child labour

People flocked to towns in search of work in the new factories, but wages were so low that families sent their children to work, too. Children were in demand because they could fit through narrow tunnels in mines and reach into gaps in factory machinery.

Child pulling a coal truck in a mine, 1840s

Essen, 1847–51

lfred Krupp perfected the process of steel casting. Steel technology was part of a second wave of the Industrial Revolution, which swept through Germany, Belgium, and Switzerland in the 1840s–70s. Essen is part of the Ruhr region, which became the centre of German industry.

NETHERLANDS

Amsterdam

Rotterdam

Essen

BELGIUM

Brussels

Liège

Cologne

Ruhr

GERMAN STATES

Hamburg

Bremen

Berlin

Poznań

POLAND

Leipzig

Prague

Pilsen

Nuremberg

AUSTRIAN EMPIRE

Liège, 1840s

he Meuse Valley round Liège in outhern Belgium as the first part of ainland Europe to ecome fully industrialized.

Karlsruhe

Stuttgart

Mulhouse

Basel

SWITZERLAND

Lyon, 1801

Here, Joseph Marie Jacquard demonstrated his invention – a loom that could weave patterned fabric.

Lyon

Industrial America

The fast-flowing Blackstone River in New England was the birthplace of America's Industrial Revolution. Hundreds of mills worked in this valley, including Slater's Mill, a water-powered cotton factory that, in 1790, was the first in America to use technology from Britain. Samuel Slater had smuggled out plans of Arkwright's water frame in his head, since exporting the machinery was illegal.

Slater's Mill

WORKING-CLASS BOYS IN ENGLAND WERE FORCED TO GO TO WORK.

Young Irelander Rebellion
On 29 July, Young Irelander protestors exchanged gunfire with the Irish Constabulary. The rebels were defeated.

Ballingarry

Yorkshire Chartists
After earlier protests failed, Chartists in Yorkshire took up arms and practised drills in June.

Yorkshire

Copenhagen
Danish protestors demanded greater personal freedom. This led to events in Schleswig (see box on opposite page).

Sch

London petition
In April, the Chartist Movement held a peaceful protest and asked Parliament for a people's charter, including votes for all men.

London

Rouen
In April, the working classes barricaded the streets in their fight against the aristocracy.

Rouen

Paris

Frankfurt
6

Mannheim
1

7

Karlsruhe

February Revolution
Angry mobs barricaded Paris in February, overthrowing the king and declaring a French republic. This lasted until December 1851, when Louis Napoleon declared himself emperor.

Lyon
Silk workers, called canuts, fought for workers' rights. They attacked factories that used machines rather than employing people.

Limoges

Lyon

SWITZERLAND

Milan

Limoges
Rural areas such as Limoges joined in a second wave of violent uprisings that started in Paris when the new Republican government did not provide people with jobs.

Sonderbund War
Years of unrest in Switzerland led to a 25-day war, because seven Catholic regions wanted to govern themselves. They lost the war, but the government gave people greater freedom.

Marseille

Bolo

Milan
In March, people fought against, and drove out, Austrian troops and tax collectors from the Austrian-controlled state.

Marseille
Influenced by the events in Paris, workers in the port of Marseille rose up for their rights.

1848 A year of revolutions

In 1848, people came out onto the streets to fight for their rights: for better working conditions; for democracy (votes for all men, not just the ruling classes); and, in the German and Italian states, for their states to unite into independent countries. Some revolts had short-term success, but most were put down with much bloodshed. By 1849, people had lost hope, yet in the following decades many of their goals would be achieved.

THE FRANKFURT ASSEMBLY PROPOSED USING THE REVOLUTIONARIES'

Poznań Uprising
In March, Polish states in the Prussian Empire fought for an independent Poland and an end to Prussian rule. The rebels were joined by Polish prisoners who had been freed during a successful uprising in Berlin.

Cracow
In March, Poles in Cracow, part of the Austrian Empire, protested and then revolted against Austrian rule. Like people in Poznań, they wanted an independent Poland.

Prague
Czechs in Prague wanted freedom from Austria, but did not want to be part of Germany.

Hungarian independence
In March, Hungarian nationalists fought to gain independence from the Austrian Habsburg Empire.

Venice
Influenced by revolutions in Sicily and France, Venice declared independence from Austrian rule in March.

Bologna
Rebels here fought against Austrian rule. The northern states wanted to form a united, independent Italy.

Wallachian Revolution
In June, rebels installed a provisional government in Bucharest for the Principality of Wallachia, in defiance of Russian and Ottoman authorities. The Ottoman Empire then suppressed it.

Rome
In November, the people rose up against papal rule and the pope left Rome. A Roman republic was formed in February 1849, but lasted just a few months.

...ples
...January, ...ople revolted ...ainst King ...rdinand II in support of ...independent Sicily.

Palermo
On 12 January, Sicilians in Palermo revolted against the king and central rule, and set up their own government.

GERMAN CONFEDERATION
Revolutions in the 39 independent states of the German Confederation lasted into 1849. People wanted a united Germany with freedoms for the people.

1 **February : Mannheim** An assembly of people of the state of Baden demanded a bill of rights, triggering similar demands in several other German states.

2 **March: Munich** Thousands of people met on the city's streets demanding workers' rights, such as fair pay and employment.

3 **March: Vienna** The first of several rebellions in the city caused the exile of Metternich, chief minister of the ruling Habsburg (Austrian) monarchy.

4 **March: Berlin** In an attempt to quell riots, the Prussian king offered to make Prussia the leader of a German national state.

5 **March: Schleswig** Officials in this Danish-controlled territory declared an independent government. This led to a war between Prussia, the German Confederation, and Denmark.

6 **September: Frankfurt** Riots against a new German National Assembly, created in May, were put down with help from Prussia and Austria.

7 **May 1849: Dresden, Karlsruhe** The Assembly dissolved when the king of Prussia refused to rule Germany. Riots for democracy broke out in many places, but were violently defeated by troops.

KEY
In 1848, Germany and Italy were not unified countries, but made up of separate states with their own rulers.

State borders, 1848

German Confederation (association of German-speaking states)

 Revolt or unrest

 Peaceful protest

The American frontier

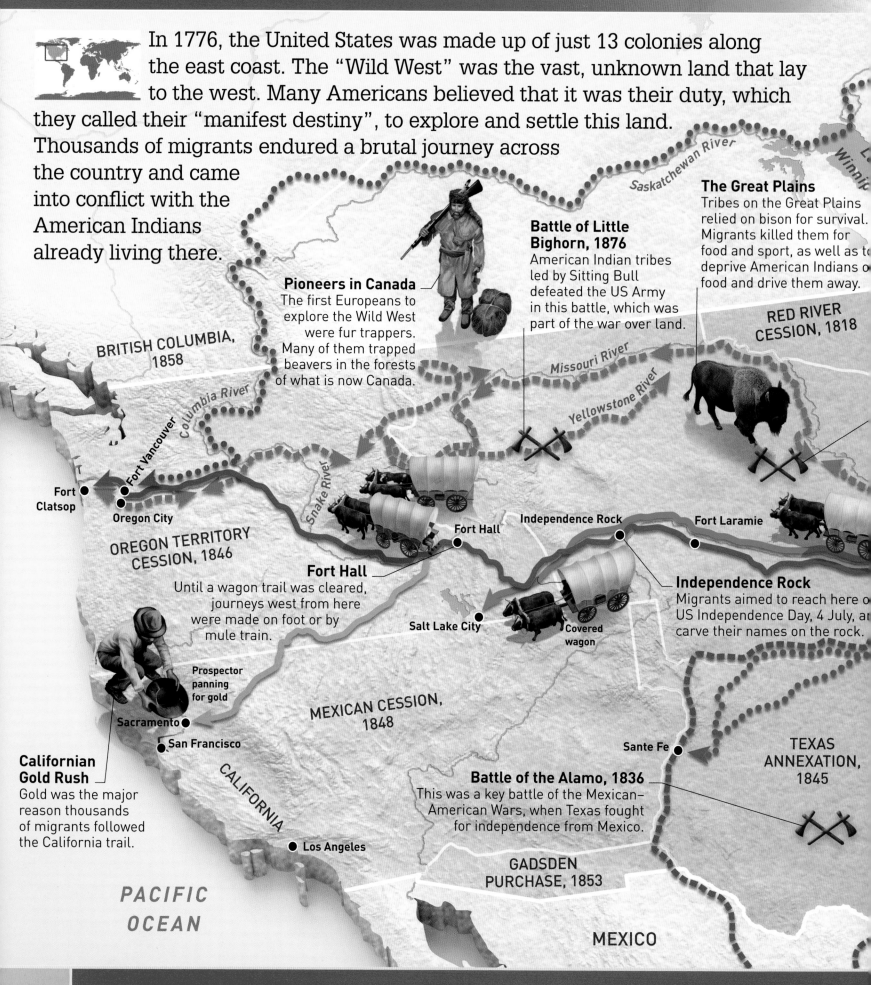

In 1776, the United States was made up of just 13 colonies along the east coast. The "Wild West" was the vast, unknown land that lay to the west. Many Americans believed that it was their duty, which they called their "manifest destiny", to explore and settle this land. Thousands of migrants endured a brutal journey across the country and came into conflict with the American Indians already living there.

Pioneers in Canada
The first Europeans to explore the Wild West were fur trappers. Many of them trapped beavers in the forests of what is now Canada.

Battle of Little Bighorn, 1876
American Indian tribes led by Sitting Bull defeated the US Army in this battle, which was part of the war over land.

The Great Plains
Tribes on the Great Plains relied on bison for survival. Migrants killed them for food and sport, as well as to deprive American Indians of food and drive them away.

Saskatchewan River

L Winnip

RED RIVER CESSION, 1818

BRITISH COLUMBIA, 1858

Columbia River

Missouri River

Yellowstone River

Snake River

Fort Vancouver

Fort Clatsop

Oregon City

OREGON TERRITORY CESSION, 1846

Fort Hall
Until a wagon trail was cleared, journeys west from here were made on foot or by mule train.

Fort Hall

Independence Rock

Fort Laramie

Independence Rock
Migrants aimed to reach here o US Independence Day, 4 July, ar carve their names on the rock.

Salt Lake City

Covered wagon

Prospector panning for gold

MEXICAN CESSION, 1848

Sacramento

San Francisco

Sante Fe

TEXAS ANNEXATION, 1845

Californian Gold Rush
Gold was the major reason thousands of migrants followed the California trail.

CALIFORNIA

Battle of the Alamo, 1836
This was a key battle of the Mexican–American Wars, when Texas fought for independence from Mexico.

Los Angeles

GADSDEN PURCHASE, 1853

PACIFIC OCEAN

MEXICO

IN 1860–61, CALIFORNIA WAS LINKED BY THE "PONY EXPRESS" SERVICE,

Hudson Bay

● York Factory

York Factory
The Hudson's Bay Company, which controlled the fur trade and sent trappers to explore the land, had its headquarters here.

Plight of the Indians
As the American people expanded west to find freedom and a better life, the American Indians found their lands invaded, their freedom taken away, and their culture almost entirely destroyed. Wars between Indians and the US lasted for over a century. Sioux leader Sitting Bull led resistance until he and his family were made prisoners of war in 1881.

Sitting Bull and family overlooked by a US cavalryman, 1882

RUPERT'S LAND (OWNED BY THE HUDSON BAY COMPANY), 1870

LOWER CANADA, 1791

Wounded Knee Massacre, 1890
The Sioux tribe was almost wiped out in this last key encounter between American Indians and the US army.

UPPER CANADA, 1791

Mississippi River

ADDITIONAL UNITED STATES TERRITORY, 1783

LOUISIANA PURCHASE, 1803

Nauvoo

Trail of Tears
In 1830, the US government passed the Indian Removal Act, which allowed it to force American Indians from the southeast and northeast, and resettle them west of the Mississippi River. The journey became known as the Trail of Tears.

St Joseph
St Louis
Independence

KEY

● Key location

⚔ Battleground

RED RIVER CESSION, 1818 — Territory, with the year it was established

EXPEDITIONS
◄ **Lewis–Clark Expedition** Goverment trip to explore and map the country in 1803–04.

◄ **Pike expeditions** Zebulon Pike sent by US to find the sources of three major rivers.

PIONEER TRAILS
◄ **Oregon Trail** Earliest migrant trail, crossing 3,200 km (2,000 miles) of territory.

◄ **California Trail** Key migrant trail used to access the Gold Rush in 1849.

◄ **Mormon Trail** Used by Mormons – religious refugees looking for a new home.

TRADE AND POSTAL ROUTES
◄ **Sante Fe Trail** Great trade route opened in 1821. Used by US to invade Mexico.

◄ **York Factory Express** Trade route chiefly used by the fur trade to access sea ports.

Indian Territory
Plains tribes, such as the Pawnee, were among the many peoples resettled in Indian Territory – now part of Oklahoma. In their homeland of the Great Plains, the Pawnee had lived in tents called tepees during bison hunts.

THE THIRTEEN COLONIES, 1776

Natchitoches
Mississippi River

PURCHASE OF FLORIDA, 1819

Antonio

Gulf of Mexico

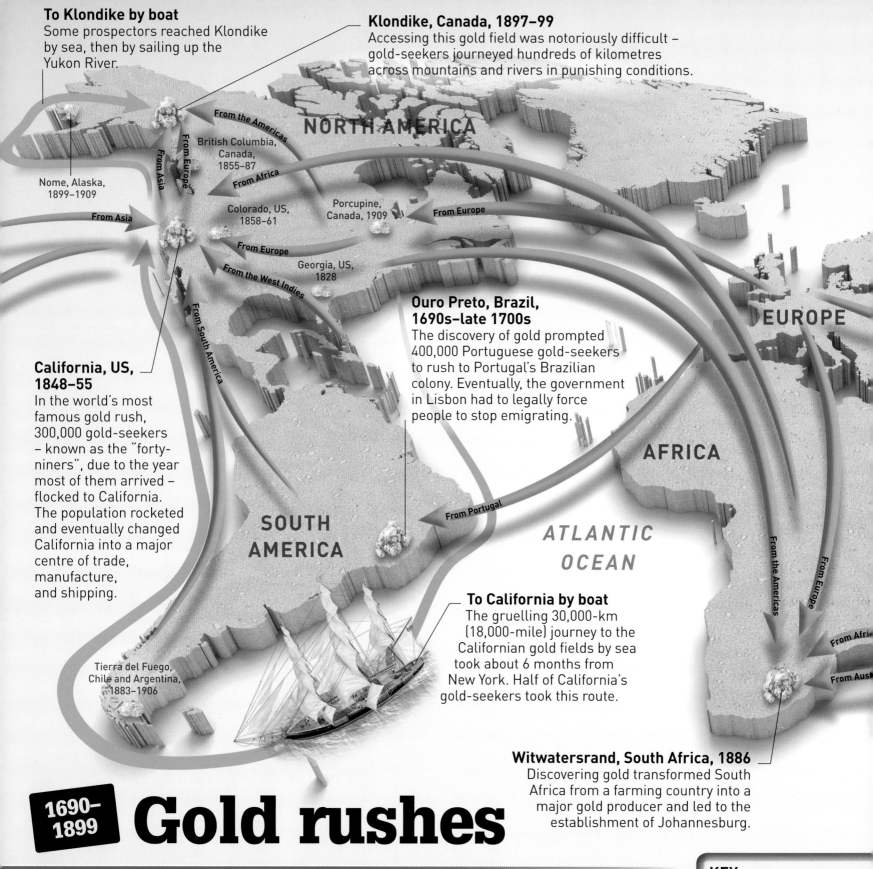

To Klondike by boat
Some prospectors reached Klondike by sea, then by sailing up the Yukon River.

Klondike, Canada, 1897–99
Accessing this gold field was notoriously difficult – gold-seekers journeyed hundreds of kilometres across mountains and rivers in punishing conditions.

From the Americas

NORTH AMERICA

British Columbia, Canada, 1855–87

From Europe

From Asia

From Africa

Nome, Alaska, 1899–1909

Colorado, US, 1858–61

Porcupine, Canada, 1909

From Europe

From Asia

From Europe

Georgia, US, 1828

From the West Indies

Ouro Preto, Brazil, 1690s–late 1700s
The discovery of gold prompted 400,000 Portuguese gold-seekers to rush to Portugal's Brazilian colony. Eventually, the government in Lisbon had to legally force people to stop emigrating.

EUROPE

From South America

California, US, 1848–55
In the world's most famous gold rush, 300,000 gold-seekers – known as the "forty-niners", due to the year most of them arrived – flocked to California. The population rocketed and eventually changed California into a major centre of trade, manufacture, and shipping.

SOUTH AMERICA

AFRICA

From Portugal

ATLANTIC OCEAN

From the Americas

From Europe

Tierra del Fuego, Chile and Argentina, 1883–1906

From Afri

To California by boat
The gruelling 30,000-km (18,000-mile) journey to the Californian gold fields by sea took about 6 months from New York. Half of California's gold-seekers took this route.

From Aus

Witwatersrand, South Africa, 1886
Discovering gold transformed South Africa from a farming country into a major gold producer and led to the establishment of Johannesburg.

1690–1899 # Gold rushes

Since the end of the 17th century, finding gold in a new region has triggered gold rushes – global migrations of thousands of people in search of fortune. Some gold rushes happened on a grand scale, bringing lasting prosperity to an area, as populations soared and trade thrived. However, such wealth came to only a small number of those who flocked to find it.

KEY
Icons show the locations of history's greatest gold rushes.

 Major gold rush

Minor gold rush

→ Direction of migration

→ Route by boat

Striking it rich

Gold rushes are linked with wealth and good fortune, yet the reality was very different. Gold-seekers endured hard journeys, and if they reached the gold fields, they faced high living costs and often had to pay to pan for gold. Of the many who set out, few ever found gold, and fewer still made any money.

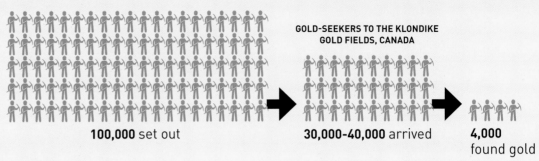

GOLD-SEEKERS TO THE KLONDIKE GOLD FIELDS, CANADA

100,000 set out → **30,000-40,000** arrived → **4,000** found gold

"Gold! **Gold!** Gold from the **American River!**"

Samuel Brannan, American merchant and entrepreneur, stirring up gold fever to boost trade, 1848

ARCTIC OCEAN

ASIA

From Asia

INDIAN OCEAN

Victoria, Australia, 1851–60s
Australia's first major gold rush increased the country's population from 430,000 in 1851 to 1.7 million in 1871.

PACIFIC OCEAN

From boomtown to ghost town

Boomtowns were settlements that grew rapidly as a result of the gold rushes. Once the rushes were over, some continued to thrive, but others were quickly abandoned. Many of these ghost towns still exist as a desolate reminder of the quest for riches.

From Europe

From China

From the Americas

From India

AUSTRALASIA

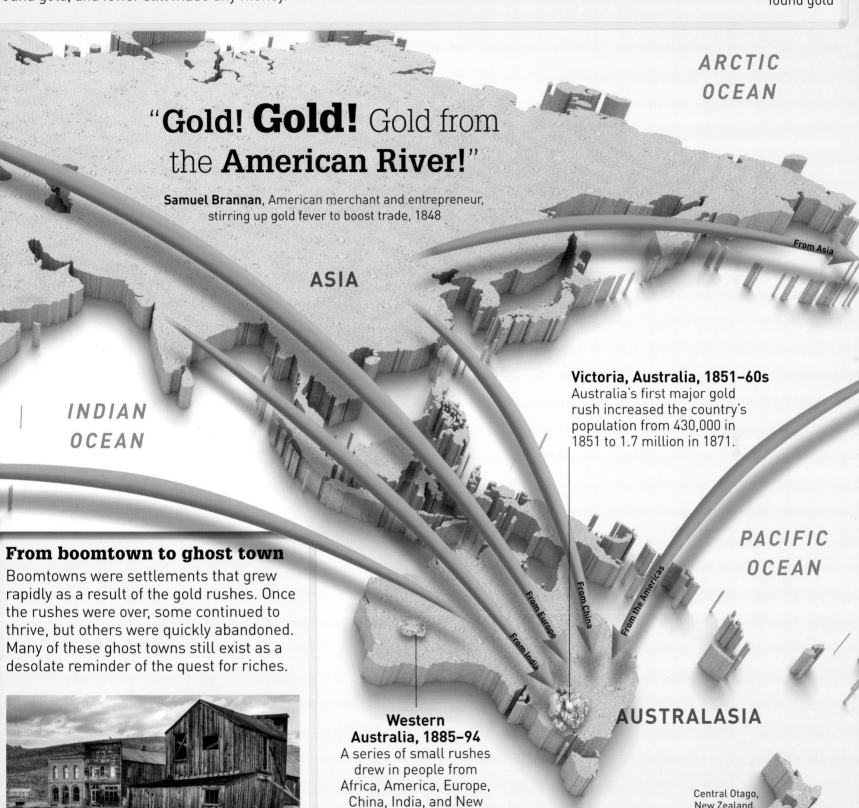

Bonie, California

Western Australia, 1885–94
A series of small rushes drew in people from Africa, America, Europe, China, India, and New Zealand, as well as from the mining areas of eastern Australia.

Central Otago, New Zealand, 1861

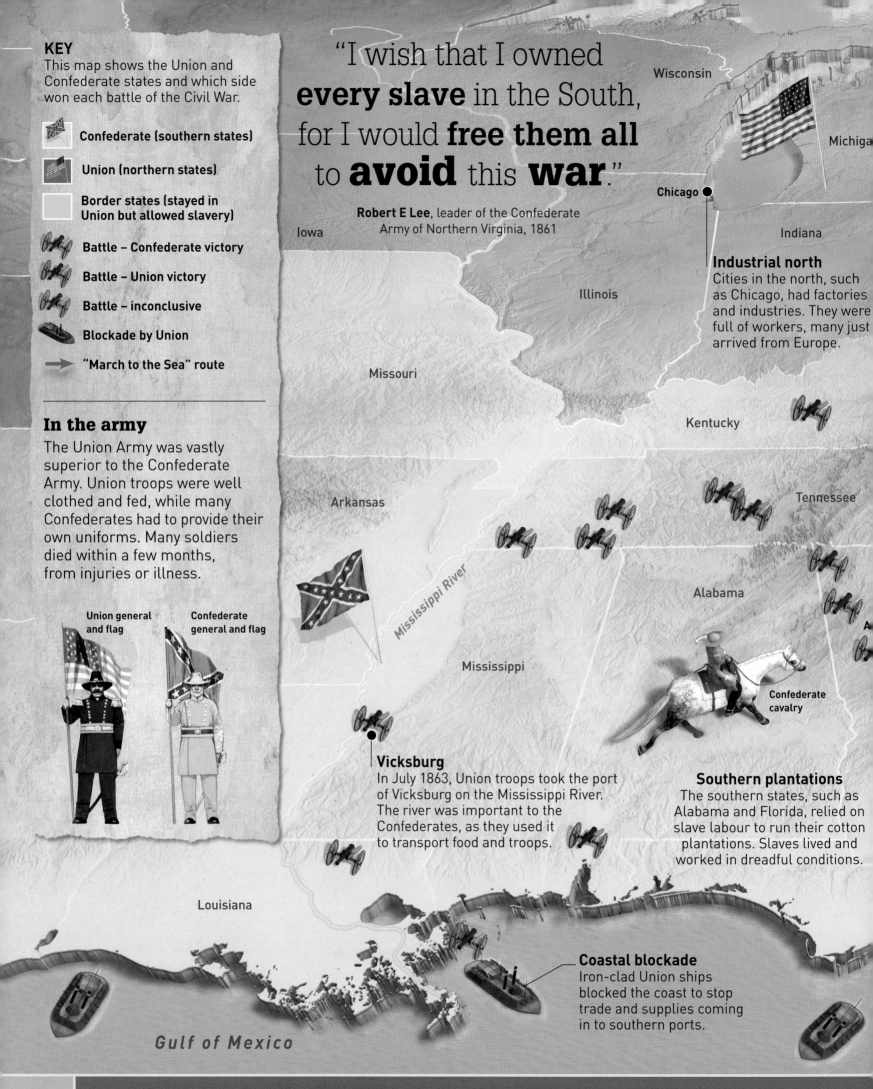

KEY

This map shows the Union and Confederate states and which side won each battle of the Civil War.

Confederate (southern states)

Union (northern states)

Border states (stayed in Union but allowed slavery)

Battle – Confederate victory

Battle – Union victory

Battle – inconclusive

Blockade by Union

"March to the Sea" route

In the army

The Union Army was vastly superior to the Confederate Army. Union troops were well clothed and fed, while many Confederates had to provide their own uniforms. Many soldiers died within a few months, from injuries or illness.

Union general and flag

Confederate general and flag

"I wish that I owned **every slave** in the South, for I would **free them all** to **avoid** this **war**."

Robert E Lee, leader of the Confederate Army of Northern Virginia, 1861

Wisconsin

Michigan

Chicago

Iowa

Indiana

Industrial north
Cities in the north, such as Chicago, had factories and industries. They were full of workers, many just arrived from Europe.

Illinois

Missouri

Kentucky

Arkansas

Tennessee

Mississippi River

Alabama

Mississippi

Confederate cavalry

Vicksburg
In July 1863, Union troops took the port of Vicksburg on the Mississippi River. The river was important to the Confederates, as they used it to transport food and troops.

Southern plantations
The southern states, such as Alabama and Florida, relied on slave labour to run their cotton plantations. Slaves lived and worked in dreadful conditions.

Louisiana

Coastal blockade
Iron-clad Union ships blocked the coast to stop trade and supplies coming in to southern ports.

Gulf of Mexico

WHILE MOST OF THE SOLDIERS WERE VOLUNTEERS, HUNDREDS OF

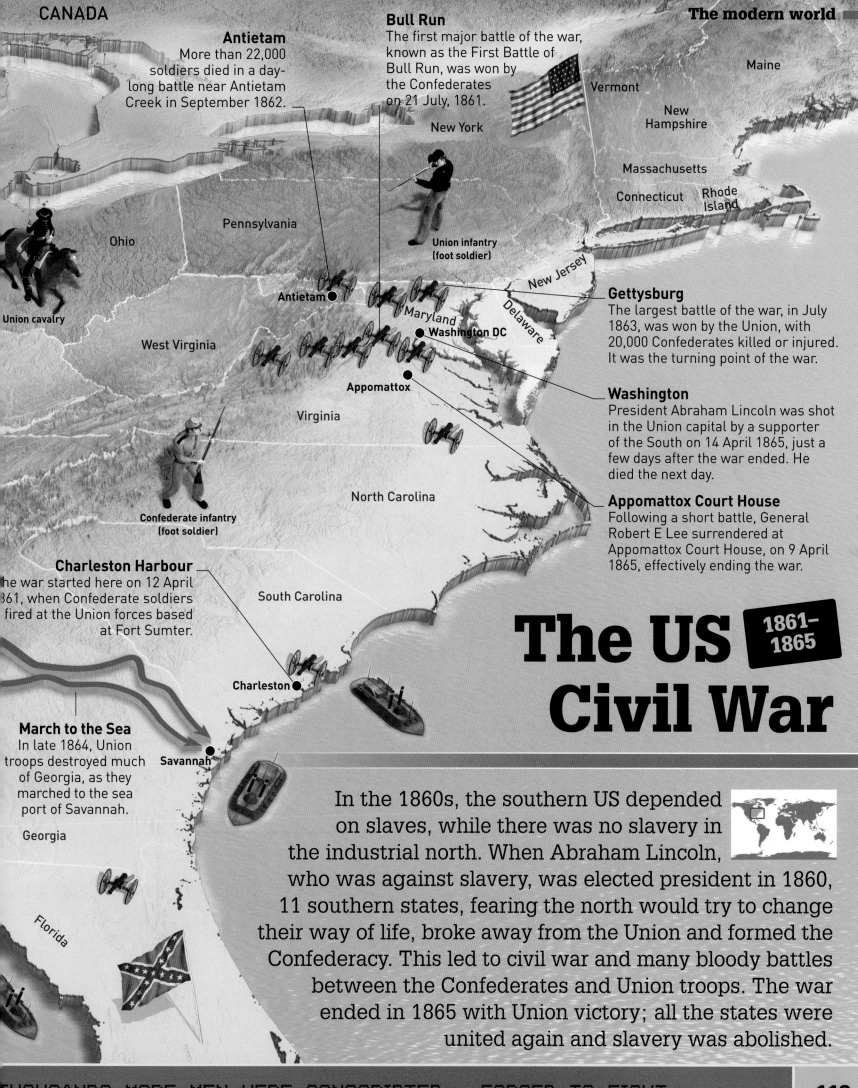

Antietam
More than 22,000 soldiers died in a day-long battle near Antietam Creek in September 1862.

Bull Run
The first major battle of the war, known as the First Battle of Bull Run, was won by the Confederates on 21 July, 1861.

Maine

Vermont

New Hampshire

New York

Massachusetts

Connecticut

Rhode Island

Union infantry (foot soldier)

Pennsylvania

Ohio

Union cavalry

West Virginia

Antietam

Maryland

New Jersey

Delaware

Washington DC

Gettysburg
The largest battle of the war, in July 1863, was won by the Union, with 20,000 Confederates killed or injured. It was the turning point of the war.

Appomattox

Virginia

Washington
President Abraham Lincoln was shot in the Union capital by a supporter of the South on 14 April 1865, just a few days after the war ended. He died the next day.

Confederate infantry (foot soldier)

North Carolina

Appomattox Court House
Following a short battle, General Robert E Lee surrendered at Appomattox Court House, on 9 April 1865, effectively ending the war.

Charleston Harbour
The war started here on 12 April 1861, when Confederate soldiers fired at the Union forces based at Fort Sumter.

South Carolina

Charleston

The US Civil War 1861–1865

March to the Sea
In late 1864, Union troops destroyed much of Georgia, as they marched to the sea port of Savannah.

Savannah

Georgia

Florida

In the 1860s, the southern US depended on slaves, while there was no slavery in the industrial north. When Abraham Lincoln, who was against slavery, was elected president in 1860, 11 southern states, fearing the north would try to change their way of life, broke away from the Union and formed the Confederacy. This led to civil war and many bloody battles between the Confederates and Union troops. The war ended in 1865 with Union victory; all the states were united again and slavery was abolished.

Japan faces the future

For more than 200 years, outsiders were forbidden from setting foot in Japan and Japanese people could not travel abroad. Japan traded only with certain neighbours. That changed in 1854 when the United States forced Japan's shogun (military leader) to sign an unfair international trade agreement. This caused civil war in Japan, which led to the emperor being restored to power in place of the shogun. In the Meiji Period that followed, Japan raced to catch up and overtake the West's industry and technology, so that the country could once again be proudly independent.

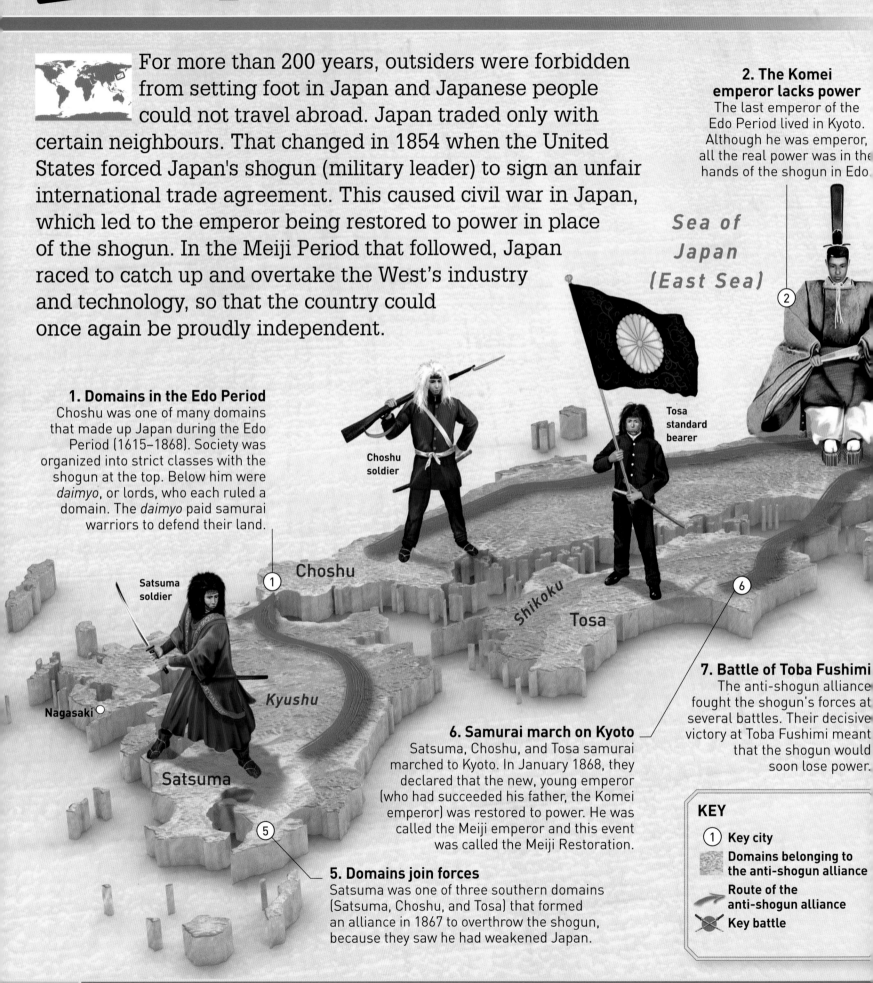

2. The Komei emperor lacks power
The last emperor of the Edo Period lived in Kyoto. Although he was emperor, all the real power was in the hands of the shogun in Edo.

Sea of Japan (East Sea)

Tosa standard bearer

1. Domains in the Edo Period
Choshu was one of many domains that made up Japan during the Edo Period (1615–1868). Society was organized into strict classes with the shogun at the top. Below him were *daimyo*, or lords, who each ruled a domain. The *daimyo* paid samurai warriors to defend their land.

Choshu soldier

Satsuma soldier

Choshu

Shikoku

Tosa

7. Battle of Toba Fushimi
The anti-shogun alliance fought the shogun's forces at several battles. Their decisive victory at Toba Fushimi meant that the shogun would soon lose power.

Kyushu

Nagasaki

6. Samurai march on Kyoto
Satsuma, Choshu, and Tosa samurai marched to Kyoto. In January 1868, they declared that the new, young emperor (who had succeeded his father, the Komei emperor) was restored to power. He was called the Meiji emperor and this event was called the Meiji Restoration.

Satsuma

5. Domains join forces
Satsuma was one of three southern domains (Satsuma, Choshu, and Tosa) that formed an alliance in 1867 to overthrow the shogun, because they saw he had weakened Japan.

KEY
- ① Key city
- Domains belonging to the anti-shogun alliance
- Route of the anti-shogun alliance
- Key battle

9. Battle of Hakodate
The last stronghold of the shogun's army was Hakodate, where it held out for 6 months against the anti-shogun forces, before surrendering in 1869.

Hokkaido

Hakodate

"Oitsuke, oikose."
("Catch up, overtake.")

Meiji Period slogan

3. The shogun rules
During the Edo Period, Japan was ruled from Edo by a military leader called the shogun.

Sendai

Nagaoka

Aizu

J A P A N

Utsunomiya

Edo
(Tokyo)

Koshu
Katsunuma

Honshu

4. Black ships sail into Edo
In 1853, US Commodore Matthew Perry sailed into Edo with four iron warships (called "Black Ships" in Japan), bristling with the latest guns. He forced the shogun into an unfair trade agreement, which benefitted the US and other foreign powers.

8. Edo is renamed Tokyo
The new emperor visited Edo in 1868 and renamed the city Tokyo. In 1889, Tokyo became Japan's capital.

Meiji industry

The Meiji emperor was only 15 years old when he was swept to power. Far from keeping Japan traditional, as some samurai had hoped, his rule saw sweeping changes. The class system, including the samurai class, was abolished. Japan raced to become an industrial nation, exporting factory-made products to the West. In some countries, including Britain, there was also a craze for traditional Japanese products, such as silk, pottery, and fans.

KEY

Industrial areas

Exports

Manufacturing

Chemicals

Machinery

Fans

Yahata

Kyoto

Osaka

Tokyo

Silk and textiles

Ceramics

North

(7,000 MILES) OF RAILWAY AND BUILT MORE THAN 1,500 STEAMSHIPS.

115

Canadian Pacific Railway, 1885
This railway helped to strengthen Canada against the powerful neighbouring United States, by connecting its east and west provinces.

Locomotion No.1, 1825

NORTH AMERICA

Vancouver

Montreal

Council Bluffs, Iowa

Sacramento, California

CP No. 60 *Jupiter*, 1868

First Transcontinental Railroad, 1869
This railway was finished when the Central Pacific Railroad from California met the Union Pacific Railroad from Iowa. Builders from each end had raced towards the middle in only 6 years.

Stockton–Darlington Railway, 1825
The world's first public steam railway carried coal and passengers. The railway's first locomotive was the *Locomotion*, designed by British engineer George Stephenson.

Stockton, Darlington
London
Paris

Orient Express, 1883
This luxury passenger train ran between Europe and the East. Its first route ran between Paris and Istanbul.

Railways in Africa, 1854–1900
European colonial powers introduced railways to Africa. Often, tracks ran in from the coast, but did not join up to create a network.

AFRICA

How rail changed the world
As well as allowing convenient travel, railways helped develop many areas of work and daily life.

SOUTH AMERICA

Lima

Railway time
Time was slightly different in each town before the railways. Standard railway time (the same everywhere) was established so that trains could run without colliding.

Farming
Fresh produce could be carried great distances without spoiling, which helped farmers and improved diets.

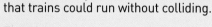
Industry and employment
Railways created jobs and boosted industry, as materials were needed to build tracks, and coal was needed to fuel the engines.

Postal Services
Mail carriages were added to trains, and letters were delivered in days, not months.

Trade
Railways transported goods faster than roads or canals. Global trade improved as goods travelled quickly to ports for export.

Military
Railways transported soldiers and their equipment quickly during times of war, which made rail vital to military success.

Callao, Lima, and Oroya Railway, 1870–1908
Built to cross the Andes mountains in Peru, linking Pacific ports with the interior of the country, this was the highest railway in the world for the next 100 years.

"By **building the Union Pacific**, you will be the **remembered man** of your generation."

US President Abraham Lincoln, to industrialist Oakes Ames, 1865

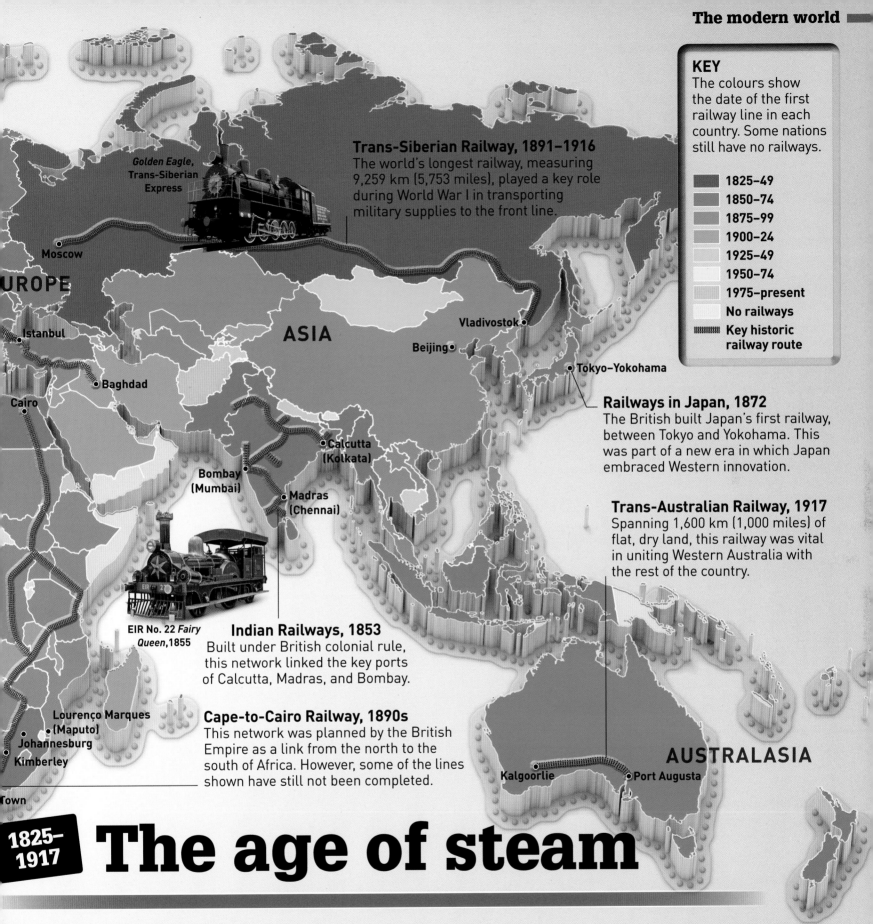

KEY
The colours show the date of the first railway line in each country. Some nations still have no railways.

	1825–49
	1850–74
	1875–99
	1900–24
	1925–49
	1950–74
	1975–present
	No railways
	Key historic railway route

Trans-Siberian Railway, 1891–1916
The world's longest railway, measuring 9,259 km (5,753 miles), played a key role during World War I in transporting military supplies to the front line.

Golden Eagle, Trans-Siberian Express

Moscow

EUROPE

ASIA

Istanbul

Baghdad

Cairo

Vladivostok

Beijing

Tokyo–Yokohama

Railways in Japan, 1872
The British built Japan's first railway, between Tokyo and Yokohama. This was part of a new era in which Japan embraced Western innovation.

Calcutta (Kolkata)

Bombay (Mumbai)

Madras (Chennai)

Trans-Australian Railway, 1917
Spanning 1,600 km (1,000 miles) of flat, dry land, this railway was vital in uniting Western Australia with the rest of the country.

EIR No. 22 Fairy Queen,1855

Indian Railways, 1853
Built under British colonial rule, this network linked the key ports of Calcutta, Madras, and Bombay.

Lourenço Marques (Maputo)
Johannesburg
Kimberley

Cape-to-Cairo Railway, 1890s
This network was planned by the British Empire as a link from the north to the south of Africa. However, some of the lines shown have still not been completed.

AUSTRALASIA

Kalgoorlie
Port Augusta

Town

1825–1917 The age of steam

The opening of the first passenger steam railway in Britain in 1825 revolutionized transport. Soon, people and goods would travel huge distances – even abroad – quickly and easily. Railways soon spread to Europe and North America, then across the world. They connected cities, provided jobs, and improved trade. Within a few years, rail had become the world's most important means of transport.

MOUNTAINS AT AN ALTITUDE OF UP TO 4,818 M (15,806 FT).

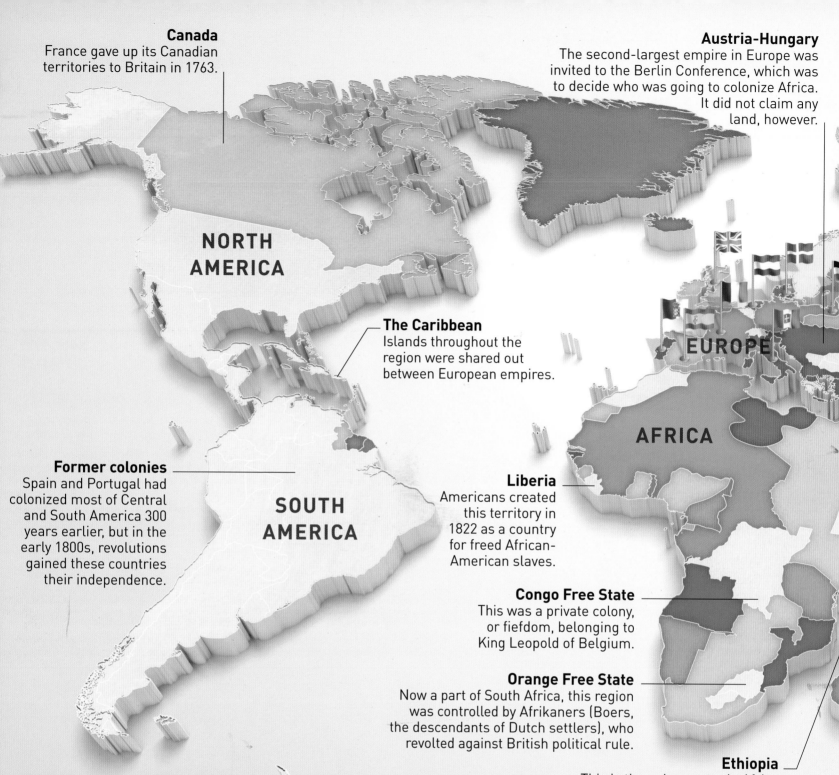

Canada
France gave up its Canadian territories to Britain in 1763.

Austria-Hungary
The second-largest empire in Europe was invited to the Berlin Conference, which was to decide who was going to colonize Africa. It did not claim any land, however.

NORTH AMERICA

EUROPE

The Caribbean
Islands throughout the region were shared out between European empires.

AFRICA

Former colonies
Spain and Portugal had colonized most of Central and South America 300 years earlier, but in the early 1800s, revolutions gained these countries their independence.

SOUTH AMERICA

Liberia
Americans created this territory in 1822 as a country for freed African-American slaves.

Congo Free State
This was a private colony, or fiefdom, belonging to King Leopold of Belgium.

Orange Free State
Now a part of South Africa, this region was controlled by Afrikaners (Boers, the descendants of Dutch settlers), who revolted against British political rule.

Ethiopia
This is the only country in Africa never to have been colonized.

The Scramble for Africa
When Europeans entered Africa to help end the slave trade, they took the chance to occupy territory. This turned into a scramble for wealth and glory, so the Berlin Conference of 1884–1885 was organized to govern it. Africa was split between seven European powers, giving them land if they flew their nation's flag there and made treaties with local leaders. These treaties, however, were mostly made by force.

A French political cartoon passes comment on the Berlin Conference. It shows the German Chancellor cutting up African territory like a cake.

"His majesty's **dominions**, on which the **Sun never sets**."

Christopher North (pen name of writer John Wilson), describing the British Empire, 1829

BY 1902, EUROPEANS CONTROLLED 90 PER CENT OF AFRICA, BUT

Europe's empires

By 1900, the major powers in Europe had empires that stretched across the world. (There were other imperial powers too, including China, Japan, and the US.) The European powers gained global importance and also wealth – by taking it from their colonies. The fiercest competition of the time was for control of Africa.

ASIA

Russia
Three-quarters of the Russian Empire was in Asia, with one quarter in Europe. It included around 200 small nations in addition to Russia.

India
British rule, or Raj, divided India into eight provinces, each with its own governor.

China
The last dynasty of China – the Qing – ruled a huge empire including Mongolia and Tibet.

Japan
Japan's empire building accelerated after 1900, and the country annexed Korea in 1910.

...oman Empire
...e of the world's ...gest-running empires, ...s Islamic empire lasted ...re than 620 years, until 1922.

Siam
Known today as Thailand, Siam was one of the few countries not to be colonized by a European power.

Kaiser-Wilhelmsland
The furthest outpost of the German Empire was named after the emperor Wilhelm II. It is now the northern part of Papua New Guinea.

...KEY

...his map shows the extent of ...he European empires in 1900.

- Britain and possessions
- France and possessions
- Netherlands and possessions
- Portugal and possessions
- Spain and possessions
- Germany and possessions
- Russian Empire
- Italy and possessions
- Denmark and possessions
- Ottoman Empire

AUSTRALASIA

Australia
Australia was made up of six independent British colonies. In 1900, they chose to become a federation, which remained a part of the British Empire.

Telephone, 1876
Scotsman Alexander Graham Bell developed his telephone in Boston, US. The first person he spoke to with his invention was his assistant, Watson.

Factory, 1771
When Richard Arkwright opened his water-powered mill in Cromford, England, he became the first person to combine several stages of production under one roof.

Anaesthetic, 1846
American dentist William Morton was the first person to use anaesthetic succesfully during surgery.

NORTH AMERICA

Air conditioning, 1902
American Willis Carrier created the modern air-cooling machine, which controlled both air temperature and humidity.

Steam locomotive, 1804
Invented by Briton Richard Trevithick, the first locomotive ran on the road. By 1804, Trevithick had built and run locomotives designed for railway tracks.

Vaccine, 1796
English scientist Edward Jenner injected a vaccine (weakened or killed germs) into a patient's body to encourage it to fight the disease smallpox. It led to the development of vaccinations for other diseases.

Light bulb, 1879
Although bulbs had already been invented earlier, US inventor Thomas Edison developed a type of bulb that could safely glow for up to 50 hours, making it suitable for home use.

EUROPE

Cinema, 1895
The cinématographe was invented by French brothers August and Louis Lumière. The device was a combined camera and film projector, and it played a moving picture for several minutes at a public screening in Paris.

Radio, 1895
Italian Guglielmo Marconi transmitted and received radio signals at a distance of 2.4 km (1.5 miles).

Aeroplane, 1903
American brothers Orville and Wilbur Wright developed the first powered aeroplane, whose maiden flight lasted for 12 seconds and covered 36 m (120 ft).

AFRICA

SOUTH AMERICA

Pasteurization, 1865
Frenchman Louis Pasteur discovered that liquid foods could be heated to destroy harmful bacteria without affecting their food value.

Piano, 1709
Italian Bartolomeo Cristofori developed the piano. Compared to earlier keyboard instruments, it allowed musicians much greater control of the loudness of notes, and it became a mainstay of Western music.

Rubber, 1735
During an expedition to Ecuador, Frenchman Charles-Marie de la Condamine came across rubber. The material became famous back in Europe, and in 1770, Englishman Joseph Priestley discovered that it could rub out pencil marks. He called his invention the "rubber".

ALTHOUGH MODERN TINNED FOOD DATES BACK TO 1810, PEOPLE OPENED

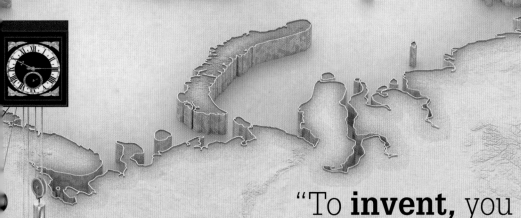

The Industrial Revolution

Between the late 1700s and 1850, Britain transformed itself into the world's first industrial power. It gained a huge commercial and technological head start over the rest of the world. This achievement was helped by many inventions made in Britain, including the steam locomotive, the factory, the spinning jenny for spinning thread, the tin can for preserving food, and the underground railway. This period is known as the Industrial Revolution.

A coloured engraving showing the inside of an English factory during the late 18th century.

Pendulum clock, 1657
Dutchman Christiaan Huygens built the first pendulum clock, which vastly improved the accuracy of timekeeping.

"To **invent,** you need a good **imagination** and a **pile of junk**."

Thomas A Edison, US inventor, 1847–1931

Electric train, 1879
Werner von Siemens exhibited the first electric train in Berlin, Germany. It carried 20–25 people and reached a speed of 6 kph (4 mph).

ASIA

Motor car, 1886
German engineer Karl Benz demonstrated the first car, the Motorwagen, which had three wheels and was powered by a small engine.

1500–1900 Modern inventions

The modern period (1500–1900) was a time of great development in Europe and North America. The Industrial Revolution in Britain saw the birth of the factory, as well as many machines for manufacturing. There were also major advances in the fields of transport, science, and medicine, with inventions that would eventually transform people's lives throughout the world.

The 20th and 21st centuries

Into space
The most recent chapter of Earth's history hasn't taken place entirely on our planet, as people explored space for the first time in the 20th century. Here, NASA astronauts (Greg Chamitoff, shown; and Mike Fincke, reflected in the visor) make a space walk to repair the International Space Station in 2011.

RADIO ACROSS THE ATLANTIC (1901) Radio pioneer Gugliemo Marconi sends the first radio signals from England to Canada.

SOUTH POLE (1911) Norwegian explorer Roa Amundsen becomes the first person to reach the South Pole. »pp126–27

1900

THE WRIGHT FLYER (1903) The first powered, controlled flight takes place at Kitty Hawk, North Carolina, US. »pp132–33

TITANIC DISASTER (1912) The luxury cruise ship *Titanic* is sunk by an iceberg, killing more than 1,500 passengers and crew.

Wright *Flyer*
Brothers Orville and Wilbur Wright's plane had a wooden frame covered in muslin cloth.

WAR IS OVER (1945) The war ends in August with Victory over Japan Day, following Victory in Europe day in May. »pp140

Soviet Ilyushin Il-2 "Shturmovik" anti-tank aircraft

US JOINS WORLD WAR II (1941) The US joins the wa after Japan attacks the American naval base at Pearl Harbour. »pp138–39

NORTH AND SOUTH KOREA (1945) Korea is divided into the Soviet-controlled North and the US-occupied South.

D-DAY (1944) British, US, and Canadian troops land on French beaches to gain access to German-held territory. »pp142–43

GERMANY INVADES THE SOVIET UNION (USSR) (1941) The war's largest invasion, on the Eastern Front, changes the course of the war. »pp140–41

WORLD WAR II (1939–45) England and France declare war on Germany after it invades Poland. »pp138–43

Mohandas Gandhi spinning cotton in defiance of British law

SUPERSONIC FLIGHT (1947) The Bell X-1 rocket plane is the first manned aircraft to fly faster than sound. »pp132–33

THE STATE OF ISRAEL (1948) The State of Israel is declared, following a United Nations vote to partition British-controlled Palestine.

AMERICAN CIVIL RIGHT (1955–68) Martin Luther King Jr rallies African-Americans to rise up against racial segregatio

INDIAN INDEPENDENCE (1947) Gandhi inspires the end of British rule in India, and the country is divided into Hindu-majority India and Muslim-majority Pakistan. »pp144–45

APARTHEID (1948–94) South African apartheid law severely restricts the rights of black people. It is abolished in 1994.

MOUNT EVEREST (1953) Sir Edmund Hillary and Sherpa Tensing Norgay conquer the world's highest mountain.

VIETNAM WAR (1956–75) North and South Vietnam are united in 1975 after the US lose the war to stop Communism in the South.

CHINA POWER (2013) China becomes the largest trading nation in the world, overtaking the US. »pp154–55

END OF THE COLD WAR (1991) Aggression between the US and USSR finishes as Communist government ends and the USSR splits up.

EMAIL (1971) Computer programmer Ray Tomlinson sends the first email. »pp152–53

WALKING ON THE MOON (1969) US astronaut Neil Armstrong becomes the first person to walk on the Moon. »pp150–51

WORLD WIDE WEB (1991) British scientist Tim Berners-Lee creates a system of interlinked pages on the Internet and calls it the World Wide Web. »pp152–53

ARPANET (1969) Computers are connected in a network for the first time. The network, in California, US, is called ARPAnet and is an early version of the Internet. »pp152–53

ABORIGINAL RIGHTS (1967) The Australian government recognizes Aboriginal People as full Australian citizens.

IN 2008, 978 MILLION PEOPLE WATCHED THE BEIJING OLYMPICS'

PRODUCTION LINE (1913)
The Ford motor company introduces assembly-line mass production, making cars faster and cheaper to produce.

WORLD WAR I (1914–18)
After the assassination of Archduke Franz Ferdinand, Austro-Hungary declares war on Serbia. »pp128–29

TANK WARFARE (1916)
The first battle tanks are used by the British army during World War I. »pp128–29

Net connection
The white lines on the globe represent Internet connections between cities.

RUSSIAN REVOLUTION (1917–22) The Bolsheviks (later known as Communists) take control of the Russian Empire. »pp130–31

IN THE AIR (1915)
World War I sees the first air battles. Airships drop bombs and planes battle in dogfights. »pp128–29

British Whippet tank, World War I

AMELIA EARHART (1937)
Aviation pioneer Amelia Earhart disappears in the Pacific when trying to fly around the world. »pp132–33

THE GREAT DEPRESSION (1929–39) A global economic crisis is fuelled by companies losing value and unemployment rising disastrously. »pp134–35

END OF THE WAR (1918)
A temporary truce was agreed to end World War I, with a formal peace treaty signed in 1919. »pp128–29

CHINA'S LONG MARCH (1934–35) The rebel Chinese Communist army marches for 1 year and 3 days to escape Nationalist forces. »pp136–37

AMRITSAR MASSACRE (1919) The British army fires on 6,000 protestors for Indian rights in Amritsar, India, killing hundreds. »pp144–45

AMERICA JOINS WORLD WAR I (1917) Outraged by German bombing of their ships, the US joins World War I. »pp128–29

SPUTNIK IN SPACE (1957)
The Soviet Union (USSR) launches *Sputnik I* – the first artificial satellite to orbit the Earth. »pp148–49

NASA's
Space Shuttle

TO THE MOON (1959)
Luna 2, sent by the Soviet Union (USSR), becomes the first spacecraft to land on the Moon. »pp150–51

Beyond 1900

THE CUBAN MISSILE CRISIS (1962) The US asks the Soviet Union to remove its missiles from Cuba. The world waits for war, but it doesn't come. »pp146–47

The 20th century saw the fast development of many forms of technology, from radio and television to space exploration and computing. Technology had a major impact on wars, but also made the world smaller: every continent has been explored, thanks to improvements in transport, and every part of the world is connected, thanks to a revolution in telecommunication.

THE BERLIN WALL (1961–89) Communist East German authorities build a wall to stop people escaping from Communist East Berlin into West Germany.

The race to the South Pole

By the early 20th century, the South Pole was exploration's last great challenge and British explorer Robert Falcon Scott was determined to meet it. But as he and his team made their way to the Antarctic in 1910, he heard that Norwegian Roald Amundsen also had his eye on the prize. What followed was a race that captivated and shocked the world.

Antarctica

The coldest place on Earth, with a lowest ever temperature of -89.2°C (-128.6°F), Antarctica is also the most remote, the windiest, the highest, and the least-known continent on the planet.

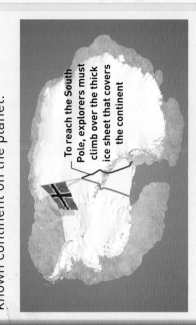

To reach the South Pole, explorers must climb over the thick ice sheet that covers the continent

Roald Amundsen

After discovering the Northwest Passage (a sea route from the Atlantic Ocean to the Pacific) in 1903–06, Norwegian Roald Amundsen was already a celebrated explorer. Well used to the polar conditions, he led his team to the South Pole and back in 99 days.

Robert Falcon Scott

Robert Falcon Scott was a naval officer and a veteran of the 1901–04 *Discovery* Expedition to Antarctica, and he returned to the Antarctic in 1911 "to reach the South Pole". However, Amundsen's team beat his to the pole, and Scott and his men died on their return journey.

6. Amundsen reaches the pole
Amundsen's team became the first to reach the South Pole on 14 December 1911. The journey to the pole took them 56 days.

5. Butchering the dogs
Of the 45 dogs that climbed the Axel Heiberg Glacier, only 18 made the final assault on the South Pole. The rest were killed for food.

4. Climbing the glacier
Amundsen's team started their climb of a glacier (which they called Axel Heiberg Glacier) to the Polar Plateau. They had crossed

e. Scott reaches the pole
Scott's team reached the South Pole 34 days behind Amundsen on 17 January 1912. They set off on their return journey the same day.

f. First casualty
Teddy Evans, of Scott's team, died on 7 February 1912.

South Pole

6 e

e

Polar Plateau (Antarctic Ice Sheet)

Last Depot 14 Jan 1912

1½° Depot 10 Jan 1912

3° Depot 31 Dec 1911

Upper Glacier Depot 21 Dec 1911

Last Depot 8 Dec 1911

Devil's Glacier Depot 29 Nov 1911

Butcher's Shop Depot 21 Nov 1911

5

4

Main Depot 17 Nov 1911

85°

Heiberg

AMUNDSEN LEFT NO MARGIN FOR ERROR: THE FOOD SUPPLIES IN HIS

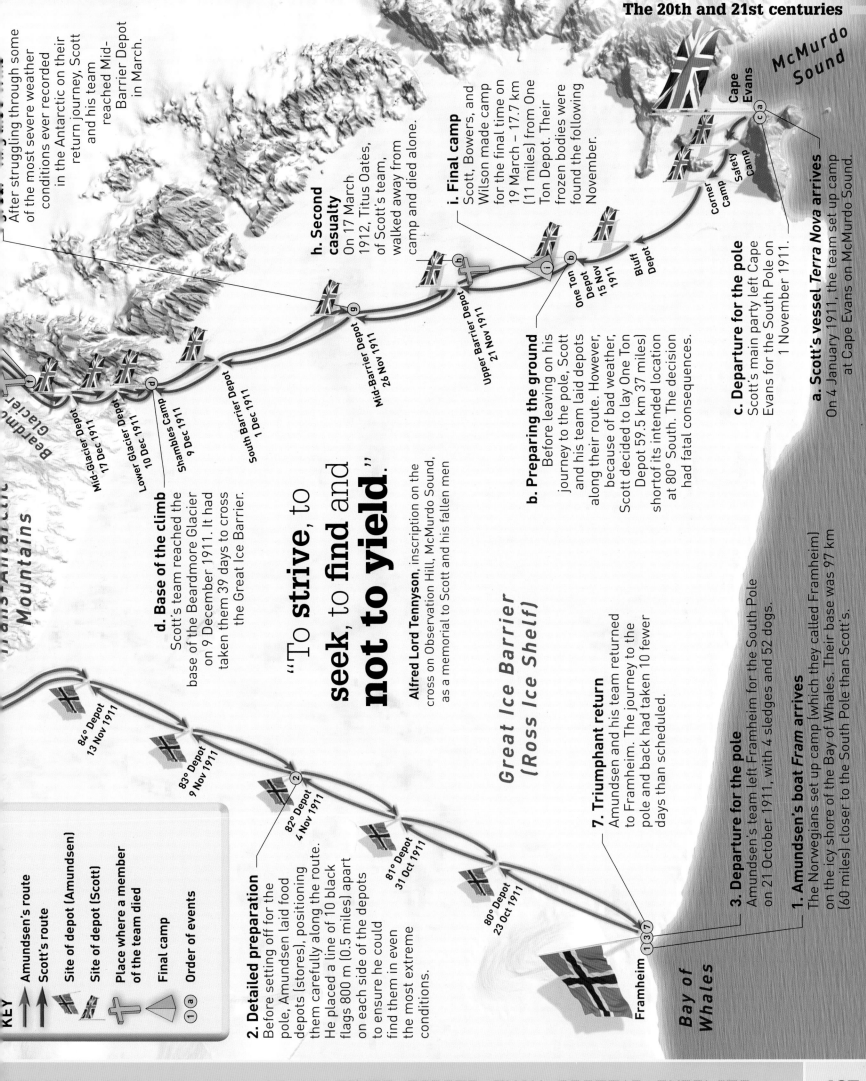

McMurdo Sound

After struggling through some of the most severe weather conditions ever recorded in the Antarctic on their return journey, Scott and his team reached Mid-Barrier Depot in March.

Transantarctic Mountains

Beardmore Glacier

Mid-Glacier Depot 17 Dec 1911

Lower Glacier Depot 10 Dec 1911

Shambles Camp 9 Dec 1911

d. Base of the climb
Scott's team reached the base of the Beardmore Glacier on 9 December 1911. It had taken them 39 days to cross the Great Ice Barrier.

South Barrier Depot 1 Dec 1911

h. Second casualty
On 17 March 1912, Titus Oates, of Scott's team, walked away from camp and died alone.

Mid-Barrier Depot 26 Nov 1911

i. Final camp
Scott, Bowers, and Wilson made camp for the final time on 19 March – 17.7 km (11 miles) from One Ton Depot. Their frozen bodies were found the following November.

Upper Barrier Depot 21 Nov 1911

One Ton Depot 15 Nov 1911

Bluff Depot

Corner Camp

Safety Camp

Cape Evans

c. Departure for the pole
Scott's main party left Cape Evans for the South Pole on 1 November 1911.

a. Scott's vessel *Terra Nova* arrives
On 4 January 1911, the team set up camp at Cape Evans on McMurdo Sound.

b. Preparing the ground
Before leaving on his journey to the pole, Scott and his team laid depots along their route. However, because of bad weather, Scott decided to lay One Ton Depot 59.5 km (37 miles) short of its intended location at 80° South. The decision had fatal consequences.

"To **strive**, to **seek**, to **find** and **not to yield**."

Alfred Lord Tennyson, inscription on the cross on Observation Hill, McMurdo Sound, as a memorial to Scott and his fallen men

Great Ice Barrier (Ross Ice Shelf)

7. Triumphant return
Amundsen and his team returned to Framheim. The journey to the pole and back had taken 10 fewer days than scheduled.

84° Depot 13 Nov 1911

83° Depot 9 Nov 1911

82° Depot 4 Nov 1911

2. Detailed preparation
Before setting off for the pole, Amundsen laid food depots (stores), positioning them carefully along the route. He placed a line of 10 black flags 800 m (0.5 miles) apart on each side of the depots to ensure he could find them in even the most extreme conditions.

81° Depot 31 Oct 1911

80° Depot 23 Oct 1911

3. Departure for the pole
Amundsen's team left Framheim for the South Pole on 21 October 1911, with 4 sledges and 52 dogs.

1. Amundsen's boat *Fram* arrives
The Norwegians set up camp (which they called Framheim) on the icy shore of the Bay of Whales. Their base was 97 km (60 miles) closer to the South Pole than Scott's.

Framheim

Bay of Whales

KEY
Amundsen's route
Scott's route
Site of depot (Amundsen)
Site of depot (Scott)
Place where a member of the team died
Final camp
Order of events

UNITED KINGDOM

London ●

U-boats
German submarines (undersea boats, or U-boats) attacked mercha[nt] ships, battleships, and even passenger and hospital ships belonging to Britain and America. This finally prompted the US to join the war, in April 1917.

Drowning in mud
Heavy rains made the mud on the Passchendaele battlefield so deep that injured soldiers drowned in it.

Gas attack
In 1915, gas was used as a weapon for the first time, by German forces against French soldiers at Ypres.

Zeppelin air raids
From 1915, German airships attacked London and other British towns, as well as Paris.

British hospital ship

Football at Christmas
An unofficial cease fire on Christmas Day 1914 allowed troops from the two sides to meet. Some even played football in no-man's land.

The Hundred Days
A successful Allied offensive at Amiens in August 1918 started the "Hundred Days" of victories that pushed Germany out of France.

Tank warfare
The first tanks were invented to push beyond the trenches over rough terrain. The Allies had the first tanks, and the greatest number of them – thousands against the Germans' 20.

KEY
This map shows the Western Front of World War I.

— The 1914–1916 front line

✳ Major battle

— National border

● Town

Ypres, 1915

Passchendaele, 1917

Messines, 1917

Lys, 1918

Loos, 1915

Cambrai, 1917

Arras, 1917

Somme, 1916

Battle of the Som[me]
More than 1 million soldiers were killed or wounded in this 4-month-long battle

Amiens, 1918

River Somme

Compiègne

Chemin des Dames, 1917

British Whippet tank

River Oise

River Seine

In the trenches
Living in a trench gave soldiers some protection from gunfire, but trenches were muddy, water-logged, disease-ridden, and infested with rats and lice. Both sides dug trenches on their side of the front line. The space between the trenches was unclaimed and was called "no-man's land". No soldier wanted to go there – they would be too likely to be killed.

Versailles ●

● Paris

River Marne

Chateau Thierry, 1918

Paris attacked
In 1918, the French capital was shelled by a newly invented German long-range gun. Hundreds of people died.

Treaty of Versailles
A peace treaty was finally signed here in June 1919. Germany had to give up territory and pay a fine to make up for the losses and damage caused by the war.

FRANCE

The end of the war
An armistice (truce) was signed in a railw[ay] wagon at Compiègne, and fighting came to [an] end at the 11th hour [of] the 11th day of the 1[1th] month of 1918. The w[ar] would not officially e[nd] until the peace treat[y] was signed in 1919.

"**Hell** cannot be this **dreadful**."
Albert Joubaire, French soldier, Verdun, 1916.

River Loire

AROUND 60 MILLION TROOPS FOUGHT IN WORLD WAR I: 8 MILLION

1914–1918 World War I

NETHERLANDS

River Scheldt

Antwerp, 1914

BELGIUM

The first battle
The Belgian city of Liège fell to the Germans in 1914, in the first battle of the war.

Mons, 1914

River Meuse

Charleroi, 1914

Liège, 1914

German Fokker Dr.I

British Sopwith Camel

Allied breakthrough
A massive offensive by the US army in 1918 broke through the German defensive line.

LUXEMBOURG

GERMANY

River Moselle

Argonne, 1918

Verdun, 1916

Marne, 1914, 1918

The front line
The border between the two sides did not move much from this position between 1914 and 1916.

St Mihiel, 1918

German troops
German troops made advances into France and Belgium in 1914. Germany was one of the leading nations of the Central Powers, along with Austria-Hungary and the Ottoman Empire (Turkey).

Battle of Verdun
The fierce battle in 1916 for this fortified French town lasted 10 months and left more than 300,000 soldiers dead.

Allied troops
French and British troops (including Commonwealth troops, such as Australian, Canadian, and Indian) fought on the Allied side of the Western Front. Along with Russia, these powers were known as the "Triple Entente".

Battles of the Marne
Two major battles were fought here. The first, in September 1914, stopped the German advance on Paris. The second, in July 1918, stopped another German offensive and turned the tide in the Allies' favour.

In July 1914, Austria-Hungary declared war on Serbia. This triggered a wider war between the Central Powers and the Triple Entente, two rival European military alliances (groups of countries). Over time, more nations joined in, including the US. Battles were fought across the world, but the most crucial fighting was in western Europe. New weapons such as machine guns, planes, and tanks made this one of the bloodiest wars in history.

Dogfights
Fighter planes were first used during this war. In air battles known as dogfights, skilled pilots tried to shoot enemy planes down while dodging incoming fire.

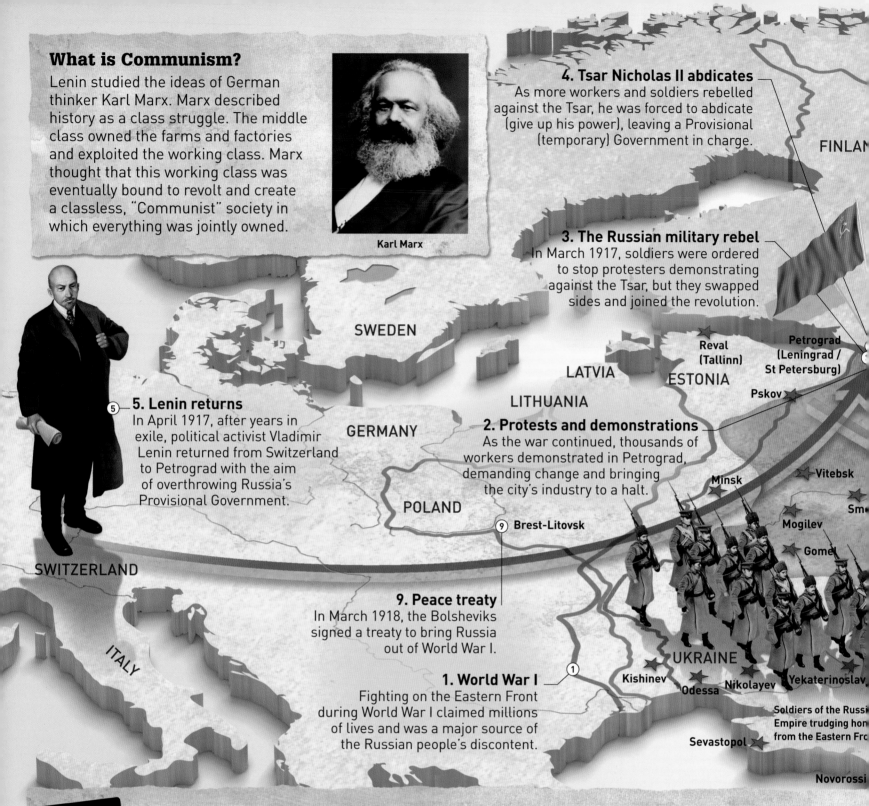

What is Communism?

Lenin studied the ideas of German thinker Karl Marx. Marx described history as a class struggle. The middle class owned the farms and factories and exploited the working class. Marx thought that this working class was eventually bound to revolt and create a classless, "Communist" society in which everything was jointly owned.

Karl Marx

4. Tsar Nicholas II abdicates
As more workers and soldiers rebelled against the Tsar, he was forced to abdicate (give up his power), leaving a Provisional (temporary) Government in charge.

FINLAN

3. The Russian military rebel
In March 1917, soldiers were ordered to stop protesters demonstrating against the Tsar, but they swapped sides and joined the revolution.

SWEDEN

Reval (Tallinn)

Petrograd (Leningrad / St Petersburg)

LATVIA

ESTONIA

Pskov

LITHUANIA

5. Lenin returns
In April 1917, after years in exile, political activist Vladimir Lenin returned from Switzerland to Petrograd with the aim of overthrowing Russia's Provisional Government.

GERMANY

2. Protests and demonstrations
As the war continued, thousands of workers demonstrated in Petrograd, demanding change and bringing the city's industry to a halt.

Minsk

Vitebsk

POLAND

Sm

Mogilev

9 Brest-Litovsk

Gomel

SWITZERLAND

9. Peace treaty
In March 1918, the Bolsheviks signed a treaty to bring Russia out of World War I.

UKRAINE

ITALY

1. World War I
Fighting on the Eastern Front during World War I claimed millions of lives and was a major source of the Russian people's discontent.

1

Kishinev

Odessa

Nikolayev

Yekaterinoslav

Soldiers of the Russi Empire trudging hom from the Eastern Fro

Sevastopol

Novorossi

1917–1922 The Russian Revolution

World War I caused food shortages, and life for the working people of Russia was brutal. The tsar, who once ruled with absolute power, stepped down, but this was not enough. Workers' councils, called soviets sprang up all over the country. These and the Bolshevik party organized a people's revolution that led to the establishment of the world's first Communist state.

Soviet Union

In 1922, the triumphant Bolsheviks united most of the former Russian Empire under Communist rule, creating the Soviet Union. This included Ukraine, Belarus, Georgia and other areas, as well as Russia itself.

The symbol on the Soviet Union's flag was a hammer, standing for industrial workers, crossed with a sickle, standing for farm labourers. The star stood for the Communist Party.

KEY
■ Soviet Union

. Bolsheviks take ower in Petrograd

On 25 October 917, under Lenin's ommand, the Bolsheviks seized ontrol of Petrograd's elegraph systems, ridges, and ailway stations.

7. Storming of the Winter Palace

Later on 25 October, armed Bolsheviks entered the Winter Palace and arrested the Provisional Government.

8. Communist government

After taking power, Lenin and the Bolsheviks set up a Communist government. Despite their ideals, they soon established a ruthless dictatorship.

10. Exile and execution

After his abdication, the tsar and his family were placed under house arrest in a remote retreat near Yekaterinburg. They were shot by their Bolshevik captors in July 1918.

BOLSHEVIK RUSSIA

Tsar Nicholas II and family

Archangel
Petrozavodsk
rod
Vologda
Kostroma
Tver
Yaroslavl
Moscow   Ivanovo
Vyatka
Nizhny Novgorod
Kaluga
Mogilev
Kazan
Izhevsk
Orel   Tambov   Penza
kov
Samara
Ufa
Saratov
Yekaterinburg (Sverdlovsk)
Novocherkassk
Orenburg
-on-Don   Tsaritsyn (Stalingrad / Volgograd)

11. Ongoing conflict

The Bolsheviks, renamed the Communists in 1918, met with immediate resistance to their leadership. They controlled the large area shown here in 1919, but civil war raged until 1922.

KEY

▬ Border of Russian Empire, 1914
▬ Eastern Front of World War I, 1917
➤ Movement of Tsar Nicholas II
➤ Movement of Lenin
✶ **Towns under Bolshevik control, 1918**
Having seized power in Petrograd, the Bolsheviks fought for control in other areas.

▢ **Area under Bolshevik control by 1919**
By 1919 the Bolsheviks had retreated, but kept control of Russia's heartland.

▬ **Border of Soviet Union, 1922**
By 1922, the Bolsheviks had Russia under Communist rule, although they lost Finland, Poland, Estonia, Latvia, and Lithuania.

① Key event

"History will **not forgive us** if we do not **assume power now**."

Vladimir Lenin, in a letter to Bolshevik leaders in Petrograd and Moscow, 12–14 September 1917

The story of flight

Until the 20th century, flying was a hobby of a few adventurous balloonists. In 1903, however, the Wright brothers made the first controlled, powered flight in an aeroplane. Within a few years, planes were being used both as vehicles taking paying passengers and as weapons of war.

Newfoundland–Ireland, 1919
Alcock and Brown flew a Vickers Vimy across the Atlantic in 16 hours, receiving a £10,000 prize from the *Daily Mail* newspaper and knighthoods from the king of England.

Connecticut–Ohio, 1942
The first mass-produced helicopter, the Sikorsky R-4, flew 1,225 km (761 miles) on a test flight.

California, 1947
The Bell X-1 rocket plane, piloted by Chuck Yeager, became the first manned aircraft to travel faster than sound in level flight.

Clifden

Wenatchee

St John's

California, 1976
The SR-71A Blackbird became the fastest and highest jet aircraft.

Edwards Air Force Base

Kitty Hawk, North Carolina, 1903
The Wright brothers made the first-ever controlled flight in a powered aeroplane.

New York–London, 1970
The Boeing 747 heralded the age of wide-bodied airliner which carry hundred of passengers each

California, 2013
SpaceShipTwo – the world's first commercial passenger spacecraft – made its first powered test flight.

Round the world (California–California), 1986
Dick Rutan and Jeana Yeager flew the Rutan Model 76 *Voyager* non-stop around the world. The flight took 9 days, 3 minutes, and 44 seconds.

Tampa Bay, Florida, 1914
The St Petersburg–Tampa Airboat Line, launched the world's first passenger service to use winged aircraft.

Paris–Rio de Janeiro, 1976
An Air France Concorde made one of the world's first two supersonic scheduled passenger flights. The other, on the same day, was by a British Airways Concorde from London to Bahrain.

KEY

The arrows on this map show non-stop flight milestones.

- First non-stop flight across the Atlantic
- First non-stop flight across the Pacific
- First non-stop flight around the world

Frankfurt–Rio de Janeiro, 1936
The zeppelin LZ-127 *Hindenburg* began to take passengers on scheduled flights across the Atlantic.

THE FIRST AIRLINE WAS FOUNDED IN 1909 AND FLEW ZEPPELINS

Southeast England, 1940
The Battle of Britain was the first major campaign fought entirely by air forces.

Paris, 1783
Pilâtre de Rozier and the Marquis d'Arlandes became the world's first pilots, flying the Montgolfier hot-air balloon.

Yorkshire, England, 1853
George Cayley developed a manned glider that flew across the valley in front of his home.

Lichterfelde, Germany, 1896
Otto Lilienthal launched himself from his own manmade hill in a series of homemade hang-gliders.

Rostock, Germany, 1939
The experimental Heinkel He 178 was the first jet-engine-powered aircraft to fly.

Japan–US, 1931
Clyde Pangborn and Hugh Herndon crossed the Pacific in 41 hours, in their Bellanca Skyrocket, *Miss Veedol*.

Lake Constance, Germany, 1900
LZ-1 launched the era of zeppelins – rigid airships filled with hydrogen or helium.

Mediterranean, 1942
The first production helicopter, the Flettner Fl 282 Kolibri, was deployed in World War II.

Moscow, 1932
The TsAGI-1EA – the first successful helicopter with a single rotor for creating lift – took off.

Moscow–Almaty, 1975
The supersonic Tupolev Tu-144 went into service, flying mail and freight to Alma-Ata (now Almaty) in Kazakhstan.

Sabishiro Beach

Round the world (Switzerland–Egypt), 1999
Breitling *Orbiter 3* was the first balloon to fly around the world without landing.

Somewhere in the Pacific, 1937
Pioneering female pilot Amelia Earhart and her navigator disappeared on their round-the-world flight.

Sydney–Singapore, 2007
The Airbus 380 – the heaviest-ever airliner – made its first passenger flight.

"There is **no sport equal** to … being carried through the air on **great white wings**."

Wilbur Wright, 1905

California–Australia, 2001
The unmanned aircraft *Global Hawk* flew unaided across the Pacific.

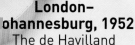

London–Johannesburg, 1952
The de Havilland Comet became the first jet airliner to fly with passengers.

Great Plains, 1930
An ongoing drought led to severe dust storms, which spread across North America's Great Plains, ruining the livelihood of farmers. The affected area was known as the Dust Bowl.

Britain, 1936
People marched against poverty and unemployment in northeast England.

NASSAU ST.
WALL ST.

NORTH AMERICA

○ Seattle

Dust Bowl

Detroit ○

UNITED STATES OF AMERICA

○ New York

New York, 1929
The value of shares on the Wall Street stock market fell rapidly, which marked the start of the depression.

Seattle, 1932
One of the largest "Hoovervilles" (see key) sprang up near the port of Seattle.

Detroit, 1930
Businesses across the US laid off workers, including those in the car-making industry in Detroit.

France, 1934
Riots broke out in Paris as people tried to bring down what they believed was a corrupt government.

JARROW CRUSADE
UK
FRAN
SPAIN

Migration to California, 1932
Thousands of farmers migrated from the Dust Bowl to find work in California.

Spain, 1936–39
War broke out between a government that wanted to combat poverty, and the army and landowners, who wanted to keep things as they were.

ALGERIA

How did it happen?
During the 1920s, the economy of the world expanded greatly, as farmers, factories, and other businesses produced more and more, believing there was an ever-growing market for their goods. Meanwhile, lots of people in the US bought stocks and shares in those businesses, hoping that they would earn a share of the profits. But eventually the expansion slowed, producers found they could not sell their goods, and companies started going bankrupt. This led to job losses and poverty.

BRAZIL

Algeria, 1937
A famine affected landless peasants displaced by European settlers; 1937 is still remembered as the "Year of Great Hunger".

Chile, 1930
Out-of-work tin miners queued outside "soup kitchens", which were handing out free food.

SOUTH AMERICA

Brazil, 1937
The depression caused the price of coffee to fall. This forced the government to burn some of it in order to increase its scarcity and its value.

Santiago ○

An American family left homeless by the depression

CHILE

> "I see nothing to give ground **to hope** – **nothing** of man."

Calvin Coolidge, US president, 1923–29, speaking during the Great Depression in 1932

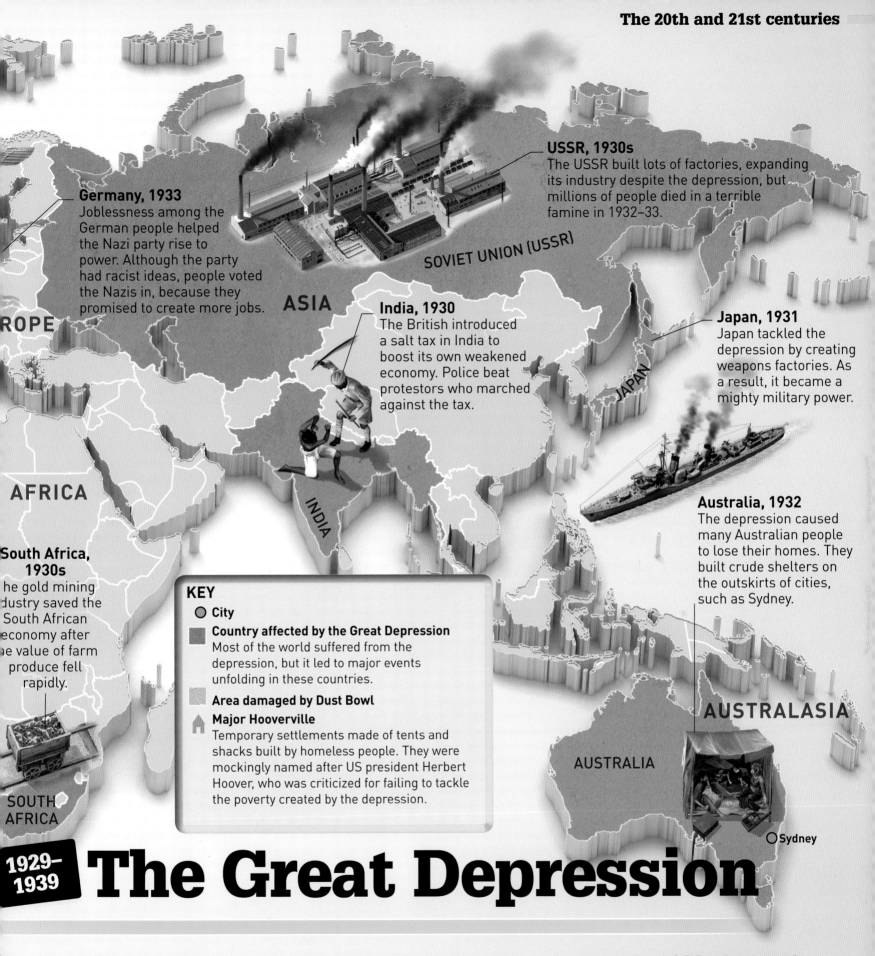

USSR, 1930s
The USSR built lots of factories, expanding its industry despite the depression, but millions of people died in a terrible famine in 1932–33.

SOVIET UNION (USSR)

Germany, 1933
Joblessness among the German people helped the Nazi party rise to power. Although the party had racist ideas, people voted the Nazis in, because they promised to create more jobs.

ASIA

India, 1930
The British introduced a salt tax in India to boost its own weakened economy. Police beat protestors who marched against the tax.

Japan, 1931
Japan tackled the depression by creating weapons factories. As a result, it became a mighty military power.

ROPE

JAPAN

AFRICA

INDIA

South Africa, 1930s
he gold mining dustry saved the South African economy after he value of farm produce fell rapidly.

Australia, 1932
The depression caused many Australian people to lose their homes. They built crude shelters on the outskirts of cities, such as Sydney.

KEY

○ **City**

⬛ **Country affected by the Great Depression**
Most of the world suffered from the depression, but it led to major events unfolding in these countries.

⬛ **Area damaged by Dust Bowl**

🏠 **Major Hooverville**
Temporary settlements made of tents and shacks built by homeless people. They were mockingly named after US president Herbert Hoover, who was criticized for failing to tackle the poverty created by the depression.

AUSTRALASIA

AUSTRALIA

SOUTH AFRICA

○Sydney

1929–1939 # The Great Depression

The Great Depression was the biggest economic crisis in history. In 1929, the stock market in the United States crashed. Banks lost money, factories closed, and trade collapsed across America, and then the rest of the world. The depression led o poverty, hunger, and mass unemployment, and lasted for about a decade.

BANKS IN THE UNITED STATES. BY 1933, ABOUT 11,000 HAD FAILED.

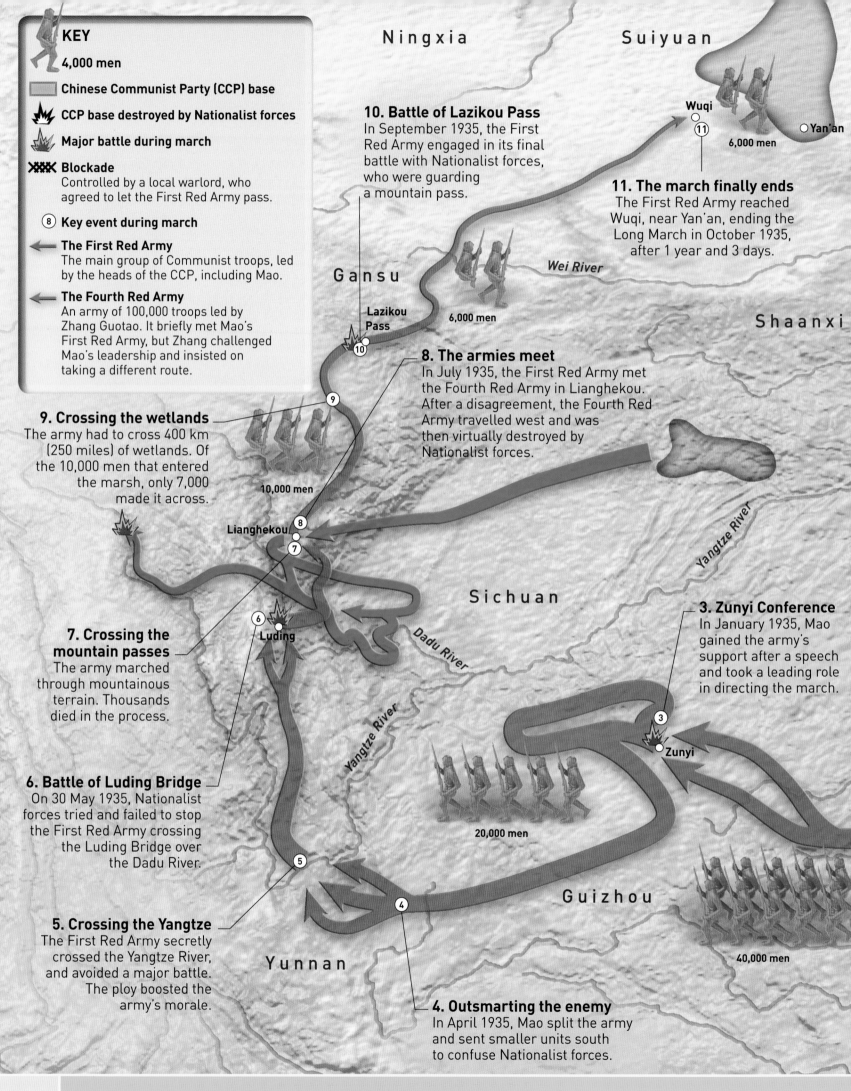

KEY

🚶 4,000 men

▢ Chinese Communist Party (CCP) base

💥 CCP base destroyed by Nationalist forces

💥 Major battle during march

✕✕✕ **Blockade**
Controlled by a local warlord, who agreed to let the First Red Army pass.

⑧ **Key event during march**

← **The First Red Army**
The main group of Communist troops, led by the heads of the CCP, including Mao.

← **The Fourth Red Army**
An army of 100,000 troops led by Zhang Guotao. It briefly met Mao's First Red Army, but Zhang challenged Mao's leadership and insisted on taking a different route.

Ningxia

Suiyuan

10. Battle of Lazikou Pass
In September 1935, the First Red Army engaged in its final battle with Nationalist forces, who were guarding a mountain pass.

Wuqi
⑪
6,000 men
Yan'an

11. The march finally ends
The First Red Army reached Wuqi, near Yan'an, ending the Long March in October 1935, after 1 year and 3 days.

Gansu

Wei River

6,000 men

Lazikou Pass
⑩

8. The armies meet
In July 1935, the First Red Army met the Fourth Red Army in Lianghekou. After a disagreement, the Fourth Red Army travelled west and was then virtually destroyed by Nationalist forces.

Shaanxi

⑨

9. Crossing the wetlands
The army had to cross 400 km (250 miles) of wetlands. Of the 10,000 men that entered the marsh, only 7,000 made it across.

10,000 men

Lianghekou
⑧
⑦

Yangtze River

Sichuan

7. Crossing the mountain passes
The army marched through mountainous terrain. Thousands died in the process.

⑥
Luding

Dadu River

3. Zunyi Conference
In January 1935, Mao gained the army's support after a speech and took a leading role in directing the march.

③
Zunyi

6. Battle of Luding Bridge
On 30 May 1935, Nationalist forces tried and failed to stop the First Red Army crossing the Luding Bridge over the Dadu River.

Yangtze River

20,000 men

⑤

5. Crossing the Yangtze
The First Red Army secretly crossed the Yangtze River, and avoided a major battle. The ploy boosted the army's morale.

Yunnan

④

Guizhou

40,000 men

4. Outsmarting the enemy
In April 1935, Mao split the army and sent smaller units south to confuse Nationalist forces.

DURING THE LONG MARCH, THE FIRST RED ARMY OF THE COMMUNIST

1934–1935 China's Long March

In the 1930s, China was ruled by a Nationalist government that wanted to crush the rebel Chinese Communist Party. To escape destruction, the First Red Army of the Communist Party marched 10,000 km (6,000 miles) across some of the harshest territory in China. Guided by their future leader Mao Zedong, about 6,000 soldiers made it to their new base in Yan'an, from where they eventually took over China.

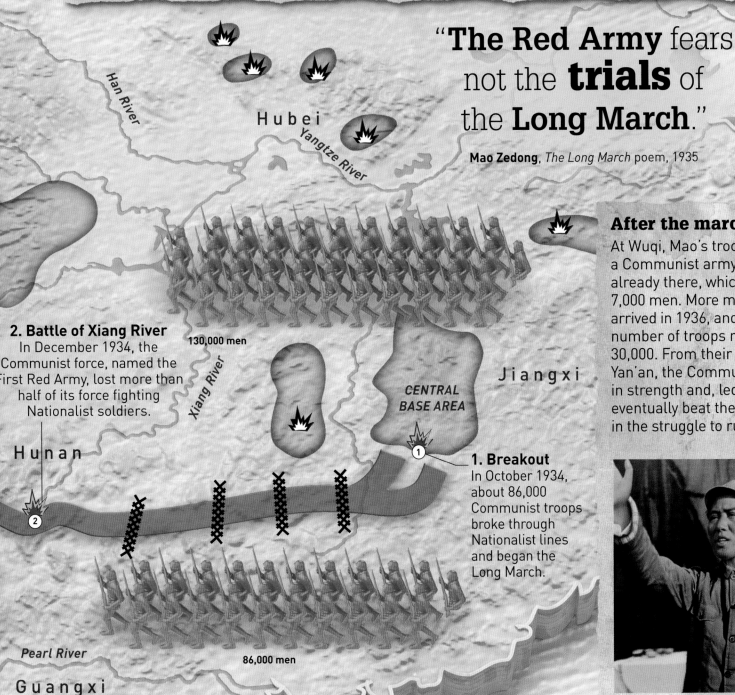

Han River

Hubei

Yangtze River

> **"The Red Army** fears not the **trials** of the **Long March**."
>
> **Mao Zedong**, *The Long March* poem, 1935

After the march
At Wuqi, Mao's troops joined a Communist army that was already there, which numbered 7,000 men. More marching units arrived in 1936, and the total number of troops rose to about 30,000. From their new base at Yan'an, the Communists grew in strength and, led by Mao, eventually beat the Nationalists in the struggle to rule China.

2. Battle of Xiang River
In December 1934, the Communist force, named the First Red Army, lost more than half of its force fighting Nationalist soldiers.

130,000 men

Xiang River

Jiangxi

CENTRAL BASE AREA

Hunan

1. Breakout
In October 1934, about 86,000 Communist troops broke through Nationalist lines and began the Long March.

Pearl River

86,000 men

Guangxi

Mao Zedong

Battle of Britain
British planes fought German aircraft above Britain in 1940, preventing a German invasion.

The Blitz
For 37 weeks in 1940–41, German bombers targeted British towns with night-time air raids.

Flash invasion
Hitler invaded and conquered most of western Europe, including France, in only 3 months in 1940.

D-Day
In 1944, Allied troops landed in Normandy to free Europe from German control (see pp142–43).

Battle of the Atlantic
German submarines sank thousands of ships carrying supplies to Britain, until the Allies stopped them in 1943, using better radar and anti-submarine ships.

Fighting in the desert
As the war spread to North Africa in 1940, Axis and Allied forces fought with tanks, planes, and mines in the desert heat.

Allied bombing raids
From 1942, the Allies started bombing German cities.

Nazi persecution
The German Nazi party forced Jewish people to wear a yellow star badge. From 1942, Jews and other victims were killed in extermination camps, mainly in Poland.

Battle of Stalingrad
German expansion into eastern Europe was halted in January 1943, when their troops surrendered Stalingrad (see p141).

EUROPE

ASIA

AFRICA

The Eastern Front
Germany and the Soviet Union pushed the border back and forth in eastern Europe as they fought ferocious battles (see pp140–41).

Battle of Anzio
After Italy's leader, Mussolini, was removed from office in 1943, the Allies fought German troops for control of the country during 1944.

China in the war
China had been partly invaded by Japan before the war, but the unoccupied part of the country joined the Allies. More civilians died here than in any other country.

AU

1939–1945 # World War II

Battle of Darwin
The biggest attack on Australia was a Japanese air-strike of 242 planes over Darwin, in February 1942.

When Germany's dictator, Adolf Hitler, invaded Poland in 1939, Britain and France declared war. As more countries joined in, the world was divided into Axis powers, led by Germany, Italy, and Japan; and the Allies, led by Britain, the US, and the Soviet Union. By the time war ended in 1945, millions of people had suffered and died, some while fighting, some from bombing raids at home, and others through the Holocaust (Hitler's killing of certain groups, especially Jews).

DURING THE WAR, MANY CHILDREN HAD TO LEAVE THEIR HOMES – AS

KEY

This map shows the world divided in mid-1942, at the height of Axis power.

- Axis nation
- Axis-controlled country
- Allied nation
- Allied-controlled country
- Neutral country
- Major battle or fighting
- Eastern Front

The Holocaust

Adolf Hitler convinced many of his Nazi supporters that other peoples, such as Jews, were inferior to the German people. In countries under Nazi occupation, Jewish people were herded into tightly packed city districts called ghettos. In 1942, Hitler ordered the Final Solution – the murder of all Jews. He set up extermination camps, where 11 million Jews, Roma (Gypsies), disabled people, and members of other groups were killed in a horrific campaign now known as the Holocaust. In a final outrage, camp workers collected the personal possessions of the victims for recycling.

Artificial limbs of Holocaust victims, preserved as a memorial in a museum that was once an extermination camp.

NORTH AMERICA

Hiroshima and Nagasaki

In August 1945, US bombers dropped two atomic bombs on these Japanese cities. Japan surrendered a week later.

Battle of Midway

An Allied victory in this 1942 sea battle ended Japanese expansion.

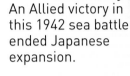

Pearl Harbor

A Japanese surprise attack in 1941 destroyed this US navy base in Hawaii, prompting the US to join the war.

War in the Pacific

From 1941, Allied forces tried to stop Japanese expansion in the Pacific. Battles were fought at sea and on the many small islands. The war continued here for almost 3 months after it ended in Europe.

Battle of the Coral Sea

Fought in 1942, this was the first sea battle ever fought between planes from aircraft carriers, rather than between ships.

SOUTH AMERICA

Brazil enters the war

Most of South America stayed neutral, but Brazil declared war on the Axis countries in 1942, after its ships were sunk.

ASIA

Leaders of the Allied nations

Winston Churchill Prime Minister of Great Britain

Joseph Stalin Dictator of the Soviet Union (USSR)

Franklin D Roosevelt President of the United States of America

Leaders of the Axis nations

Benito Mussolini Head of government of Italy

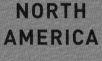

Hirohito Emperor of Japan

Adolf Hitler Führer (dictator) of Germany and leader of the Nazi (National Socialist) party

"My God, what have we done?"

Robert Lewis, copilot of *Enola Gay*, the plane that dropped the atomic bomb on Hiroshima, 1945

EVACUEES ESCAPING BOMBS, OR REFUGEES FLEEING ENEMY OCCUPATION.

End of the war in Europe
Victory in Europe (VE) Day, the end of the war, was celebrated on 8 May 1945. The loss of many Axis troops on the Eastern Front contributed to Hitler's suicide and the German surrender.

"The time for **retreating** is over. **Not one step back**!"

Soviet leader **Joseph Stalin**, part of Order Number 227 issued to the Soviet armed forces, July 28, 1942

Leningrad (St Petersburg)

Siege of Leningrad, 1941–44
The Soviet city was under siege for 900 days from September 1941. By Christmas, 52,000 people had starved to death.

GERMANY

Berlin

German Panzer III tanks

Minsk

Berlin bunker, 1945
German leader Hitler didn't spend much time in the German capital city during the war, but from January 1945, he made his headquarters here in a bunker.

German Focke-Wulf Fw 190 fighters

Warsaw

German Junkers Ju 88 bomber

MAY 1941

Battle of Kiev, 1941
In September 1941 German troops trapped and slaughtered four Soviet Red Army groups in Kiev. The Red Army lost nearly two-thirds of its total numbers.

1941–1943

The Eastern Front

In 1941, Hitler launched Operation Barbarossa – a surprise attack on the Soviet Union. In June–December 1941, the German army and its allies advanced steadily eastwards. As Soviet counterattacks pushed the front line west again, it became a brutal battleground with many killed on both sides. German defeat at Stalingrad in 1943 was the beginning of the end of World War II in Europe, as German forces were eventually pushed back to Berlin in 1945.

AROUND 4 MILLION AXIS TROOPS AND 3,500 TANKS LINED THE

Soviet Ilyushin
Il-2 "Shturmovik"
anti-tank aircraft

Battle of Moscow , 1941
Stalin, leader of the Soviet Union, declared Moscow to be under siege in October 1941, but the German advance was hampered by savage weather. After a Soviet counterattack, Germany withdrew in December and Moscow was saved.

KEY
This map shows the changing position of the Eastern Front, as German troops made advances and the Soviets made counterattacks. This key explains the advances in the order they happened.

Major battle   ● Key town

German advances in June–December 1941
These pushed the front east

Soviet counterattack in December 1941–May 1942
This pushed back the front in the north

German advances in 1942
These pushed the front further east in the southern part

German/Axis border, May 1941

Eastern Front, December 1941

Eastern Front, November 1942

Soviet T-34 tanks

Moscow

Soviet Lavochkin La-5 fighter

SOVIET UNION

nsk

Battle of Kursk , 1943
The largest tank battle of the war took place here in July 1943. It resulted in another German defeat after Stalingrad.

German
Panzer III tank

Kursk

Battles in Kharkov, 1941–43
This city saw four battles, from the first German capture of the city in October 1941 to the final liberation by the Red Army of the Soviet Union in August 1943.

German Junkers Ju 87 "Stuka" dive-bombers

Kharkov

DECEMBER 1941

Siege of Stalingrad, 1942–43
It took four attacks, including a two-day aerial bombardment and weeks of fighting, from August to October 1942, for the Germans to break into Stalingrad. In November additional Soviet troops outside the city launched a massive attack. The 330,000 German troops in the city were trapped and under siege. At the end of January 1943, the Germans surrendered Stalingrad.

Stalingrad (Volgograd)

Rostov

German Junkers Ju 88 bomber

NOVEMBER 1942

German Panzer IV tanks

Sevastopol

Sevastopol bombardment, 1942
From 2 June 1942, the Germans bombarded this city, launching 1,000 air strikes a day. The city was evacuated after 24 days of fighting.

At dawn on 6 June 1944, 600 warships, 4,000 landing craft, and 156,000 Allied troops launched a surprise attack on the coast of Normandy, France. It was codenamed D-Day, and was the start of Operation Overlord – the plan to free mainland Europe from German occupation. The Allies suffered huge losses. Some landing craft sank, soldiers were drowned, and they were under German artillery fire all the time. Yet by the evening, they had secured five beaches and were on their way to victory.

> "This **operation** is planned as a **victory**, and **that's** the way it's **going to be**."

General Dwight D Eisenhower, Supreme Commander of the Allied Forces in Europe, 1944

Warships
As well as transporting the troops, ships provided gunfire support before and during the landings. They also worked as floating hospitals.

English Channel

Floating tank
Sherman tanks were launched at sea. A canvas "skirt" helped them stay afloat to reach the shore.

US 4th Infantry Division

LCM Landing Craft

Coast guard
German gun emplacements (bunkers) lined the coast at Normandy.

US P-38 Lightning fighters

UTAH

US infantry

Sainte-Mère-Église

River Douvre

Support from the air
Around 1,900 planes and gliders made 10,750 flights during D-Day. Many, such as the Douglas C-47, dropped paratroopers, while others were fighter or bomber planes.

Cherbourg

US 82nd Airborne Division

Douglas C-47 transports

US 101st Airborne Division

US paratroopers
Soldiers were parachuted in before dawn to attack the Germans from behind their coastal defences.

KEY
- ○ Town
- ▢ Areas liberated by Allies (British, Canadian, and US troops) by evening of 6 June
- ▢ Area liberated by Allies by 12 June
- → Troops arriving by air
- → Troops arriving by sea
- ☆ US troops
- ◉ British and Canadian troops

Barrage balloon

Horsa glider transport

British 6th Airborne Division

DUCW

Landing craft
Special flat-bottomed boats were built to take the troops from the ships to the shore.

British 3rd Infantry Division

Canadian 3rd Infantry Division

Higgins Boats

British 50th Infantry Division

and US 1st Infantry Division

SWORD

Saint-Aubin-sur-Mer

Ouistreham

German infantry

JUNO

Courseulles-sur-Mer

GOLD

Arromanches-les-Bains

Caen

Longues-sur-Mer

River Orne

OMAHA

Sainte-Honorine-des-Pertes

Bayeux

Vierville-sur-Mer

Pointe du Hoc

British infantry

German infantry

River Vire

an

UK paratroopers
British soldiers were dropped here to take control of an important bridge over the River Orne, to stop German reinforcements arriving.

German defence
Only one German tank unit was in place to counterattack the Allies. The German command planned to have tanks along the coast in case of attack, but it was not able to get them there.

Landing craft
Different types of landing craft were used on D-Day. The Higgins Boat, LCI (Landing Craft, Infantry, shown right), and LCA (Landing Craft, Assault) were basic, flat-bottomed craft that could transport soldiers all the way to the beach; while the amphibious DUKW, nicknamed "Duck", was like a boat with wheels that could also be driven as a truck. Even tanks were made to float with a canvas "skirt" designed to keep the water out, but many sank by Omaha Beach as they were swamped by high waves.

OCCUPIED FRANCE

Gandhi and Indian independence

PERSIA

India won its freedom from British colonial rule in 1947, after many decades of struggle. Mohandas Gandhi joined the fight for independence in 1914 and helped the cause with his philosophy of non-violent resistance called *satyagraha*. His dedication to Indian freedom earned him the name *Mahatma*, meaning "Great Soul".

5. Dandi Salt March
When in 1930, Britain began forcing Indians to buy salt from the British at high prices, Gandhi protested by making a 24-day march, ending in the salt-manufacturing town of Dandi. There, he broke the law by picking up a fistful of salt.

Dandi

7. Quit India Movement
In 1942, Gandhi made a stirring speech in Bombay, demanding that the British leave the country immediately. Gandhi was thrown in jail once again. This led to more protest marches, but he was only released in 1944.

Bombay (Mumbai)

Pune

6. Spinning to defy the British
While imprisoned in Pune's Yerwada Jail, in 1932, Gandhi made his own clothes, to encourage the Indian people to weave at home instead of buying clothes from the British. The spinning wheel became a symbol of the independence movement.

KEY

Key sites of non-violent resistance

Route of the Dandi Salt March

1 Key location in the story of the Indian struggle for self-rule

CEYLON

Partition of India, 1947
Gandhi wanted India to be independent as a single state in which different religions would live at peace, but many Muslims wanted their own state. After fighting broke out between Muslims and Hindus, the British divided India into two states. Muslim-majority areas became Pakistan, divided into East and West parts, and the rest became Hindu-majority India.

WEST PAKISTAN

EAST PAKISTAN

INDIA

IN 1943, BEING HELD AS A POLITICAL PRISONER, GANDHI WENT

"In a **gentle way**, you can **shake the world**."

Mohandas Gandhi, speaking in 1942

AFGHANISTAN

SOVIET UNION (USSR)

2. Amritsar massacre
On April 13, 1919, British General Dyer ordered troops to open fire on 6,000 Indian protestors, killing hundreds. The act strengthened Gandhi's determination to liberate India.

Amritsar

4. Chauri Chaura incident
In 1922, a non-violent protest turned nasty when angry people set fire to a police station killing 22 policemen. The government blamed Gandhi for inciting the violence and imprisoned him for 2 years.

INDIA

CHINA

1. Champaran *satyagraha*
In 1917, Gandhi organized protests on behalf of farmers in Champaran who were forced to grow indigo dye instead of food crops. They also had to pay taxes, even in time of famine. Gandhi refused to leave the village until the British authorities dropped their demands.

NEPAL

Chauri Chaura

Champaran

hi addresses his
orters in Bengal

8. Gandhi's triumph
Britain finally granted India independence in February, 947. Speaking during a tour f the Bengal region, Gandhi called it "the noblest act of the British nation".

BHUTAN

Bengal

Calcutta (Kolkata)

Non-cooperation Movement
aunched in Calcutta in 1920, the campaign attracted millions of followers who stopped buying British goods and in doing so, refused to be part of the British-led economy.

Burma

WITHOUT FOOD FOR 21 DAYS AS A PROTEST AGAINST BRITISH RULE.

The Cold War

DEW Line (Distant Early Warning)
The US set up radar installations in a line measuring nearly 10,000 km (6,200 miles) to detect incoming Soviet bombers.

After World War II, the US and USSR (the Soviet Union, including Russia) emerged as two superpowers – rich countries capable of influencing international events. They became bitter rivals with contrasting political ideas about how the world should live. For almost 50 years, the two countries threatened each other by amassing enough nuclear weapons to wipe out the planet. However, aware of the fatal results of actually using these weapons, the US and USSR chose instead to fight one another indirectly by taking sides in conflicts in other countries. This period was called the Cold War.

CANADA

UNITED STATES OF AMERICA

Intercontinental Ballistic Missiles (ICBMs)
These missiles were designed to launch nuclear weapons that were capable of destroying cities thousands of kilometres (thousands of miles) away.

Cuban Missile Crisis
In 1962, the US and USSR threatened each other in an argument over the Soviet plan to station nuclear weapons in Cuba.

GUATEMALA
1954

EL SALVADOR
1979–92

NICARAGUA
1981–90

CUBA
1961,
1962

DOMINICAN REPUBLIC
1965–66

GRENADA
1983

KEY

This map shows the total number of military vehicles, hardware, and other weapons held by the US and the Soviet Union in 1985.

US	USSR	
		50 ICBM warheads
		10 warships (including battleships, cruisers, destroyers, frigates, and aircraft carriers)
		20 submarines
		500 combat-capable aircraft
		1,000 main battle tanks

NATO (North Atlantic Treaty Organisation)
The US and its allies (as they were in 1985).

The Warsaw Pact
The USSR and its allies (as they were in 1985).

Cold War conflict

Dew Line

Iron Curtain
An imaginary line dividing the two sides, so called because it was difficult to cross and hid what was beyond.

IN 1963, THE US AND USSR INSTALLED A HOTLINE, ENABLING THEIR

"The **Cold War** ... is **burning** with a **deadly heat**."

Richard Nixon, US President, 1969–74, speaking in 1964

Korean War
Backed by the USSR and China, North Korea fought against the US and its allies in an attempt to occupy South Korea.

KOREA
1950–53

UNION OF SOVIET SOCIALIST REPUBLICS (USSR, OR SOVIET UNION)

EAST GERMANY
1948–49, 1953, 1958–62

POLAND
1956, 1980–81

CZECHOSLOVAKIA
1948, 1968

HUNGARY
1956

Iron Curtain

Vietnam War
The US entered the war in Vietnam in 1957 to stop the army of North Vietnam from spreading Communism in the South. The North claimed victory 2 years after the US withdrew in 1973.

TAIWAN
1958

TURKEY
1945–47

YUGOSLAVIA
1948–53

GREECE
1945–49

EGYPT
1956, 1957, 1973

IRAN
1945–46, 1951–53

IRAQ
1958

LEBANON
1958

AFGHANISTAN
1979

INDIA
1962

LAOS
1953–75

SOUTH VIETNAM
1946–54, 1957–75

CAMBODIA
1969–75

YEMEN
1962–70

ETHIOPIA
1977–78

gaden War
Ethiopia)
When US-backed
omalia invaded
gaden in Ethiopia,
he USSR and
uba helped
thiopia to
eclaim
he region.

SOMALIA
1970S, 1980S

CONGO
1960–61

MOZAMBIQUE
1977–92

ANGOLA
1975–90

The Berlin Airlift 1948–49

After World War II, Germany's capital, Berlin, was divided into four zones, each separately controlled by the US, France, Britain (the Allies), and the Soviet Union. In June 1948, the Soviets closed all Allied routes into Allied-occupied Berlin, leaving the people trapped. For more than a year, the Allies supplied the people food, medicine, and fuel by air. This was the first clash of the Cold War.

Berlin children cheer a US cargo plane bringing supplies to the besieged city.

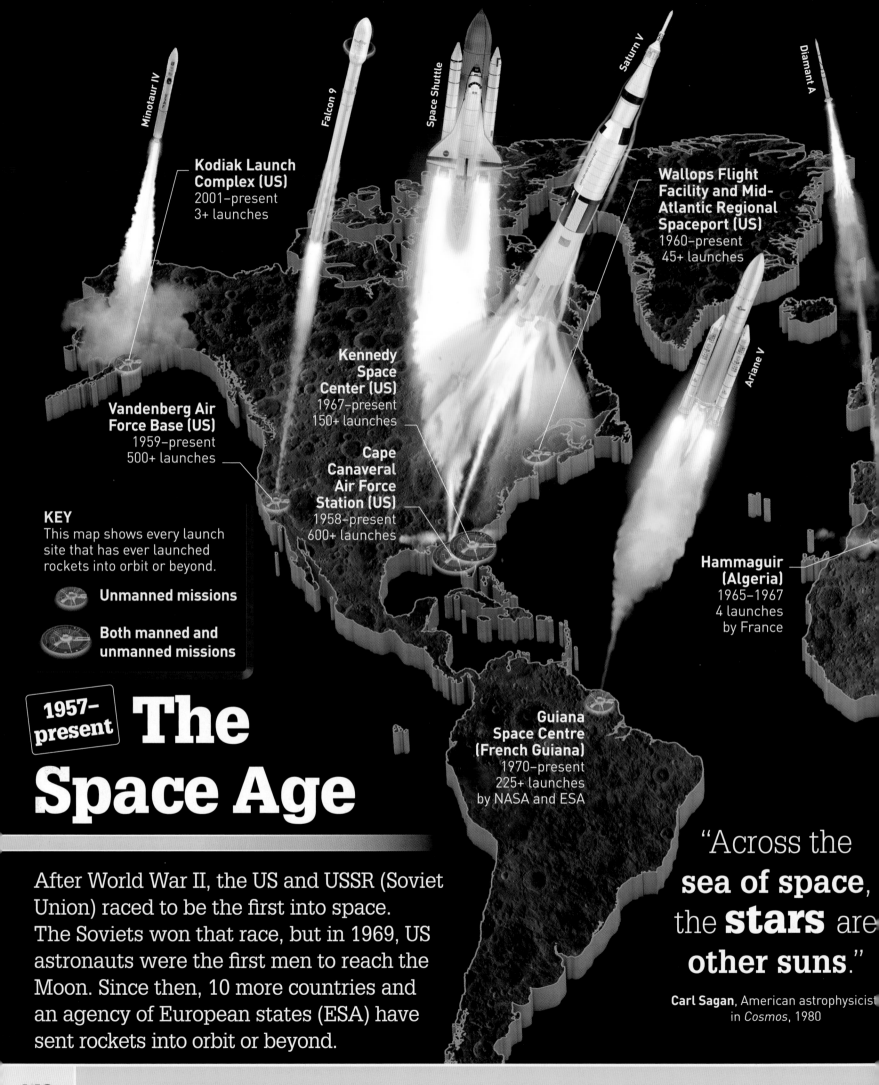

Minotaur IV

Falcon 9

Space Shuttle

Saturn V

Diamant A

Ariane V

Kodiak Launch Complex (US)
2001–present
3+ launches

Wallops Flight Facility and Mid-Atlantic Regional Spaceport (US)
1960–present
45+ launches

Kennedy Space Center (US)
1967–present
150+ launches

Cape Canaveral Air Force Station (US)
1958–present
600+ launches

Vandenberg Air Force Base (US)
1959–present
500+ launches

Hammaguir (Algeria)
1965–1967
4 launches by France

KEY
This map shows every launch site that has ever launched rockets into orbit or beyond.

🛸 **Unmanned missions**

🛸 **Both manned and unmanned missions**

Guiana Space Centre (French Guiana)
1970–present
225+ launches by NASA and ESA

1957–present The Space Age

After World War II, the US and USSR (Soviet Union) raced to be the first into space. The Soviets won that race, but in 1969, US astronauts were the first men to reach the Moon. Since then, 10 more countries and an agency of European states (ESA) have sent rockets into orbit or beyond.

"Across the **sea of space**, the **stars** are **other suns**."

Carl Sagan, American astrophysicist in *Cosmos*, 1980

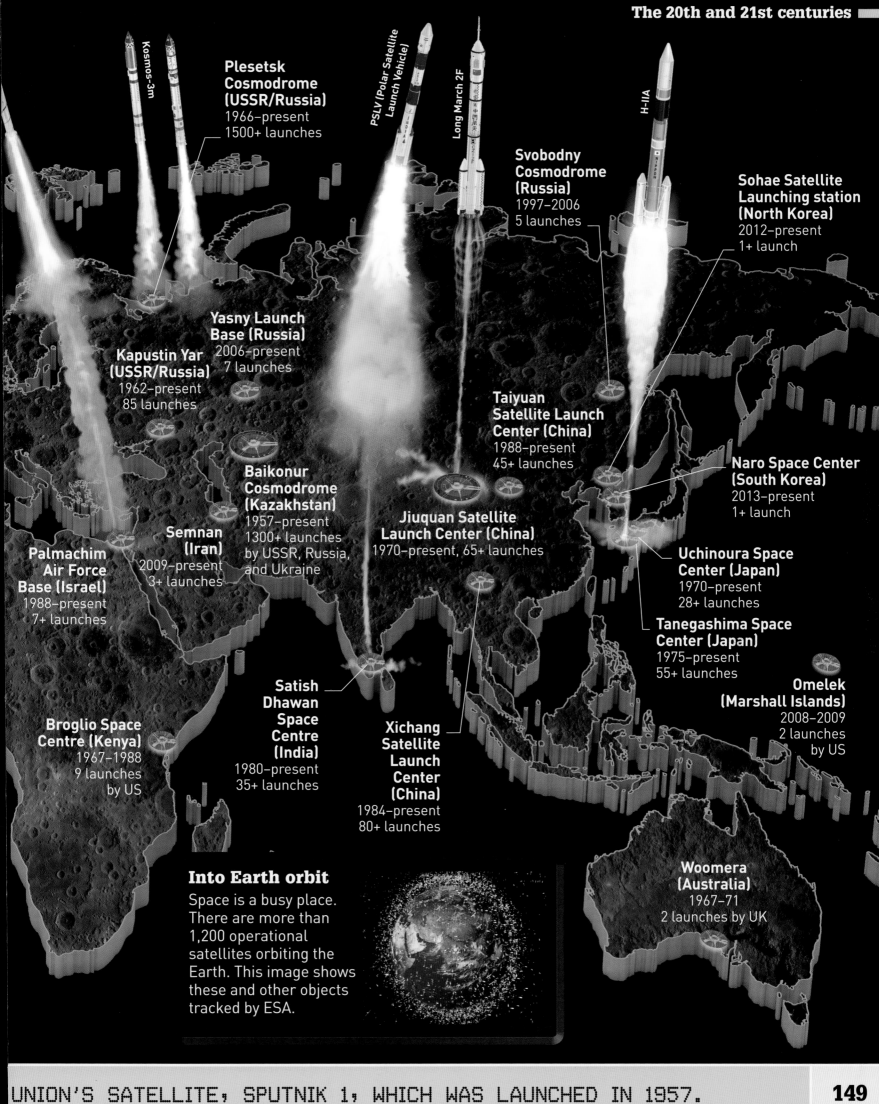

Kosmos-3m

**Plesetsk
Cosmodrome
(USSR/Russia)**
1966–present
1500+ launches

PSLV (Polar Satellite Launch Vehicle)

Long March 2F

H-IIA

**Svobodny
Cosmodrome
(Russia)**
1997–2006
5 launches

**Sohae Satellite
Launching station
(North Korea)**
2012–present
1+ launch

**Yasny Launch
Base (Russia)**
2006–present
7 launches

**Kapustin Yar
(USSR/Russia)**
1962–present
85 launches

**Taiyuan
Satellite Launch
Center (China)**
1988–present
45+ launches

**Naro Space Center
(South Korea)**
2013–present
1+ launch

**Baikonur
Cosmodrome
(Kazakhstan)**
1957–present
1300+ launches
by USSR, Russia,
and Ukraine

**Semnan
(Iran)**
2009–present
3+ launches

**Jiuquan Satellite
Launch Center (China)**
1970–present, 65+ launches

**Uchinoura Space
Center (Japan)**
1970–present
28+ launches

**Palmachim
Air Force
Base (Israel)**
1988–present
7+ launches

**Tanegashima Space
Center (Japan)**
1975–present
55+ launches

**Omelek
(Marshall Islands)**
2008–2009
2 launches
by US

**Broglio Space
Centre (Kenya)**
1967–1988
9 launches
by US

**Satish
Dhawan
Space
Centre
(India)**
1980–present
35+ launches

**Xichang
Satellite
Launch
Center
(China)**
1984–present
80+ launches

Into Earth orbit

Space is a busy place.
There are more than
1,200 operational
satellites orbiting the
Earth. This image shows
these and other objects
tracked by ESA.

**Woomera
(Australia)**
1967–71
2 launches by UK

UNION'S SATELLITE, SPUTNIK 1, WHICH WAS LAUNCHED IN 1957.

Moon landings

The USSR had already landed a spacecraft on the Moon when, in 1961, President Kennedy of the US announced that his country would launch manned lunar missions before the end of the decade. Sure enough, between 1969 and 1972, 12 American astronauts walked on the Moon's surface, during a total of six Apollo voyages. Since 1972, however, the Moon has been explored only by unmanned probes and rovers.

KEY

This map shows the landing sites of 30 successful Moon missions. The first ones aimed simply to crash on the Moon to study the accuracy of rockets. Later, engineers designed robotic spacecraft (probes) that would make safe, "soft" landings. Since the era of manned exploration in 1969–72, there have been only three more of these soft landings – the Soviet Luna 21 (1973) and 24 (1976), and the Chinese Chang'e 3 (2013).

 Probe crash-landing on the Moon

 Probe soft-landing on the Moon

 Probe soft-landing on the Moon and returning rock samples to Earth

 Manned spacecraft landing

 Apollo Lunar Roving Vehicle

 Lunokhod rover

 Yutu rover

Chang'e 3
Chinese mission to land a probe and rover, Yutu, 2013. Chang'e 3 aimed to study the lunar soil down to 30 m (98 ft) deep.

Chang'e 3

Luna 17

Luna 17
First spacecraft to deploy a lunar rover, Lunokhod 1, 1970. This Soviet rover worked for 322 days and travelled 10 km (6 miles).

Luna 13

Luna 9
First spacecraft to make a controlled landing, 1965. This Soviet craft also sent back the first photos of the Moon's surface.

Luna 9

Surveyor 1

Surveyor 3   Apollo 12

Apollo 14

Ranger 7

Surveyor 1
First US spacecraft to make a controlled landing, 1966. It tested the lunar surface's temperature and hardness to prepare for manned landings.

SMART-1 (ESA)

Surveyo

LCROSS
One of a series of craft searching for frozen water that might be trapped in the dark corners of craters near the Moon's South Pole. It was sent by the US in 2009.

"That's **one small step** for man, **one giant leap** for **mankind**."

Neil Armstrong, on setting foot on the Moon during the Apollo 11 mission, 1969

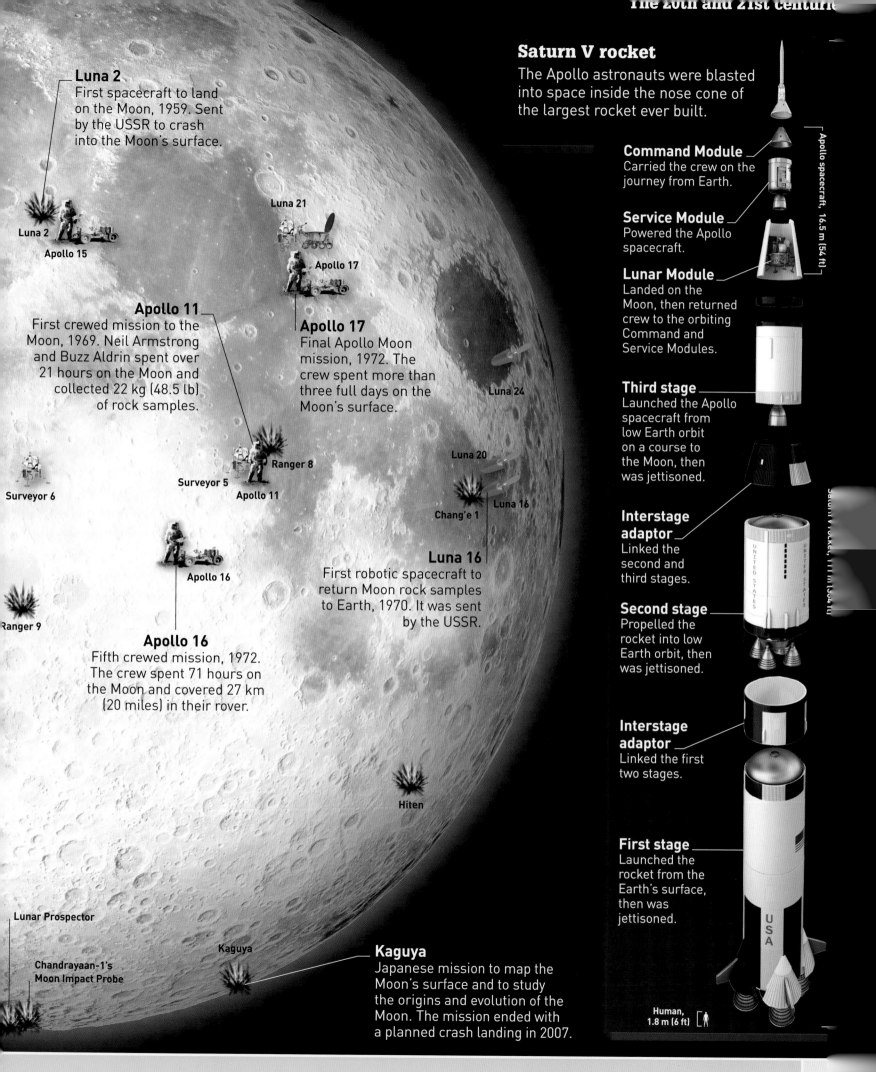

Luna 2
First spacecraft to land on the Moon, 1959. Sent by the USSR to crash into the Moon's surface.

Luna 2

Apollo 15

Luna 21

Apollo 17

Apollo 11
First crewed mission to the Moon, 1969. Neil Armstrong and Buzz Aldrin spent over 21 hours on the Moon and collected 22 kg (48.5 lb) of rock samples.

Apollo 17
Final Apollo Moon mission, 1972. The crew spent more than three full days on the Moon's surface.

Surveyor 6

Surveyor 5

Ranger 8

Apollo 11

Luna 24

Luna 20

Luna 16

Chang'e 1

Luna 16
First robotic spacecraft to return Moon rock samples to Earth, 1970. It was sent by the USSR.

Ranger 9

Apollo 16

Apollo 16
Fifth crewed mission, 1972. The crew spent 71 hours on the Moon and covered 27 km (20 miles) in their rover.

Hiten

Lunar Prospector

Chandrayaan-1's Moon Impact Probe

Kaguya

Kaguya
Japanese mission to map the Moon's surface and to study the origins and evolution of the Moon. The mission ended with a planned crash landing in 2007.

Saturn V rocket
The Apollo astronauts were blasted into space inside the nose cone of the largest rocket ever built.

Command Module
Carried the crew on the journey from Earth.

Service Module
Powered the Apollo spacecraft.

Lunar Module
Landed on the Moon, then returned crew to the orbiting Command and Service Modules.

Third stage
Launched the Apollo spacecraft from low Earth orbit on a course to the Moon, then was jettisoned.

Interstage adaptor
Linked the second and third stages.

Second stage
Propelled the rocket into low Earth orbit, then was jettisoned.

Interstage adaptor
Linked the first two stages.

First stage
Launched the rocket from the Earth's surface, then was jettisoned.

Apollo spacecraft, 16.5 m (54 ft)

Saturn V rocket, 111 m (364 ft)

UNITED STATES

USA

Human, 1.8 m (6 ft)

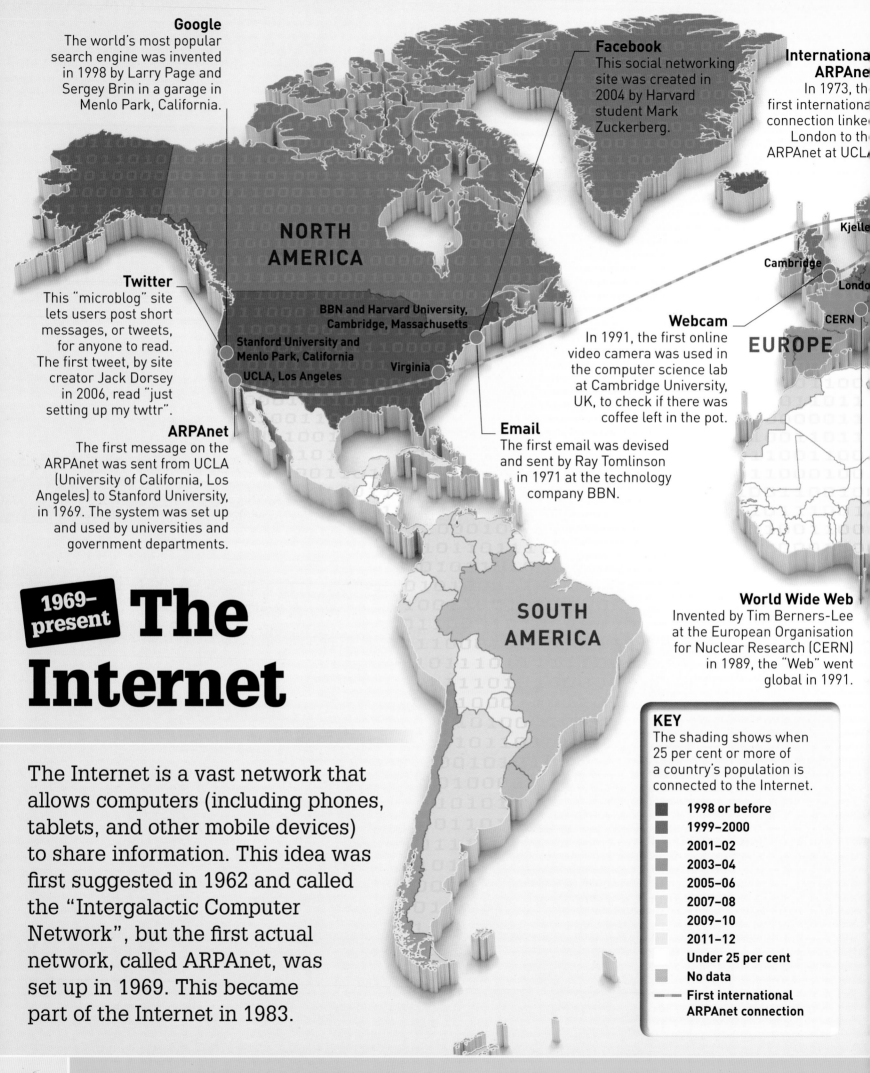

Google
The world's most popular search engine was invented in 1998 by Larry Page and Sergey Brin in a garage in Menlo Park, California.

Facebook
This social networking site was created in 2004 by Harvard student Mark Zuckerberg.

International ARPAnet
In 1973, the first international connection linked London to the ARPAnet at UCLA.

NORTH AMERICA

Kjelle

Cambridge

Londo

Twitter
This "microblog" site lets users post short messages, or tweets, for anyone to read. The first tweet, by site creator Jack Dorsey in 2006, read "just setting up my twttr".

BBN and Harvard University, Cambridge, Massachusetts

Stanford University and Menlo Park, California

UCLA, Los Angeles

Virginia

Webcam
In 1991, the first online video camera was used in the computer science lab at Cambridge University, UK, to check if there was coffee left in the pot.

EUROPE

CERN

ARPAnet
The first message on the ARPAnet was sent from UCLA (University of California, Los Angeles) to Stanford University, in 1969. The system was set up and used by universities and government departments.

Email
The first email was devised and sent by Ray Tomlinson in 1971 at the technology company BBN.

SOUTH AMERICA

World Wide Web
Invented by Tim Berners-Lee at the European Organisation for Nuclear Research (CERN) in 1989, the "Web" went global in 1991.

1969–present

The Internet

The Internet is a vast network that allows computers (including phones, tablets, and other mobile devices) to share information. This idea was first suggested in 1962 and called the "Intergalactic Computer Network", but the first actual network, called ARPAnet, was set up in 1969. This became part of the Internet in 1983.

KEY
The shading shows when 25 per cent or more of a country's population is connected to the Internet.

- 1998 or before
- 1999–2000
- 2001–02
- 2003–04
- 2005–06
- 2007–08
- 2009–10
- 2011–12
- Under 25 per cent
- No data
- First international ARPAnet connection

THE FIRST MESSAGE EVER SENT OVER THE ARPANET WAS "LOGIN".

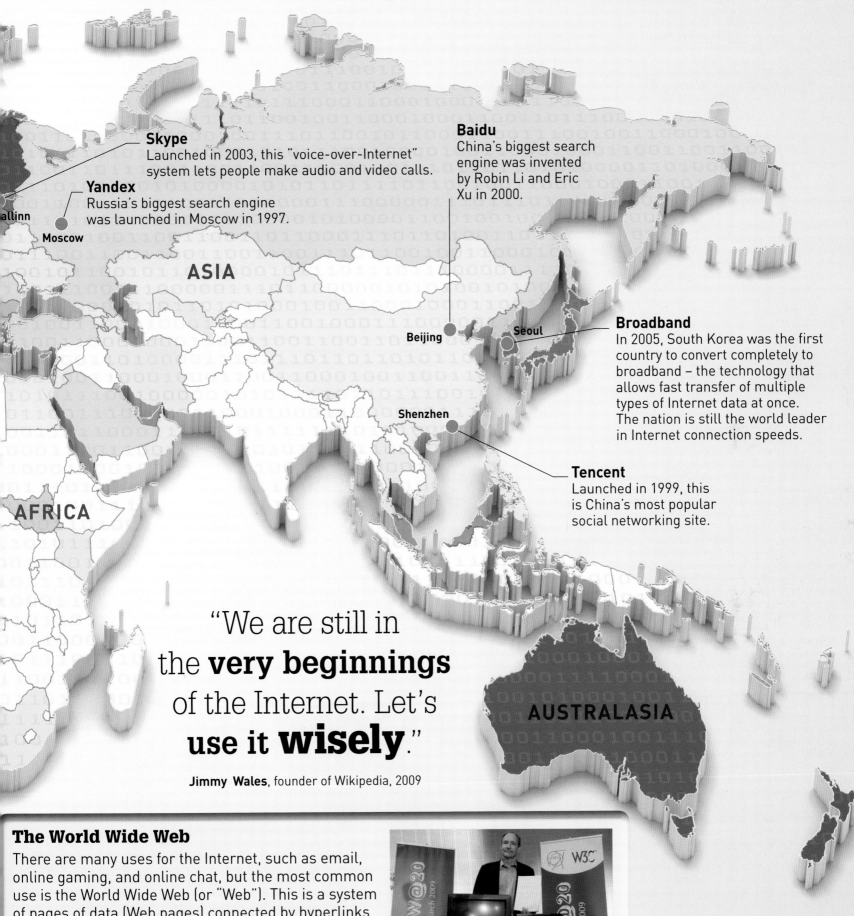

Skype
Launched in 2003, this "voice-over-Internet" system lets people make audio and video calls.

Yandex
Russia's biggest search engine was launched in Moscow in 1997.

Baidu
China's biggest search engine was invented by Robin Li and Eric Xu in 2000.

Broadband
In 2005, South Korea was the first country to convert completely to broadband – the technology that allows fast transfer of multiple types of Internet data at once. The nation is still the world leader in Internet connection speeds.

Tencent
Launched in 1999, this is China's most popular social networking site.

allinn

Moscow

ASIA

Beijing

Seoul

Shenzhen

AFRICA

AUSTRALASIA

"We are still in the **very beginnings** of the Internet. Let's use it **wisely**."

Jimmy Wales, founder of Wikipedia, 2009

The World Wide Web

There are many uses for the Internet, such as email, online gaming, and online chat, but the most common use is the World Wide Web (or "Web"). This is a system of pages of data (Web pages) connected by hyperlinks (links that take the reader to more, related information on other pages). There were 1 trillion pages of Web content by 2008. Search engines help readers by scouring the Web for any word or phrase entered.

Inventor Tim Berners-Lee shows the first Web server on the World Wide Web's 20th birthday.

THE L AND O ARRIVED, BUT THE SYSTEM CRASHED ON THE LETTER G.

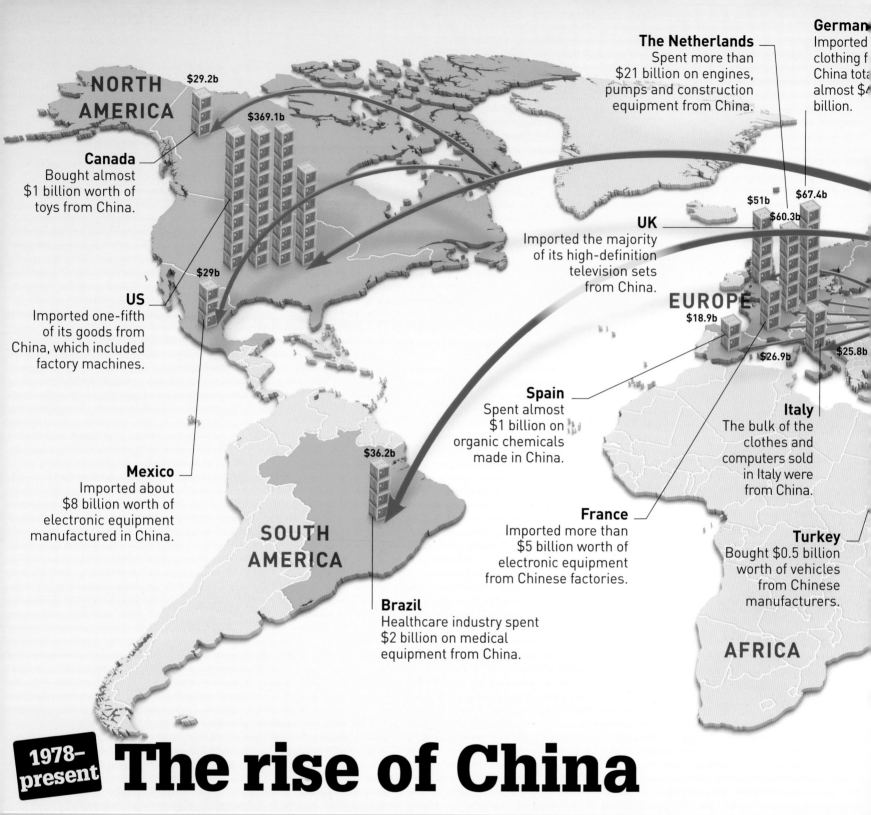

NORTH AMERICA $29.2b

Canada
Bought almost $1 billion worth of toys from China.

$369.1b

US
Imported one-fifth of its goods from China, which included factory machines.

$29b

Mexico
Imported about $8 billion worth of electronic equipment manufactured in China.

SOUTH AMERICA

$36.2b

Brazil
Healthcare industry spent $2 billion on medical equipment from China.

The Netherlands
Spent more than $21 billion on engines, pumps and construction equipment from China.

German
Imported clothing f China tota almost $ billion.

$51b $67.4b
$60.3b

UK
Imported the majority of its high-definition television sets from China.

EUROPE

$18.9b

$26.9b $25.8b

Spain
Spent almost $1 billion on organic chemicals made in China.

Italy
The bulk of the clothes and computers sold in Italy were from China.

France
Imported more than $5 billion worth of electronic equipment from Chinese factories.

Turkey
Bought $0.5 billion worth of vehicles from Chinese manufacturers.

AFRICA

1978–present

The rise of China

Since the late 1970s, China's wealth has increased at an incredible rate. It is now the world's largest trading nation after overtaking the US in 2013. One of the main reasons China is becoming richer is that it sells more goods to the world than any other country. In 2013, China sold produce worth $1.2 trillion ($1,200 billion), in US dollars, to its top 20 customers.

KEY

Country that is among the top 20 importers of Chinese goods

US $10 billion worth of Chinese goods imported in 2013

Export of Chinese goods

IN 2000–10, CHINA'S ECONOMY GREW SEVEN TIMES FASTER THAN THAT

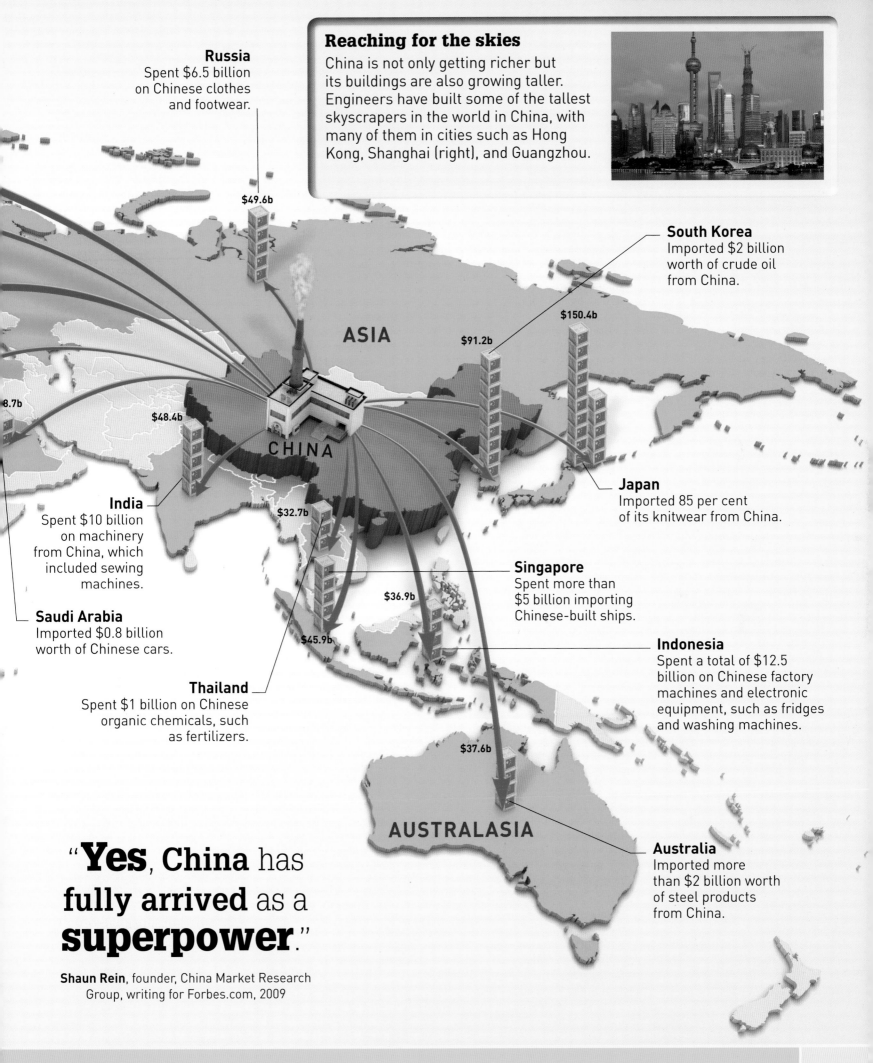

Russia
Spent $6.5 billion on Chinese clothes and footwear.

Reaching for the skies
China is not only getting richer but its buildings are also growing taller. Engineers have built some of the tallest skyscrapers in the world in China, with many of them in cities such as Hong Kong, Shanghai (right), and Guangzhou.

$49.6b

South Korea
Imported $2 billion worth of crude oil from China.

$150.4b

$91.2b

ASIA

8.7b

$48.4b

CHINA

India
Spent $10 billion on machinery from China, which included sewing machines.

$32.7b

Japan
Imported 85 per cent of its knitwear from China.

Singapore
Spent more than $5 billion importing Chinese-built ships.

$36.9b

Saudi Arabia
Imported $0.8 billion worth of Chinese cars.

$45.9b

Indonesia
Spent a total of $12.5 billion on Chinese factory machines and electronic equipment, such as fridges and washing machines.

Thailand
Spent $1 billion on Chinese organic chemicals, such as fertilizers.

$37.6b

"Yes, China has fully arrived as a superpower."

Shaun Rein, founder, China Market Research Group, writing for Forbes.com, 2009

AUSTRALASIA

Australia
Imported more than $2 billion worth of steel products from China.

Index